TRUMP'S
WAR ON
CAPITALISM

TRUMP'S WAR ON CAPITALISM

DAVID A. STOCKMAN

FOREWORD BY ROBERT F. KENNEDY JR.

HOT BOOKS

Hot Books may be purchased in bulk at special discounts for sales promotion,
corporate gifts, fund-raising, or educational purposes. Special editions can also
be created to specifications. For details, contact the Special Sales Department,
Skyhorse Publishing, 307 West 36th Street, 11th Floor, New York, NY 10018
or info@skyhorsepublishing.com

Hot Books® and Skyhorse Publishing® are registered trademarks of
Skyhorse Publishing, Inc.®, a Delaware corporation.

Visit our website at www.skyhorsepublishing.com.

Please follow our publisher Tony Lyons on Instagram @tonylyonsisuncertain

10 9 8 7 6 5 4 3 2 1

Library of Congress Cataloging-in-Publication Data is available on file.

ISBN: 978-1-5107-7932-7
eBook: 978-1-5107-7933-4

Cover design by Brian Peterson

Printed in the United States of America

For my grandchildren, Isabelle, Benjamin, and Zia

Contents

Foreword by

Robert F. Kennedy Jr.

———

Occupying a senior role in the Administration of President Reagan, David Stockman was a powerhouse of energy and creativity. He was Director of the Office of Management and Budget—the most controversial ever. His budget slashing at EPA made him my personal nemesis. While I disagreed with many of his proposals and ideas, I never doubted he was doing what he believed was right.

Fortunately, he still is.

Stockman has become one of the nation's most steadfast and eloquent crusaders against the corrupt merger of state and corporate power. I confess my addiction to his weekly Substack. I find exhilarating Stockman's clear-minded excoriation of the corporate kleptocracy that has eclipsed America's once-exemplary democracy. Stockman articulates, more persuasively than almost any critic I know, how corporate capture of the Pentagon and intelligence apparatus by military contractors transformed America into a warfare state that has weakened America's national defense, made it less safe to be American at home and abroad, while bankrupting us both economically and morally. Meanwhile, the capture of the Fed by Wall Street and the big banks has financialized our economy and shifted wealth upward, while annihilating our industrial base and the American middle class. Stockman continually reminds his readers that the warfare state is both a cause and a symptom of the Fed's money printing addiction. As galloping money printing undermined the strength of the US dollar, eternal wars, weapons sales, and global hegemony—reinforced by eight hundred military bases abroad—became the substitutes for economic efficiency and productivity at home. The war machine, as Stockman shows, keeps the dollar afloat. Only global military domination protects the dollar's value, allowing the Fed to continuously pleasure Wall Street with cheap gambling chips under the phony guise of promoting growth, jobs, and an inoculation against incipient deflationary entropy.

Finally, Stockman is that rare Republican willing to denounce, as gaslighting, President Donald Trump's most pervasive brag: that he created a great economic boom for America. Stockman shows that the opposite is true.

Though President Trump now says the pandemic was the only thing that ruined "the greatest economy in the history of the world," Stockman slices and dices that argument. He reminds readers that it was Donald Trump who locked down the country, destroying 3.3 million businesses overnight. Some of these were built on multiple generations of sweat and equity. Around 40 percent of Black-owned businesses will never reopen.

Stockman argues that President Trump shoulders the blame for the overwhelming share of the $6.5 trillion of Covid spending—the stimulus checks to 90 percent of the public, the added weekly unemployment toppers, the massive corporate giveaways of the Paycheck Protection Program, and the flood of Covid money into local governments. All of these ruinous initiatives were directly linked to President Trump's useless and harmful lockdowns. President Trump did more than all the preceding presidents, back to George Washington, to saddle our children with a $33 trillion debt. The small business closures under President Trump shifted $4 trillion of wealth north into the pockets of a new oligarchy of billionaires, creating approximately five hundred new billionaires in five hundred days. The closure of all those small concerns proved the final nail in the coffin for the American middle class.

Stockman also gives us hope in the form of a blueprint for how to revive American democracy and restore our nation to global financial and moral leadership. His remedies begin with cuts in military spending (to levels matching those at the height of the Cold War), reining in the Fed to stop showering Wall Street with ultra-cheap credit and nearly limitless liquidity, closing the border and ensuring legal immigration sufficient to meet job demand, prodigious investment in plants and equipment, and other policies to foster a powerful burst of entrepreneurial energy and invention.

Even the reluctant *Washington Post* has said of Stockman, "He's a truth-teller," and he tells the truth in these pages—by the numbers.

Robert F. Kennedy Jr.

Chapter One

The Myth of the MAGA Economy

The GOP primary season has come alive, and the state of play is abysmal. Front and center there is Donald Trump, while everyone else, including a few real Republicans and several neo-con fakers, stumble along far in the rear.

And that's a terrible shame. America desperately needs a return to old-fashioned GOP governance, yet Donald Trump is not remotely a conservative, let alone even a half-assed Republican. As it is, he fluked into the Oval Office in November 2016 and proceeded to wantonly abandon Republican economic doctrine and badly tarnish the brand. But rather than showing him the door, the floundering remnants of the Republican Party have rallied to the banner of one of the most bombastic, egomaniacal, unfit mountebanks ever to appear on the American political scene.

So, what are the good people of the GOP thinking?

To be clear, we have no objection to The Donald's relentless and frequently unhinged attacks on the ruling elites of Washington, Wall Street, the mainstream media and the Fortune 500. Indeed, his one abiding virtue is that he has all the right enemies. That is, the Washington political class and the likes of the *New York Times*, CNN, the broadcast networks, the foreign policy think tanks, and the liberal Silicon Valley billionaires.

These are the very people, in fact, whose policies and ideologies threaten the future of America.

But while Trump has the right enemies, he has been hopelessly wrong on the substance of policy. Indeed, when it comes to what the GOP's core mission should be amidst the ongoing tussle of democratic governance—standing up for free markets, fiscal rectitude, sound money, personal liberty, and small government at home and non-intervention abroad—Donald Trump has overwhelmingly come down on the wrong side of the issues.

Yet the situation is now so far gone that the election of a true conservative leader in 2024 is the only hope remaining. The very future of constitutional democracy and capitalist prosperity in America is literally at stake. These foundational threats simply cannot endure another four years of Donald Trump in the White House. Nor can it tolerate another election where a woebegone Democrat like Joe Biden wins by default, owing to the simple fact that they are not Donald Trump.

Indeed, the calamity of Joe Biden's wars, inflation, corruption, and relentless assaults on liberty and constitutional rights is so blatant that the American people will surely be looking to drum the Dems out of office in 2024. So, the chance must not be wasted. It is imperative that well-meaning Republicans and conservatives understand Trump's miserable record as a big spender, easy money-man, hard-core protectionist, immigrant-basher, militarist, and all-around Big Government statist, and look elsewhere for a standard-bearer.

The Donald's abysmal policy failings are documented in detail and at length in the pages that follow; but first, the myth of the great MAGA Economy should be debunked. A lot of Republican voters, though misguided, are willing to overlook all his egregious egotism, petty bombast, and endless departures from conservative economic principles based on the claim that he delivered the Greatest Economy Ever.

In a word, he didn't. Not remotely. On the bread-and-butter matters of growth, jobs, inflation, productivity, savings and investment, in fact, his record is among the worst of modern presidents, not the best. Indeed, the US economy's faltering performance during The Donald's tenure was worse than that of every one of his modern Democratic predecessors going all the way back to Truman.

To be sure, the very idea that America's infinitely complex, deeply cyclical, and globalized $26 trillion economy can be assessed by statistical outcomes realized during the arbitrary forty-eight calendar months of a presidential term is deeply faulty. That's because economic cycles and trends begin and end on calendars wholly unrelated to presidential terms. So the overwhelming bulk of economic policy claims by all presidents amount to partisan talking points, not credible economic analysis.

For instance, years of bad Fed policy brought the US economy into a thundering tailspin in 2008. So any statistical measure of results for George W. Bush's tenure has a dismal endpoint, which was largely not his doing.

By the same token, Barack Obama was sworn in at the very bottom of the worst recession in post-war history and subsequently benefited from the natural regenerative forces of market capitalism. His economic growth and jobs numbers, therefore, couldn't help but be brighter. Yet Obama's policies had precious little to do with these outcomes—well, except to thwart what might have been a far stronger recovery.

In fact, the overwhelming bulk of economic outcomes during these four-year presidential intervals reflect the combined action of tens of millions of workers, entrepreneurs, managers, investors, consumers, savers, and speculators operating on the (quasi) free market. And that's even as compromised as the private economy has become owing to government intervention and central bank manipulation.

Indeed, when it comes to the big picture, presidential policy is, by and large, overrated. And in the particular period of 2017 through 2020, The Donald inherited the positive momentum of a ripening business cycle that was overwhelmingly not his doing.

Nevertheless, even if you give Trump credit owed to broader cyclical and historical trends, the facts still leave little room for doubt. Real economic growth averaged just 1.52 percent per annum during Trump's forty-eight months in the Oval Office. Literally, you can't find anything that weak over the course of a presidential term since the Korean War!

Of course, circumstances, cycles, and even demographics change so much over long periods of time that reaching way back for comparisons has its limits. Still, real growth over the sixty-two-years between 1954 and 2016 averaged 3.04 percent per annum. That's exactly *twice*—to the second decimal point—what materialized during The Donald's term.

As it happened, that extended sixty-two-year interval encompassed nine recessions, eleven presidents, numerous wars, and a goodly number of domestic and international crises. So it's a fair representation of modern history, not distorted by short-run fluctuations owing to cyclical timing factors or aberrations like the Great Financial Crisis (GFC). And yet, and yet. The Donald's ballyhooed MAGA economy grew at just half the rate of what might fairly be called the modern growth norm.

Moreover, when dialed in closer to the present time during which both demographics and long-term policy constraints weakened the underlying growth trend, the most apt comparison of the Trump years is with Obama's second term. Both of which were all part of the extended post-financial crisis recovery cycle, and occurred under a monetary and regulatory regime that was broadly continuous over the eight years in question.

The economic growth rate during Obama's second term wasn't anything to write home about, either. But it still computed to 2.18 percent per annum—a rate 40 percent higher than that on The Donald's watch.

It should be noted here that real final sales of domestic product are used as a proxy for economic growth for the purpose of consistent comparisons. That's because it has the analytical virtue of removing from the data short-term inventory fluctuations that are irrelevant to growth over any reasonable period but can badly distort beginning and end points when measuring growth rates via the conventional real GDP series.

With the economic growth data smoothed in this manner, there is no room for doubt. If you want to brag about outcomes during the artificial interval of a presidential term, The Donald and his MAGA partisans should remain as quiet as church mice. They have the worst record ever compiled!

Per Annum Change in Real Final Sales Since 1954:
- Kennedy/Johnson 1960–1968: 4.97 percent.
- Clinton 1992–2000: 3.75 percent.
- Reagan 1980–1988: 3.44 percent.
- Carter 1976–1980: 3.37 percent.
- Eisenhower 1954–1960: 2.92 percent.
- Nixon/Ford 1968–1976: 2.73 percent.
- George H. W. Bush 1988–1992: 2.22 percent.
- George W. Bush 2000–2008: 2.00 percent.
- Obama 2008–2016: 1.74 percent.
- *Trump 2016–2020: 1.52 percent.*
- All Presidents, 1954–2016: *3.04 percent.*

Trump's defenders, of course, will claim that the great Covid pandemic knocked his record into a cocked hat, and that he shouldn't be tagged with the economic plunge of 2020 that originated in China. You can get that argument from The Donald's own tweet of August 2020 after the economy had been flushed into the ditch by the lockdowns and White House–fueled Covid hysteria:

> . . . My Administration and I built the greatest economy in history, of any country, **turned it off,** saved millions of lives, and now am building an even greater economy than it was before. Jobs are flowing, NASDAQ is already at a record high, the rest to follow. Sit back & watch!

We will refute that bit of nonsense below, but suffice it to note here that the economic contractions of 2020 were due to the sweeping Washington-imposed lockdowns, not the virus itself. And as it happened, Trump was the very author of those lockdowns and the related self-quarantining of a frightened population. All this disruptive Washington interference with normal economic function was announced and promoted week-after-week from the bully pulpit at the Trump White House.

Measured through Q1 2020, thereby discarding the big April-June GDP plunge, brings the average economic growth rate to just 2.10 percent, a figure still near the bottom of the above rankings. So even when you set the lockdown mayhem aside, you still can't make an economic silk purse out of the sow's ear which was the MAGA economy.

Jobs The Donald Didn't Create

Nor does the claim that The Donald was a great jobs creator wash, either. For crying out loud, presidents don't create jobs—capitalists and businessmen do. And while most presidents are unwilling to give the free market its due, the egomaniacal poseur otherwise known as Donald Trump was especially eager to hog the credit.

Except, there was actually no credit to boast about. There were 145,400,000 NFP (nonfarm payroll) jobs in December 2016 and just 142,475,000 in December 2020. The Donald's tenure, therefore, was the only presidential term in which private payrolls in the US economy actually shrank—and by three million jobs to boot. Well, at least since Herbert Hoover!

Again, defenders will blame it on the pandemic, but that doesn't hold up either. Even if you assume that Trump's term ended at the pre-pandemic peak in February 2020, the contrast with Obama's comparable second term is not flattering. Trump's adjusted monthly jobs growth number was 33 percent smaller than Barry's.

NFP Job Change Per Month:
- Obama: December 2012 to December 2016: +215,300
- Trump: December 2016 to February 2020: +145,000

When you translate these jobs numbers to annual growth rates, the story is much the same as it was for real economic growth.

During Obama's second term the annualized growth rate of NFP jobs was +1.86 percent, which compares to an annualized gain of, well, -0.51 percent during The Donald's term.

And, yes, we can again pretend that the Trump lockdowns and shutdown carnage never happened and stop the calculation in February 2020, but a jobs growth rate of 1.47 percent is still nothing to write home about.

In fact, the rebound of the jobs growth rate from the Great Recession peaked in early 2015 and slid downhill continuously from there—with no discernible reversal during The Donald's pre-Covid tenure. The chart below with its downward trending jobs growth rate, of course, won't be found at a MAGA literature stand. It takes the air right out of The Donald's bloated jobs claims.

Y/Y Change in Nonfarm Payroll Jobs, Jan. 2015 to Feb. 2020.

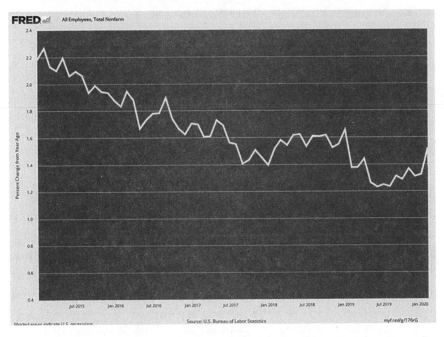

In the broader context of the last half century the job story on The Donald's watch is not much better. During the twelve presidencies between 1945 and 2016, the annualized jobs growth rate computes to 2.14 percent per annum, a figure nearly 44 percent higher than the above cited gain (1.47 percent) under Trump sans the lockdowns.

The MAGA economy thus ended up in the bottom half of the jobs league tables, even when you excise from the record the ten million jobs lost during The Donald's final ten months in the Oval Office. So the truth of the matter is that when it comes to jobs and economic growth, Trump was the Greatest Boaster Ever, not a superlative generator of economic prosperity.

Annualized Rate of Nonfarm Jobs Growth:
- Kennedy/Johnson 1960–1968: 3.22 percent.
- Carter 1976–1980: 3.11 percent.
- Clinton 1992–2000: 2.43 percent.
- Truman/Eisenhower 1945–1960: 2.14 percent.
- Reagan 1980–1988: 2.04 percent.
- Nixon/Ford 1968–1976: 1.89 percent.
- Obama 2nd Term 2012–2016: 1.86 percent.
- *Trump Dec. 2016 Thru February 2020: 1.47 percent.*
- George H. W. Bush 1988–1992: 0.60 percent.
- George W. Bush/Obama 1st Term 2000–2012: 0.15 percent.
- *Trump Dec. 2016 through Dec. 2020: -0.51 percent.*
- All Presidents 1945–2016: *2.14 percent.*

Moreover, even the job gains that did occur on the Trump watch through February 2020 were disproportionately in the low-wage or low-productivity sectors of the economy. Thus, of the 6.96 million increase of nonfarm jobs reported by the Bureau of Labor Statistics during that thirty-eight-month period, 3.7 million or 53 percent were accounted for by government, education and health services, leisure and hospitality industries, personal services, and business administrative support. By contrast, the high value-added manufacturing, construction, mining, and energy industries generated only 18 percent of the gains in payroll jobs.

One of the reasons for these tepid GDP and jobs growth figures was the fact that the core of the US economy represented by the industrial production index stalled out completely during Trump's tenure. In fact, in December 2020 it was actually 1 percent below the level he inherited in January 2017.

Ironically, the industrial production index encompasses manufacturing, mining, energy and gas and electric utility output—the very ailing sectors of the US economy that Trump claimed to champion and fix. As it happened, however, with a -0.21 percent per annum figure, he stood far in the dust compared to the average +2.9 percent per annum gain under the previous twelve presidents after WWII.

Industrial Production Index, January 2017 to December 2020.

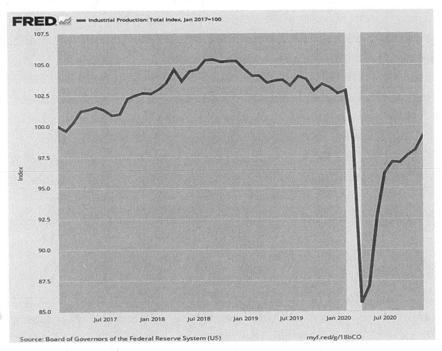

Then there is the double-fiction that the MAGA economy was not only booming, but it was inflation-free as well. The facts, of course, say otherwise.

The best measure of medium-term inflation is the 16 percent trimmed mean Consumer Price Index (CPI) because it strains out the high and low monthly outliers which can distort short-term readings. Accordingly, during Obama's second term, the inflation reading on this measure averaged 1.84 percent per annum, while the figure during The Donald's four years computes to 2.18 percent per year.

Again, inflation is cyclical and a function of Fed and other central bank monetary policies, which rarely aligns with the fixed forty-eight-month term of a US president. Still, not only was inflation accelerating during The Donald's term, but he was actually fanning the flames via constant demands on the Fed for even lower interest rates and even more inflationary policies.

Thus, in September 2019, when inflation was clearly accelerating, The Donald relieved himself of one of the most incoherent, ignorant statements on monetary policy ever uttered by a US president. And it was merely more of the same crackpottery that he had been espousing for years:

> **The USA should always be paying the lowest rate.** No Inflation! It is only the naïveté of Jay Powell and the Federal Reserve that doesn't allow us to do what other countries are already doing. A once in a lifetime opportunity that we are missing because of 'Boneheads'. . .
>
> **The Federal Reserve should get our interest rates down to ZERO, or less,** and we should then start to refinance our debt. INTEREST COST COULD BE BROUGHT WAY DOWN, while at the same time substantially lengthening the term. . .

This statement is not just a case of The Donald off on a monetary tangent. It's downright offensive to the very notion of coherent thought. That the US interest rate should always be "the lowest" on the planet, for instance, betrays The Donald's primitive mantra that winning is all that matters and that what is right is always what is first.

Self-evidently, The Donald is here confusing the Fed's policy rate target with the rates across the yield curve that the US Treasury pays on its own mountainous debt. So doing, the above comes dangerously close to saying that the key mechanism of capitalist prosperity—the price of money and capital markets securities—should be set by the Fed at ultra-low levels in order to relieve the US Treasury of debt service costs.

Indeed, the level of wild-eyed irresponsibility in the above statement would make historic American monetary quacks like William Jennings Bryan, Huey Long, Wright Patman, and John Connally turn green with envy. In fact, this Trumpian monetary humbug—and it's only a sample—is so over the top that you simply cannot talk about Trump's allegedly superior economic stewardship with a straight face.

You also can't limit the MAGA claims strictly to the calendar months of The Donald's term. That's because the Fed's monetary inflation machine was already running in high gear when he took the oath and had been running red hot for years after the so-called emergency of the Great Financial Crisis had fully abated.

So any good steward of American prosperity who chanced to land in the Oval Office in January 2017 should have been doing the opposite of the Trumpian calls for still easier money. That is to say, the vaunted "independence" of the Fed to the contrary notwithstanding, under the circumstances a sound money president would have urged them to stop the printing presses forthwith.

But The Donald doesn't have the slightest affinity for sound money, owing to reasons we develop below. He therefore has no right on that count alone to claim that he brought the Best Economy Ever to main street America. The crucial truth of the matter is that the Trumpian fiscal bacchanalia of 2020 and the massive money-printing by the Fed which accompanied it is what fueled the outbreak of forty-year high inflation directly thereafter.

For crying out loud, sound money and fiscal rectitude is the *sine qua non* of sustainable prosperity—so the stagflationary disaster which hit the US economy subsequent to The Donald's term is very much his legacy. It is the product of his noisy insistence on the most profligate Fed money-printing policies in modern times (Chapter 2), slathered with the most reckless outbreak of fiscal responsibility in all of American history (Chapter 4).

As it happened, the Fed's balance sheet grew at the staggering rate of 13 percent per annum during The Donald's term. Milton Friedman would have been rolling in his grave and would not have hesitated to say that owing to the lags in monetary policy effect, the virulent inflation that busted out in 2021 was very much gestated by the Fed during The Donald's watch and pursuant to his endless demands for still easier money.

But here's the thing. Any historic GOP president—including Bush the Younger and Bush the Elder, as RINO-tending as they were—would never have tolerated the Fed's print-a-thon, which actually started in September 2019 during the utterly unnecessary bailout of the "repo" market. Yet all the time he was roaming

Y/Y Change in the 16 Percent Trimmed Mean CPI, 2013 to 2020.

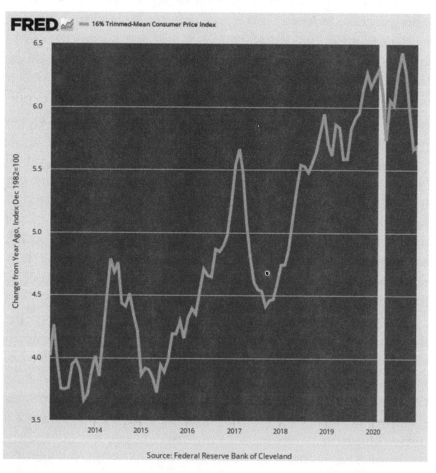

Source: Federal Reserve Bank of Cleveland

around the White House tweeting economic dumbassery and boasting about the bubble-ridden stock market, The Donald had no clue that the fundamental basis for sustainable prosperity was being savaged by America's rogue central bank.

The Lame Foundation of the MAGA Economy

Back in the day, another part of the GOP gospel focused on the crucial significance of productivity growth, which was properly understood to be the true foundation of rising living standards. Low taxes, minimal regulatory intervention, the slimmest possible claim on GDP by government spending and sound monetary policy were the means to this crucial outcome. And over the long stretch from 1954 to 2007, productivity growth did average nearly 2.1 percent per annum.

During The Donald's four years, however, there definitely was no MAGA magic on the productivity front. The growth rate was only 1.2 percent per annum or barely half of the fifty-six-year average.

Moreover, the reason is not hard to find. Historical US productivity growth has gone AWOL because the main street economy has become freighted down with public and private debt and strip-mined by corporate financial engineering enabled by the Fed.

The Donald's big spending and easy money policies did nothing to reverse these adverse trends. But suffice it here to note that what might be termed the national leverage ratio—total public and private debt as a percentage of GDP—rebounded to record levels on The Donald's watch. Compared to the solid 1.5x ratio that accompanied the nation's prosperity prior to 1970, the national leverage ratio peaked at 3.82x in 2020.

That meant, in practical terms, that the US economy was lugging around $50 trillion of incremental debt compared to what would have prevailed at the historic 1.5x leverage ratio. There is no wonder, therefore, that productivity growth during Trump's term slid into the sub-basement of modern history.

Total Public and Private Debt as Percent of GDP, 1947 to 2020.

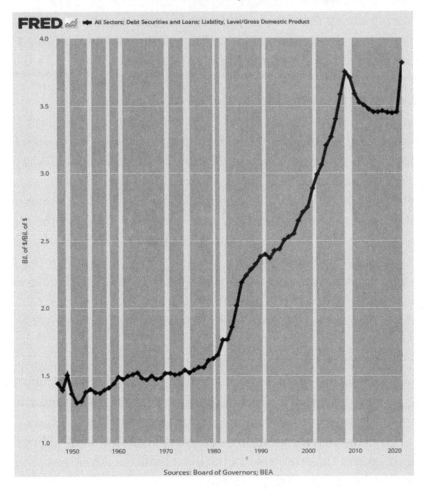

Another cornerstone of long-term growth and wealth creation is net savings from current economic output. This metric measures true economic savings, or the amount of resources left for new investment in productivity and growth after government borrowings have been subtracted from private household and business savings.

As depicted in the chart, that ratio averaged 7.5 percent to 10 percent of GDP in the economic heyday before 1980. But especially after the money-pumping era of Greenspan and his heirs and assigns commenced in the early 1990s, the net national savings ratio headed relentlessly south.

The Donald's tenure did not reverse that baleful trend, either. Indeed, it might be well and truly said that the runaway spending and borrowing of the Trump years delivered the coup de grace. By 2022 the ratio was an anemic 1.0 percent of GDP—a sheer rounding error in the sweep of post-war history.

For want of doubt, consider the absolute dollar figures embedded in the ratio chart below. The actual net national savings in 2022 at 1.0 percent of GDP was just $260 billion, but that figure would have computed to $1.960 trillion at the 7.5 percent net savings rate of the pre-1980 period.

In a word, $1.7 trillion of national savings has gone missing on an annual basis. Gross savings in the private sector have fallen

Net National Savings Rate, 1955 to 2022.

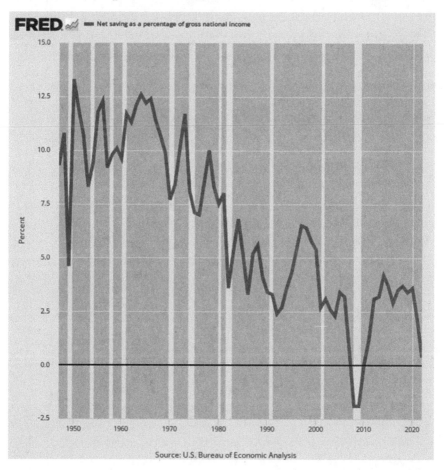

Source: U.S. Bureau of Economic Analysis

sharply, even as governments have scarfed up most of the available new private savings to fund massive, serial budget deficits.
And, yes, the Trump years comprised the very apotheosis of that
darkening trend.

As it has happened, real economic growth dropped from a
trend rate of 3.5 percent per year before the turn of the century to
barely 1.5 percent per annum since then. At the end of the day, the
reason for this severe deterioration is that real private investment
has stopped growing due to savings being channeled into private
speculation and massive public debts—the latter having become
far worse on The Donald's watch than ever before.

Indeed, since the year 2000, real net investment—which strains
out the inflation and the annual depreciation from the gross
investment figures—had dropped from $953 billion to $721 billion in 2020. Stated differently, main street experienced a deep cut
in the motor fuel of growth and rising prosperity, and the MAGA
economy did absolutely nothing to reverse that trend.

Real Net Private Investment, 2000 to 2020.

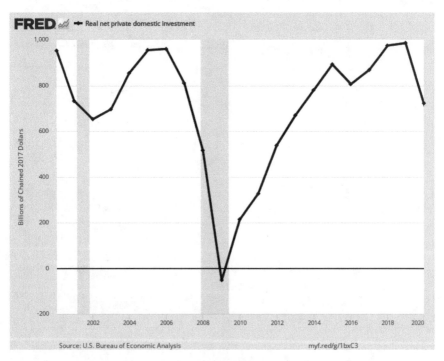

Of course, the ultimate purpose of growth, jobs, savings, productivity, and investment is to generate rising societal wealth and living standards. Yet when it comes to the key metric for that crucial objective, the MAGA economy ranks damn near the bottom of that league table, as well.

In fact, the proxy for American living standards—real GDP per capita—during Trump's term rose by only two-fifths of the average level posted over the half century after the US economy got back on a peacetime footing in 1947.

So, when it comes to The Donald's MAGA boasting, there is absolutely nothing to brag about.

Per Annum Growth in Per Capita Real GDP, 1947–2023
- Kennedy-Johnson, 1960–1968: +3.93 percent.
- Truman, 1947–1952: +3.43 percent.
- Reagan, 1980–1988: +2.62 percent.
- Clinton, 1992–2000: +2.60 percent.
- Carter, 1976–1980: +2.07 percent.
- Nixon-Ford, 1968–1976: +1.67 percent.
- Obama, 2008–2016: +1.06 percent.
- *Trump, 2016–2020: +1.03 percent.*
- Bush the Elder, 1988–1992: +0.97 percent.
- Bush the Younger: +0.91 percent.
- Eisenhower: +0.72 percent.
- *All presidents, 1947–2000: +2.45 percent.*

Chapter Two

The Illusory Foundations of Peak Trump

———

T he history books will record that peak Trump happened on February 19, 2020. That's when the S&P 500 hit 3385—a level 70 percent higher than on the day Donald Trump was sworn to office. So in the State of the Union address a few days earlier, The Donald had gone all-in embracing the most dangerous and unstable everything bubble in modern times:

> Since my election, U.S. stock markets have soared 70 percent, adding more than $12 trillion to our nation's wealth, transcending anything anyone believed was possible . . . All of those millions of people with 401(k)s and pensions are doing far better than they have ever done before with increases of 60, 70, 80, 90 and 100 percent, and even more.

But that's all she wrote, and even that was largely an illusion. Within days, the US economy was monkey-hammered by The Donald's own hand, when he unleashed Dr. Fauci and the virus patrol and sent the economy of main street America into a thundering tailspin.

We will amplify The Donald's culpability for that national disaster at length in Chapter 3. But as we have seen, the sweeping

Trump-ordered lockdowns sent his MAGA record into last place in the economic performance league tables of post-WWII presidencies and left the American economy in a condition so bruised, battered, inflated, and debt-ridden that it still hasn't recovered.

More importantly, the booming stock market Trump was celebrating in February 2020 was never real or sustainable and certainly not a tribute to Trump-O-Nomics in any way, shape, or form. To the contrary, it was the final surge of a long-running bubble fueled by the nation's rogue central bank—the real culprit behind the hollowed-out economy of Flyover America that had handed Trump a hairline Electoral College victory in 2016.

In just the eight short years between the Lehman Brothers bankruptcy filing in September 2008 and Trump's inauguration, the Fed had pumped $3.5 trillion of newly minted dollars into Wall Street. That was nearly *400 percent more* than the $920 billion the Fed had printed during the entire first ninety-four years of its existence!

The resulting immense stock market bubble which Trump inherited also came eight years after the decisive Capitol Hill

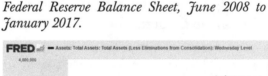

Federal Reserve Balance Sheet, June 2008 to January 2017.

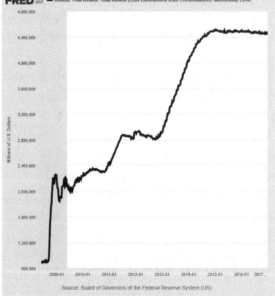

turning point of September 29, 2008. That was the date of the failed first Troubled Asset Relief program (TARP) vote in the US House of Representatives.

By a vote of 228–205, that day a majority of the US House— led by two-thirds of the GOP—had opted for honest capitalism in America and to allow Wall Street speculators who had grown rich ridding a giant financial bubble fostered by the Fed to face their just deserts.

The 700-point, 7 percent Dow drop that day, in fact, should have been just the beginning of a long overdue financial purge. But, unfortunately, it was not. Washington and Wall Street alike were more than happy to have the central bankers bailout their egregious excesses.

Indeed, excessive debt and rampant financial asset inflation had been building in the US economy ever since Tricky Dick Nixon deep-sixed the dollar's anchor to gold in August 1971, thereby ending the postwar Breton Woods system of fixed exchange rates and international financial discipline.

But the resulting financial rot had dramatically intensified in the years after Black Monday of October 1987. That's when Alan Greenspan panicked and rescued Wall Street from a bloodbath brought on by rampant speculation in a new gambling invention called stock portfolio insurance. He then went on to erect a thoroughly crooked monetary regime based on "wealth effects," which encompassed stock market price-keeping operations (implied puts and coddling of trader sentiment), systematic suppression of interest rates, and an inflationary quadrupling of the Fed's balance sheet from $200 billion to $800 billion during Greenspan's nineteen-year tenure.

This entire Bubble Finance regime had come crashing down when its most egregious Wall Street practitioner, the once venerable Lehman Brothers, shocked the world with its bankruptcy filing on September 15, 2008.

But there should have been no mystery: Lehman's $600 billion balance sheet was loaded with the toxic waste of its mortgage securitization mills, undistributed parts and pieces of its junk

bond underwritings, and far-flung speculations in leveraged real
estate. And, needless to say, Lehman Brothers was no outlier. To
the contrary, it was the poster-boy for the financial casino which
had risen up on Wall Street after 1987, where once had stood
quasi-honest and reasonably disciplined and stable capital and
money markets.

At the time of the TARP vote on September 29, 2008, in fact,
the credit default swap gambling operation that sat atop AIG's
fully solvent insurance subsidiaries had already been needlessly
bailed-out with an $85 billion lifeline from the Fed. In turn, almost
all of that fulsome pot of government money ended up being used
not for the protection of mom-and-pop insurance policy holders,
but to replenish the coffers of Goldman Sachs and other big Wall
Street and London gambling joints—thereby making them whole
for the dodgy paper they had foolishly purchased form AIG.

Likewise, by the end of September 2008, Morgan Stanley
had been totally insolvent and had been kept on life-support by
upwards of $100 billion of emergency liquidity injections from
the New York Fed; and the financial grim reaper had also been
breathing heavily on the necks of Goldman, Merrill Lynch, and
the Citigroup investment bank, too.

So then and there loomed the financial Rubicon: Wall Street
was desperate for a bailout and main street did not need one. The
overwhelming share of small- and mid-sized main street banks
and thrifts, in fact, did not own much subprime paper, had ample
FDIC insured and sticky depositor funds, and were in no danger
of failing or facing runs, despite the urban legends to the contrary
which have grown up since.

And while main street households had been lured into the
Greenspan bubble, it was not mainly for livelihood and jobs but
for a one-time spree of consumption spending that had been
financed with cash-out mortgages or MEW (mortgage equity
withdrawal). Greenspan and Bernanke had actually patted themselves on the back for inducing millions of American families to
pawn their castles in order to get a loan for a trip to Disney World
or to install a man-cave or to speculate in the stock market.

Accordingly, at the peak in 2006–2007, MEW amounted to about $600 billion per annum, which was equal to about 6 percent of PCE (personal consumption expenditure). But when the subprime mortgage bubble finally burst, the MEW gravy train dried up suddenly and completely, forcing most of main street America to return to living within its means. That was evidently unpleasant for many, but it wasn't exactly a fatal state of affairs, either.

To be sure, there were upwards of 18 million mortgage defaults over 2007–2017, but in the overwhelming share of cases, homeowners did not become homeless and without shelter; they just lost their small down payments, became renters, and perhaps learned a hard lesson about the dangers of too much leverage.

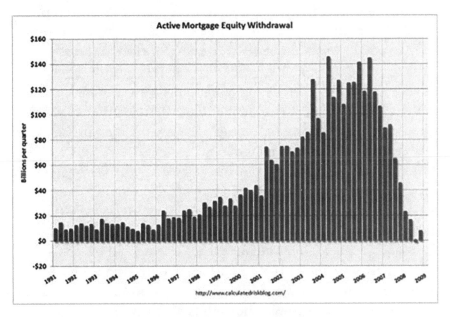

Active Mortgage Equity Withdrawal

So the truth of the Great Financial Crisis was that main street did not need a bailout. And while Wall Street's bacon was dramatically saved, main street didn't get much benefit from TARP and the Fed's massive money pumping operations, either.

Instead, the bailout funds went overwhelmingly in the first instance to the rescue of the remaining Wall Street gambling houses—Morgan Stanley, Goldman Sachs, and Citigroup directly; and also to Merrill Lynch, Wachovia, and Washington

Mutual through Washington DC arranged and lubricated shot-gun mergers.

But more importantly, the Fed's utterly insane liquidity tsu-nami in the fall of 2008 expanded its balance sheet by $1.3 trillion in *ninety-four days*. That was more than a *half billion dollars* of new money per hour!

That stopped the entire financial purge and cleansing process cold. With virtually zero interest rates on the Fed's liquidity lines and essentially no credit quality questions asked, the Wall Street gambling houses were almost instantly shored-up. And the way was paved for a massive, continuous reflation of what were already vastly overvalued financial markets.

So, what filled the bookends between the Fed's post-September 2008 doubling down on bubble finance and peak Trump in February 2020 was a dramatic worsening of the condition which gave rise to the Great Financial Crisis (GFC) in the first place. Stated differently, the braggadocio-inclined Donald Trump thought Wall Street was exuberantly cheering his performance when what was actually unfolding was only the next phase of the Fed's immense financial malignancy.

Pursuant thereto, the Wall Street bubble got far bigger and more unstable, while the Fed's systematic economic damage to main street had intensified enormously. The latter was owing to a further Fed-induced outbreak in the corporate C-suites of employ-ment and income killing financial engineering and off-shoring of production and jobs. The Fed's lopsided reflation—the robust revival of Wall Street but not main street—in the period encom-passed by these twelve-year bookends was a gigantic mistake. It further bifurcated America's economic and financial life and was so unsustainable that it was only a matter of time before the fan-tasy would unravel.

Two statistics encapsulate the story. Between the pre-crisis peak in late 2007 and The Donald's February 2020 stock market apotheosis, the inflation-adjusted NASDAQ 100 index rose by a whopping *240 percent* while industrial production gained, well, *0.0 percent*.

Inflation-Adjusted NASDAQ-100 versus Industrial Production Index, October 2007 to February 2020.

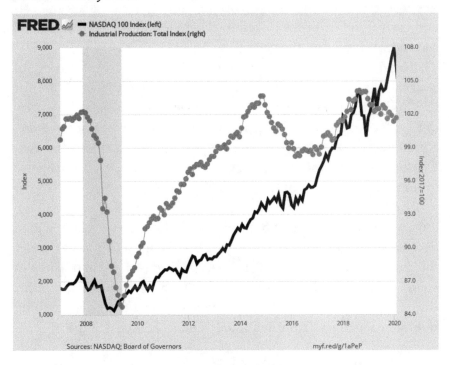

Sources: NASDAQ; Board of Governors   myf.red/g/1aPeP

That's right. The aforementioned industrial production index—speedometer of the nation's factories, mines, oil fields, and gas and electric utilities—stood at 101.6 in October 2007 and at the identical level in February 2020.

Self-evidently, twelve years of boom on Wall Street and stasis on main street could not stand as an economic matter, but there was also something more: America's democratic machinery may have become enfeebled and sidelined by Washington's permanent ruling class, yet the 2016 election proved that when things get far enough askew, the unwashed masses can still make themselves heard.

The fact is, the Trump presidency happened owing to the wrong road taken (bailouts and massive money-printing) after September 15, 2008. It also gave the Fed another decade to hammer the main street economy with its spurious 2.00 percent inflation target. The latter sent even more jobs and production offshore. At the same time, the resulting ultra-cheap debt fostered rampant Wall Street financial engineering, which strip-mined corporate balance sheets and cash flows in order to pump dividends, stock buybacks, and M&A deals back into the casino.

This second and even greater round of Bubble Finance, of course, finally sowed an even stronger tidal wave of economic hurt and social resentment in the burned-out industrial districts of Flyover America. That's why Trump had come out of nowhere, conquered the electoral college on the votes of former Rust Belt Democrats, and then had sojourned in the Oval Office loudly but to no remedial effect for the next three years.

The truth of The Donald's vaunted stock market surge, therefore, was that the crisis of September 2008 had never really ended and certainly wasn't fixed. It had just been temporarily swept under the rug by Washington's relentless violations of the requisites of sound money, fiscal rectitude, and free market financial discipline. And then it had been doubled-down upon until the everything bubble reached its Trumpian asymptote in February 2020.

That Big, Fat, Ugly Bubble

The original post-Lehman meltdown was the capstone of decades of fiscal profligacy and egregious money-pumping by the Federal Reserve. These misbegotten policies had temporarily juiced current economic results, but so doing they had also deeply impaired and capriciously bifurcated the national economy and polity.

On the one hand, soaring household debts, relentless Fed-fostered inflation of domestic costs, prices, and wages, and an addiction to destructive financial engineering in the corporate C-suites had de-industrialized much of the economic expanse of Flyover America.

These wrong-headed Washington policies had caused the off-shoring of vast amounts of America's productive base and generated enormous and chronic trade deficits. These deficits had been continuous since the late 1970s and had turned the US into the greatest debtor nation in history, owing the rest of the world nearly $18 trillion by 2020.

To be sure, Keynesian economists and the establishment commentariat always said not to worry. These figures supposedly meant that that global investors loved America so much that they wished to bring their capital here in massive dollops, even if the nation's economy was blatantly profligate!

The utter folly of that canard is addressed in much of what follows, but one economic truth cannot be gainsaid. To wit, the plunging bars in the chart below are a proxy for the devastating migration of much of America's productive industrial economy to offshore venues.

The chart therefore tracks the economic demise in those rust belt precincts of Flyover America which ultimately put Donald Trump in the White House. And it also shows that The Donald's tenure in the Oval Office did absolutely nothing to stop the decay—notwithstanding his endless boasting about the soaring stock market.

US International Net Investment Position, 1978 to 2021.

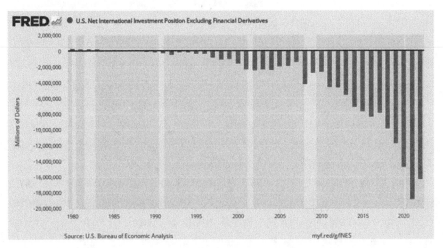

At the same time, Washington's foray into statist destruction of sound money and fiscal rectitude had capriciously conferred financialized prosperity on selective pockets of American society—mostly scattered along the coasts and sprinkled among the hinterlands.

These economic precincts have prospered mightily—albeit unsustainably—from both the vast bloating of the financial sector and the relentless inflation of assets prices, as well as from the tax-and-debt–fueled state enterprises of war, medical care, and education.

As to the financialization of the American economy, the chart below makes clear that since the 1970s—but especially after the Greenspan era of aggressive monetary expansion incepted in 1987—household assets have been winning the race with income by a country mile.

For example, the market value of household assets had soared by 31x—from $4.3 trillion in 1970 to a staggering *$133.4 trillion* as of Q4 2019. By contrast, personal income had risen by only *$18 trillion* during the same period.

What that meant, of course, is that each dollar of income has been associated with sharply rising amounts of assets. In 1970, the household sector held *$4.80* of assets for each dollar of personal income and by the time of Alan Greenspan's arrival at the Fed that figure had inched up to $5.20.

But after Greenspan figuratively discovered and deployed the printing press in the basement of the Eccles Building after October 19, 1987, when the market plunged by 22 percent in a single day, the contemporary asset bubble was off to the races. By the eve of the financial crisis in 2007 it had reached $6.80 per dollar of personal income and stood at *$7.10* as The Donald was crowing about his stock market success in the 2020 SOTU.

Actually, the more accurate ratio at that time was $8.50 of assets per dollar of personal income when you remove transfer payments from the income figures. After all, most of America's heavily transfer payment dependent households have just tiny asset holdings, if any at all.

In effect, the ratio of household assets-to-income represents the "cap rate" (i.e., PE multiple) for the aggregate economy. And, as shown below, it had been soaring for three decades at the time of Peak Trump. Yet why should it have?

If anything, the aggregate cap rate of the US economy should have been falling because the quality of household finances had been deteriorating badly. That's partially due to a much higher ratio of transfer payments to earned labor and capital income; and also due to the fact that the overall growth rate of real earned incomes has been sinking steadily since the turn of the century, as the figures presented in Chapter 1 make abundantly clear.

The truth of the matter is that this rising asset capitalization rate was phony and unsustainable. It reflected the artificial fruits of central bank money-pumping and systematic falsification of asset prices; it was the talisman of America's failed, bifurcated economy.

And yet the ginormous ego and utter economic ignorance of The Donald brooked no doubt. He claimed it as vindication of the MAGA economy when it was actually evidence of why his constituents in Flyover America had been laid so low in the first place.

Household Assets versus Personal Income, 1970 to 2020.

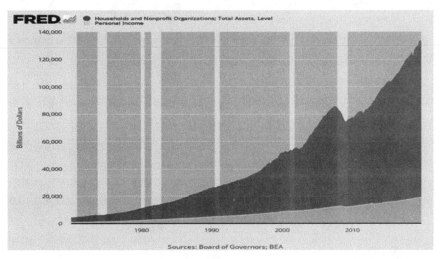

Had this $133 trillion household asset bubble been evenly distributed it would have been bad enough. The long years of the financialization party would have been shared by all—as would have the deflationary hangover when the "morning after" eventually came.

But the Fed's asset bubble had been far more perverse. As we demonstrate in the chapters ahead, it was purchased on the backs of Flyover America, but ended up in the brokerage accounts of the bicoastal elites and especially the top 1 percent, which owns more than 40 percent of all financial assets.

As is demonstrated in the chart below, on the eve of the Greenspan money-pumping era in Q4 1989, the net worth of the top 1 percent was about $4.9 trillion, while the bottom 50 percent held about $800 billion of net worth. But thereafter came the great Greenspanian bubble, perpetuated with even added gusto by his successors.

Accordingly, by the time of The Donald's arrival at the White House the top 1 percent had gained an additional $17.5 trillion of net worth, while the bottom 50 percent had picked up just $500 billion. So, the math of central bank–fueled asset bubbles is impossible to deny: To wit, the wealth of the top 1 percent was *6x* that of the bottom 50 percent in 1989, representing reasonably honest capitalism at work. But over the next quarter century the top 1 percent had gained *35x* more net worth than the bottom 50 percent of households— owing to the Fed's relentless flooding of Wall Street with easy money and repeated bailouts.

Nevertheless, at that moment in time (2016), you could not find one mainstream economist or commentator in a thousand who was aware of the data below or who thought it mattered. But the people of Flyover America knew they had been cheated. Big time.

So, they voted on November 8, 2016 with their hurt and their resentments. More crucially, the bombastic outsider from Trump Tower came out on top against all odds during the wee hours of that freakish election because he had discovered an unlikely route to power almost by accident.

Namely, he had learned after demagoguing Mexicans and immigrants in the early days of his campaign that he could channel and mobilize Flyover America's hurts and resentments by pounding relentlessly at the nefarious trade practices of foreign countries and the alleged threat to personal security and jobs posed by a purported flood of illegal immigrants pouring across the Mexican border.

Neither of these propositions were remotely true as we demonstrate in subsequent chapters, of course, and they had nothing at all to do with fixing the economic mess fostered by Washington's fiscal profligacy and monetary mayhem.

That's the part about which The Donald was utterly oblivious when he embraced from the Oval Office the very same "big, fat, ugly bubble" which he had denounced on the campaign trail in 2016.

By February 2020, of course, the ugly underside of the bubble which put him in the White House had gotten only bigger and fatter, but now he embraced it as proof positive that MAGA had been a roaring success. Of course, it was nothing of the kind, as we document below.

Net Worth of Top 1 percent versus Bottom 50 percent, 1989 to 2016.

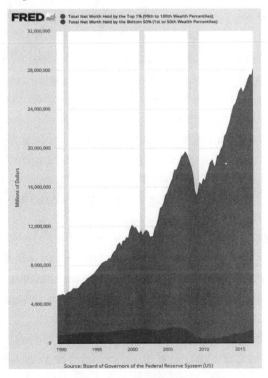

2008 Crisis Interrupted and Why It Matters

What The Donald did not remotely understand is that the crisis of September 2008 never went away. It merely represented the first down-leg of financialization coming undone, while during the subsequent decade it had actually re-emerged in an even more virulent and dangerous form.

Back when the crisis initially erupted in 2008–2009, it was essentially concentrated in the canyons of Wall Street owing to the blow-up of the securitization meth labs. In turn, these mishaps set off a contagion of falling prices for the dregs of the sliced and diced subprime mortgage pools and other dodgy assets held in investment bank inventories, of which Lehman held the most fetid collection.

These dubious assets had been accumulated during the housing and credit booms that the Fed had ignited after the dotcom crash. When soaring defaults on the underlying mortgages caused a sell-off of the securitized derivatives, the liquidation accelerated rapidly; and it was compounded by the Fed's folly of mechanically pegging and transparently telegraphing its money market (Fed funds) interest rate targets.

As was most egregiously apparent in the case of Lehman, this kind of Fed-supplied certainty about the near-term cost of overnight financing had encouraged Wall Street to recklessly fund these risky, sticky, longer-term mortgage, real estate, and junk bond assets with hideously mismatched liabilities. The latter had consisted heavily of hot, short-term money market instruments (unsecured commercial paper and overnight repo) that suddenly dried up in the summer of 2008, forcing dealers to dump even more toxic junk into the market.

Still, the fallout of the Wall Street crisis had initially penetrated Flyover America only obliquely. As indicated above, the latter was owing to the fact that the mortgage refi machine, which had been generating hundreds of billions of MEW-based middle-class spending, suddenly shut down.

Likewise, the predatory income production and housing activity generated in the mortgage broker boiler rooms, which peddled low-rate ARMS (adjustable-rate mortgages) to economically marginal households, also stopped cold. That was going to happen anyway, of course, because these marginal borrowers could not remotely hope to afford their subprime mortgages—once the ultra-low "teaser" rates reset and escalated sharply higher.

Both avenues of the housing boom came to a screeching halt when Wall Street melted-down in the fall of 2008, triggering what would otherwise have been a *mild housing-focused downturn*. But what transformed it into the so-called Great Recession's rout on main street was the corporate C-suite response to plunging stock prices in the fall and winter of 2008–2009.

By then the Fed's cancerous regime of Bubble Finance had turned the C-suites of corporate America into options-obsessed stock trading rooms and financial engineering joints. Almost instantly, a recession that was not even visible in the summer of 2008 to the Goldilocks worshiping economists of both Wall Street and Washington alike turned virulently south.

But the crash of business inventories and employment happened not for the classic reason that interest rates were soaring, and household and business credit was being crunched, but because the C-suites were desperately attempting to *propitiate the new trading gods of Wall Street in order to revive their battered stock prices.*

The sacrifices they offered consisted of sweeping so-called "restructuring" plans that amounted to shit-canning payrolls, inventories, facilities, and balance sheet assets with nearly reckless and frenzied abandon. During the brief eleven-month period after August 2008, more than *6 million* workers were tossed overboard and *$150 billion* of inventories or 10 percent of outstandings were hastily liquidated.

Even a superficial postmortem of the data shows that the Great Recession was a drastic over-reaction based on the underlying economics. Demand did not fall by anything close to what was implied by the C-suite initiated *Sturm und Drang* in response to the crash of their stock options.

But it was a godsend to the Keynesian money-pumpers at the Fed who had actually caused the subprime crash and Wall Street

Monthly Change in Inventories and Nonfarm Payrolls, August 2008 to July 2009.

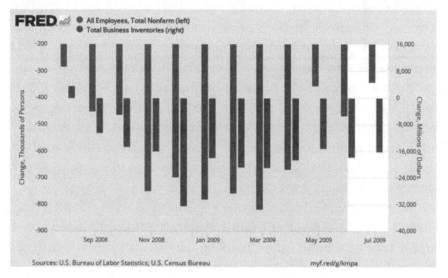

Sources: U.S. Bureau of Labor Statistics; U.S. Census Bureau   myf.red/g/kmpa

meltdown in the first place. Instead of finding themselves impaled on the hot seat of blame that they richly deserved, they swiftly turned the tables, morphing into putatively heroic economic firemen who saved the day.

Most especially, the C-suites' frenzied assault on their own employees, inventories, fixed capital, and other company operations permitted the phony Great Depression scholar and *inflationista* who had become Fed head, Professor Ben Bernanke, to run around Washington with his hair on fire.

So doing, he hysterically claimed that a reprise of the 1930s was at hand; and that extraordinary and heretofore unimaginable levels of monetary and fiscal intervention were needed to arrest a slide into Armageddon. He later even boasted that he alone had summoned the "courage to print" and had brought the rest of the government along kicking and screaming.

But the entire Bernanke-inspired narrative was unadulterated hogwash. The circumstances of 2008 were not remotely similar to those of 1930, most notably because back then America was a massive global creditor and exporter, which got monkey-hammered when the stock market crashed, and the related foreign subprime loan bubble of the day had imploded. The latter was immense, exceeding $1.5 trillion in today's economic scale.

This foreign bond market crash caused overseas demand for what had been booming US exports to crater by 80 percent, because these purchases of US goods had been financed on the margin in the New York bond market. In turn, the implosion of US exports triggered a sudden, violent plunge in previously soaring CapEx levels for what had been the urgently needed expansion of plant and equipment during the Roaring Twenties. This double whammy had further necessitated a genuine old-fashioned liquidation of excess inventories, fixed capital, labor and unsustainable bank credits after the 1929 crash.

In contrast, by 2008 America had already become a giant global debtor and importer. Washington was also a prodigious dispenser of Welfare State income and safety nets, as well as the principal financier of what had become massive domestic health care and education cartels.

Likewise, it had also become the fount of money for the nation's obscenely bloated war machine—a source of demand and economic activity that barely existed in 1930.

Accordingly, there was not a snowball's chance in the hot place that demand and domestic economic activity would have meaningfully declined owing to the liquidation of the Wall Street stock and bond bubble in the fall of 2008. Instead, massive spending for war, health care, education, retiree transfer payments, means-tested safety nets and much more, none of which existed in 1930, would have automatically proceeded apace. With these robust Welfare State and Warfare State shock absorbers in place, there was not even a remote risk that any modest main street adjustment to the overdue meltdown on Wall Street would have become a self-fueling depressionary spiral.

Bernanke's scary Great Depression 2.0 warnings, in fact, were really about the reciprocal of America's offshored economy—a Depression over there, not here. That's because the structure of the America's import-dependent and state spending-bloated economy in 2008 was upside-down from that of 1930: The "Hoovervilles" this time actually sprung-up amidst the time-immemorial poverty of the Chinese countryside.

That became apparent in the fall and winter of 2008–2009 when global production and trade swooned. In turn, that sent upwards of 100 million suddenly redundant Chinese migrant workers home from the closed-down export factories in eastern China to their family homes in the interior countryside.

But the pettifogging professor at the helm of the US central bank did not wait even a few weeks for the smoke in the canyons of Wall Street to clear after Lehman went down. Or for it to become obvious that the real recession was destined to happen in China, not the already burned-out precincts of Rust Belt America. So the Fed doubled-down into a frenzy of liquidity pumping that amounted to the financial policy crime of the century.

In early September 2008 the balance sheet of the Fed was *$905 billion,* and it had taken ninety-four years to get there from the day the Fed opened for business in 1914. Yet by early December after an insane frenzy of liquidity pumping the Fed's balance sheet stood at *$2.213 trillion.* So, in just *94 days* a run-of-the-mill Keynesian academic scribbler—who ended up on the Fed by accident because the political hatchet men around George W. Bush didn't trust Easy Al Greenspan to be easy enough (imagine that!) if electioneering so required—increased the Fed's balance sheet of plucked-from-thin-air liabilities by *145 percent more* than all his predecessors combined had done during the first *ninety-four years* of the Fed's existence.

And then, after the fact, this mountebank had the nerve to make the aforementioned boast. Actually, in printing fiat credit with reckless abandon, Bernanke had displayed something unusual—but it wasn't courage! It was arrogant monetary crack-pottery.

Bernanke's monetary crime was all the more breathtaking because it was utterly uncalled for. He and the former Dartmouth line-backer, Hank Paulson, who may or may not have worn a helmet in his collegiate football days, and who had been sent to Washington by Goldman Sachs to occupy the Secretary of Treasury's office, had single-handedly panicked Capitol Hill into

The Federal Reserve's 94-Day Balance Sheet Explosion, August to December 2008.

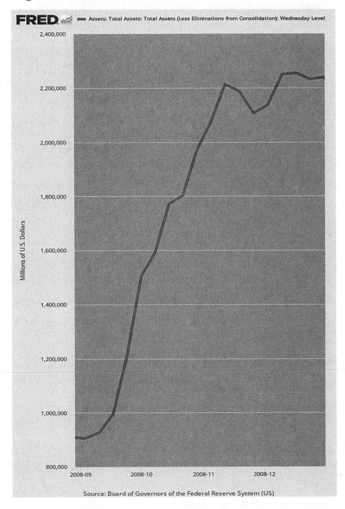

Source: Board of Governors of the Federal Reserve System (US)

resuscitating the TARP bailout after it had been courageously voted down by the House back-benchers.

In turn, the reckless act of passing a blank check $700 billion Wall Street bailout in early October 2008 further fueled the panic in the C-suites. So even more layoffs, inventory liquidations and "restructurings" ensued, and the Washington-generated Great Recession was off to the races.

Yet, save for the TARP-induced wave of fear, the C-suite panic would have otherwise quickly calmed down. And save for the insane flood of liquidity depicted above, the last remaining gambling houses on Wall Street—Merrill Lynch, Goldman Sachs, Morgan Stanley, and the Citigroup holding company—would have met their maker in the Chapter 11 courts. In turn, that would have enabled the meltdown in the canyons of Wall Street to burn-out in due course, with little spill-over to the main street economy and Flyover America.

As it happened, of course, the worst of both worlds transpired. The Washington TARP and the Fed's money pumping panic both made the Great Recession deeper and more painful than it need have been and also arrested in its tracks the liquidation of the Fed-fueled financial bubbles that had been gestating on Wall Street for more than three decades.

As indicated, the egregious reflation of the Fed-fostered asset bubbles permitted its stealth destruction of American capitalism to have an extended lease on life. That is, the Wall Street casino became red hot with reckless speculation and radical mispricing of stocks, bonds, securitized commercial real estate, and other financial assets confected by the same toxic waste labs which had brought on the home mortgage securitization fiasco.

So doing, it sucked the C-suites into even more systemic strip-mining of corporate cash flows, payrolls, investment accounts, and debt capacities in the service of financial engineering. That is, flushing cash back into Wall Street to goose stock prices and pad the value of executive stock options.

Consequently, upwards of *$15 trillion* of stock-buybacks, M&A deals and excessive dividends had pumped a tsunami of cash into the Wall Street gambling pits between 2009 and 2018. These flows, needless to say, did fuel the greatest risk asset bubble ever—even as it deeply eroded the vitality and growth capacity of the main street economy.

The Fed's decade long money-pumping spree after the 2008 meltdown also caused a "good crisis" to go to utter waste. In the immediate aftermath of the crisis, the C-suites had temporarily sobered up, sharply reducing financial engineering outlays for stock buybacks, M&A deals and dividends to a range of $500–700 billion per annum.

But year upon year of cheap debt and Fed price-keeping operations, which undergirded a relentlessly rising stock market, caused prudence to be thrown to the winds. Financial engineering outlays came roaring back, and during 2018 hit an off-the-charts $2.5 trillion. And that was especially thanks to The Donald's huge, red-inked funded corporate tax cuts.

Corporate Dividends, Share Buybacks, and Cash M&A Deals, 2010 to 2018.

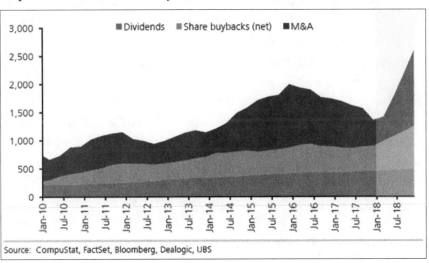

Source: CompuStat, FactSet, Bloomberg, Dealogic, UBS

Had Washington allowed Wall Street to undergo the bleeding cure it desperately needed in September 2008, the Everything Bubble would have been stopped in its tracks. And the condign justice of a Trumpified White House surely would not have materialized.

Instead, there would have been a decent opportunity for the politicians on both ends of Pennsylvania Avenue to discover that Keynesian monetary central planning was an unmitigated evil; and that the Fed's massive seizure of financial power after it was untethered from the Breton Woods gold standard by Nixon in 1971 needed to be thoroughly rescinded.

Under a shackled Fed, it is at least possible that its lunatic pursuit of domestic inflation—at no less than 2 percent per annum when deflation was called for by the competitive realities of the global economy—might have been abandoned. In turn, that might have encouraged the C-suites to get back to the business of building strong, growing, and fiercely competitive enterprises, rather than functioning as financial engineering joints devoted to the enrichment of top executives.

But that was the path not taken, and the crippling economic impairment and bifurcation of the US economy not only continued to gather force after the Lehman meltdown—it was actually intensified dramatically by the post-crisis spree of central bank money-pumping and sweeping financial asset price falsification.

This proposition bears repeating: The Fed's reckless money-printing is what put the final economic kibosh on Flyover America and thereby fostered the freakish election result of 2016. The Donald is well and truly Ben Bernanke's "gift" to America.

With a few exceptions, the lightly shaded areas of the electoral map below, representing the counties that The Donald won in 2016, are victims of the great de-industrialization wave that Washington fostered after 1971.

The economic hurt in these burned-out districts is attributable to the massive offshoring of production and jobs that occurred with malice aforethought after Greenspan thoroughly institutionalized Keynesian monetary central planning at the Fed in October 1987. This was especially true after Bernanke took it off the deep-end in response to the 2008 Wall Street meltdown.

Likewise, the sparsely scattered dark areas are overwhelmingly the beneficiaries of financialization, the casino-fueled asset inflations, and the tech and social media bubbles. They also thrive on the prodigious dispensations of America's vast Welfare State and the enormous defense, health care, and education cartels which are fed from the coffers of Imperial Washington.

In this context, The Donald's endless outbursts of economic illiteracy actually betrayed the "red" county voters. He never had a clue as to the central bank origins of the hurt and resentment he encountered in Flyover America. Nor did he proffer even a vague semblance of the policy measures that would be needed to rectify

"Red" States Speckled with a Smattering of "Blue"

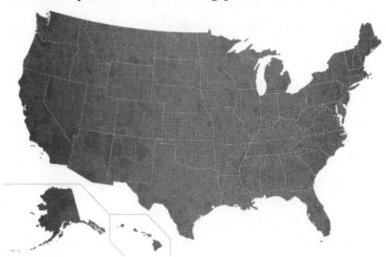

the damage and actually generate something which approximates MAGA.

Instead, The Donald simply promulgated a fake diagnosis and peddled it far and wide to the masses of Flyover America's red counties. Namely, that the cause of main street's economic decline was nefarious foreigners. By The Donald's telling, it was illegal immigrants flowing across the Mexican border and ill-paid Chinamen working for nought in the Red Ponzi's teeming export factories which had destroyed the American Dream and had stolen their once and former prosperity.

So his solution boiled down to Trade Wars and Border Wars. But no part of The Donald's diagnosis or solution was remotely true or appropriate, of course. Flyover America's prosperity was not destroyed by threats which arose from outside its borders; the whole baleful decline was fostered within the Great Washington Swamp itself.

That is, in the Warfare State complex, the bloated Welfare State, the domestic pork barrel network, the racketeering shops on K-Street, and most especially the Federal Reserve/Wall Street money axis.

The Donald thus never had a snowball's chance in hell of draining the swamp—let alone making America great again.

This should have been evident all along because from day one Trump lacked even a simulacrum of a program to rectify America's failing economy. Trump-O-Nomics wasn't even a policy, but just a slogan encompassing a dog's breakfast of populistic Trade Wars and Border Wars and about the worst combination of fiscal debauchery and monetary profligacy ever proposed.

The stock market boom that The Donald never stopped celebrating, therefore, wasn't even remotely the kind of well-considered endorsement that you can take to the bank. To the contrary, it was just one last rip of Wall Street's army of gullible speculators and momentum chasing robo-traders. The latter had been rewarded by central bank liquidity injections, financial repression, and price-keeping operations for so long that they could have probably gotten bulled-up on a plan to harvest green cheese from the far side of the moon.

In fact, what existed on the eve of the great Lockdown catastrophe in February 2020 on both main street and Wall Street were not endorsements of Trump's misbegotten policies and reckless palaver at all, but simply residual bubble momentum.

So in February 2020, the very idea of boasting about the data prints of a badly impaired 128-month-old business expansion and a speculation driven 135-month-old bull market smacked of rank egotism and stunning political naiveté. It was as if The Donald was joyfully carrying around a platter and inquiring about where exactly to place his head.

But when you are at the top of the longest business cycle in history in the context of an economy that was limping forward under an insuperable burden of $77 trillion of public and private debt and massive, destructive financial speculation, it is far past the time to be bragging about the current economy and the prosaic data flashing in the rearview mirror. But The Donald's 2020 SOTU address literally threw caution to the winds:

> Three years ago, we launched the great American comeback. Tonight, I stand before you to share the incredible results. Jobs are booming, incomes are soaring, poverty is plummeting, crime

is falling, confidence is surging, and our country is thriving and highly respected again. (Applause.) America's enemies are on the run, America's fortunes are on the rise, and America's future is blazing bright.

Needless to say, there is nothing strategic or even tactical about The Donald's foolish embrace of an aging stock market bubble and wizened economic cycle. It was just a glandular lurch—the impulsive action of an incorrigible megalomaniac grasping for anything which could be portrayed as a personal "win," including even dodgy successes (like the low U-3 unemployment rate) that were destined to implode at any moment in time.

In fact, the Trump Bubble—which The Donald had embraced with all fours—proved to be the most lunatic stock market mania of modern time. That is, until the Fed sired another, even greater bubble in response to The Donald lockdowns and massive stimmies after February 2020.

What kept the insane Trump Bubble going as long as it did, of course, was eleven years of embedded mental muscle memory in the casino. The latter held that buying the dip always—but always—resulted in a profitable gain.

And that was especially so if you were a Wall Street insider speculating with the various forms of carry trade leverage available in the options market or from the bespoke trading desks at Goldman and the other big gambling houses. Indeed, if you survived the plunge between the Lehman bankruptcy in September 2008 and the March 2009 bottom, there transpired literally fifty buyable dips in the years of fabulous riches which followed.

This one-way market, of course, was the malefic handiwork of the Fed and its global convoy of fellow-traveling Keynesian central bankers. Its extended run in financial fantasyland finally extinguished every remnant of fear in the casino.

Yet The Donald thought it was all his doing. That is, until the trading charts got eviscerated in March 2020 and the chart-monkeys went screeching out of the casino shortly thereafter.

*NASDAQ-100 Stock Index, June 2007
to February 2020.*

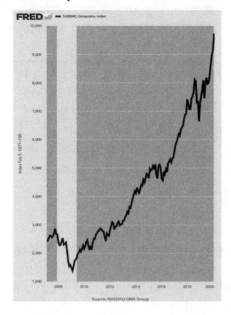

And yet, after demolishing the main street economy with sweeping lockdowns like never before in peacetime history, The Donald's insistent admonition to the Fed was to ignite yet another money flood, bigger and more destructive than ever before.

Indeed, the insane Fed money-printing of 2020 was the very hallmark of Trump's disastrous fourth year in the Oval Office. As it happened, no president has ever done so much damage to American capitalism in such a short period of time. Full stop.

Chapter Three

The Donald's Disastrous Fourth Year— But Don't Blame the Covid

The Donald's fourth year in the Oval Office was a disaster. The US economy literally collapsed after February 2020, but there is no way that Donald Trump gets a free hall pass for the Washington-instigated economic mayhem that transpired.

Trump's original sin was his whole-hearted embrace from the bully pulpit on March 16 of the "two weeks to flatten the curve" scheme, which was actually never about two weeks. It is now evident that Fauci's deputy came back from China in February 2020 singing the praises of its brutal lockdowns in Wuhan.

Consequently, Washington's incipient Virus Patrol was quickly assembled by Fauci et al. out of the bowels of the Deep State and set about imposing Chicom-style "non-pharmaceutical" policy interventions; that is, statist control schemes—across the length and breadth of America.

However, unlike any actual Republican who might have occupied the Oval Office at this crucial moment—even a RINO like George Bush Sr.—The Donald was constitutionally incapable of resisting the sweeping implementation and indefinite extension of Fauci's two-weeks ploy and the reason isn't hard to fathom. Trump was copacetic with these devastating assaults on personal liberty and private property because he accompanied them with massive fiscal and monetary relief and bailout measures. And while these egregious "stimmies" were an anathema to conservative doctrine, they were right up the middle of The Donald's philosophical fairway.

In fact, the record leaves no doubt that Trump never cared a whit about Federal spending and borrowing. Likewise, he had rarely, if ever, mentioned the words "liberty" and "limited government" in his entire adult life.

To the contrary, he had been a crude, anti-market protectionist since the 1970s and had an abiding fondness for easy money. After all, Donald Trump had literally gambled his way to (dubious) paper wealth in the real estate sector via massive accumulation of cheap debt fostered by the Fed after the mid-1990s. Without the Fed's printing press, in fact, The Donald would have never gotten out of Fred Trump's bailiwick in Queens, nor have remotely gained the opportunity to betray the GOP's core principles on Federal spending and borrowing.

As it happened, of course, Donald Trump had quickly blown his dad's fortune by the early 1990s on his New Jersey casino ventures and the Trump Shuttle, among other business failures. It was only the cheap money of Alan Greenspan and his heirs and assigns in the Eccles Building that rescued The Donald from a one-way trip to the bankruptcy courts, thereby eventually making possible his false claims to be a successful businessman who knew how to fix what ailed the American economy.

Indeed, it was this threadbare claim about his alleged business acumen that led to his freakish ascent to the Oval Office. And we do mean freakish, as in utterly unlikely.

Thus, after The Donald got out from under his casino disasters in 1995 and through 2016, the price of New York real estate rose by nearly 250 percent. At the same time, the inflation-adjusted cost of benchmark debt (ten-year UST) plunged from nearly 4.0 percent to barely 0.4 percent. So if you were speculating with tons of debt, what was not to like about the lowest interest rates that the world has ever seen for an extended period of time?

Indeed, The Donald became a rabid "low interest man" for no better reason than it had conferred upon him fabulous paper wealth for essentially doing nothing more than standing around the basket, building monuments with OPM (other people's money) to his own insatiable ego. So, he did learn something during 1995–2016—but it was the very opposite of what the GOP's historic sound money principles were based upon.

Index of New York Real Estate Prices versus Inflation-Adjusted Yield on 10-Year UST, 1995–2016.

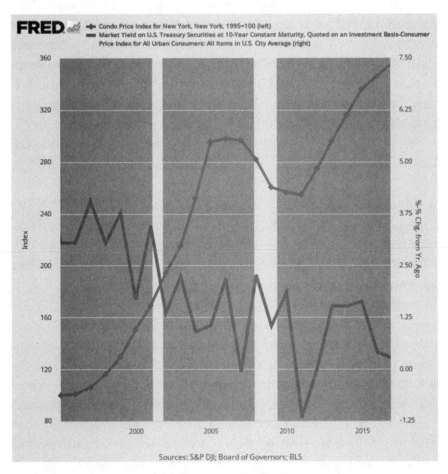

Sources: S&P DJI; Board of Governors; BLS

Artificially cheap debt, of course, is the mortal enemy of capital markets efficiency, productive investment on main street, and sustainable growth of middle-class prosperity and living standards. But it is also toxic to the financial culture, leading egomaniacal blowhards like Donald Trump to believe that they are economic geniuses.

Accordingly, "Trump-O-Nomics" was mostly about The Donald's ego-generated whims: tax cuts one day, spending boondoggles the next, a great Mexican Wall to keep out willing workers, and protectionist assaults on *"Chiiina"* for good measure.

Slaughtered in One Mighty Trumpian Fell Swoop

Consequently, in March 2020 The Donald was not about to see his "Greatest Economy Ever" go up in smoke, so he unhesitatingly embraced what should have been the unthinkable for any red-blooded conservative. To wit, what soon amounted to more than $6 trillion of Covid relief bailouts, $5 trillion of balance sheet expansion at the Fed, and hundreds of billions of government-ordered payment moratoriums for students, renters, mortgage borrowers, and other debtors.

In a word, after March 16, 2020 free market rules, personal liberty/responsibility and financial discipline got slaughtered in one mighty Trumpian fell swoop.

And there is no way that Donald Trump should be let off the hook, even for the last $2 trillion of this spending bacchanalia, which was ponied up by Joe Biden as the American Rescue Plan. After all, the heart of the Biden plan was completion of another $2,000 stimmy grant which had first been demanded by Trump himself in the run-up to the November election.

In a word, Trump-O-Nomics heavily mortgaged future taxpayers in order to buy-off what would otherwise have been a fierce political reaction to the lockdowns. Laid-off workers with a family of four, for instance, easily collected a total of $30,000 to $40,000 in stimmy checks, $600 per week unemployment toppers, child credits, and other tax breaks over the subsequent eighteen months. Likewise, nearly twelve million small businesses and self-employed entrepreneurs collected more than $800 billion in PPP (paycheck protection program) loans, of which $740 billion was forgiven!

And that's to say nothing of nearly $2 trillion of largesse which was parceled out to state and local governments, education institutions, health-care agencies, and non-profits of every way, shape and form. The amount of political acquiescence which was ulti-mately paid for with Uncle Sam's badly overdrawn credit card and the Fed's printing press money, therefore, was truly staggering. This financial bacchanalia involved orders of magnitude greater fiscal handouts and pork barrels than had ever before been dreamed about on the banks of the Potomac.

What this folly also did was drastically distort, misshape, and yo-yo the American economy in ways that will cause setbacks for years to come. And that disaster, which is the source of the present financial and economic turmoil, is the real legacy of Trump-O-Nomics.

In the meantime, the GOP needs to either throw in the towel on its traditional principles and just become the second "govern-ment party" or run like hell from Donald Trump and the baleful record they helped him compile during his term in office.

The Caesarist Danger in Plain Sight

We shouldn't mince words. Donald Trump is unfit for the Presidency (or any public office) because he is the ultimate Caesarist politician. He craves power in mega-doses purely for the satisfaction of his Brobdingnagian ego yet has virtually no policy principles that might constrain any lunge into state action that strikes his fancy.

As it has happened, today's stagflationary economic mess, shipwrecked central bank, and impending fiscal calamity are all the fruits of exactly that kind of Caesarist aggrandizement of the state. We are referring, of course, to Trump's disastrous final year in office when he endeavored to be the Great Man who vanquished the so-called Covid pandemic.

Indeed, that's how we got the hellacious lockdowns, quaran-tines, public hysteria, mask mandates, and foolhardy stampede into forced mass injections of an unproven and evidently unsafe vaccine.

To be sure, all of this Covid-fighting mayhem was cooked up by Deep State apparatchiks led by Dr. Fauci and Dr. Brix. But they got turned loose on the American economy and public only because The Donald latched onto their misbegotten schemes to "stop the spread" as an opportunity for the Great Man in the Oval Office to rescue the nation from an alleged existential threat to society.

Except, Covid wasn't a black plague at all and didn't merit extraordinary Federal intervention. Any even moderately principled conservative could have found plenty of evidence for that truth in February and March 2020 when the lockdowns and public hysteria were being unleashed.

In the first place, conservative principles would have strongly militated against even consideration of a coercive one-size-fits-all, state-driven mobilization of quarantines, lockdowns, testing, masking, distancing, surveilling, snitching, and ultimately mandated mass vaxxing. That would have been the last resort option, meaning that it would have taken overwhelming evidence of a black plague style nightmare to even table these totalitarian actions.

At the same time, the parallel excuse that "the staff made me do it" doesn't let him off the hook, either. If Donald Trump had possessed even a minimal regard for constitutional liberties and free market principles, he would never have green-lit Dr Fauci and his Virus Patrol and the resulting tyranny they erected virtually overnight. And most especially he would not have tolerated their continuing assaults as the lockdowns dragged on for weeks and months.

In this context, the one thing we learned during our days in the vicinity of 1600 Pennsylvania Avenue is that any president, at any moment in time, and with respect to any issue of public import, can call on the best experts in the nation, including those who might disagree with each other vehemently.

Yet in the early days of the pandemic—when the Virus Patrol's terrible regime was being launched—The Donald was either a willing participant or negligently passive. He made no effort at all to consult experts outside of the narrow circle of power-hungry government apparatchiks (Fauci, Birx, Collins, Adams) who were paraded into the Oval Office by his dilettantish son-in-law and knucklehead vice president.

From the very beginning of the pandemic, in fact, there were legions of pedigreed epidemiologists and other scientists like professors John Ioannidis of Stanford, Martin Kulldorff of Harvard, Sunetra Gupta of Oxford, Jay Bhattacharya of Stanford, Harvey Risch of Yale and Scott Atlas of the Hoover Institute, among countless others, who strongly opposed the lockdown and the sweeping set of public health interventions which accompanied it. Yet only Dr. Atlas made it to the vicinity of the Oval Office, and then for just a few months after August 2020 when the die was already cast.

Many of these dissenting experts later signed the Great Barrington Declaration in October 2020, which correctly held that viruses cannot be extinguished via draconian quarantines and other clumsy one-size-fits-all public health interventions.

From day one, therefore, the logical course was to allow the virus to spread its own natural immunity among the public at large, and to focus available resources on the small minority that owing to age, compromised immune systems, or comorbidities were vulnerable to severe illness.

The ultimate evidence for this proposition is that among the 4.8 million Israelis who had tested positive for the Covid thru May 2023, there has *not been a single Covid death* in the population under fifty years of age who did not have pre-existing comorbidities. Not one!

The crucial significance of this stunning fact— validated by Israeli public health authorities—cannot be gainsaid. It is flat-out impossible to claim a black plague style emergency when not a single healthy person under fifty years of age in an entire nation actually succumbed to the disease. And we are talking about a country that sits at the crossroads of human civilization, not New Zealand, stranded all by its lonesome out in the far Pacific.

In fact, that the Covid was not remotely a black plague style threat was known from the earliest days. In addition to decades of scientific knowledge about the proper management of virus-based pandemics, there existed the screaming real-time evidence from the stranded Diamond Princess cruise ship. The 3,711 souls (2,666 passengers and 1,045 crew) aboard skewed heavily to the elderly, but the survival rate known in mid-March 2020 was *99.7 percent* overall, and *100 percent* for those under seventy years of age.

That's right. As of March 10, 2020, shortly before The Donald elected to impose Chicom-style lockdowns on American society, the ship had already been quarantined for a month and 3,618 passengers and crew had been systematically tested and tracked multiple times.

Among that population, 696 or 19 percent had tested positive for Covid, but 410 or nearly three-fifths of these were asymptomatic. Among the 8 percent (286) who became ill, the overwhelming share were only mildly symptomatic. At that point, just seven passengers—all over seventy years old—had died, a figure which grew only slightly in the months ahead.

In short, just *0.19 percent* of an elderly skewed population had succumbed to the virus. These facts, which were known to the White House or certainly should have been, made absolutely clear that the Covid was no black plague type threat. In the great scheme of history, Donald Trump authorized lockdowns which amounted to tearing up the constitution and ripping apart daily economic life for a public health matter that did not remotely approach the status of an existential threat to society's survival.

To the contrary, from the beginning it was evident to independent scientists that the Covid-19 spread was an intensive but manageable challenge to America's one-at-a-time doctor/patient health-care system. The CDC, FDA, NIH, and state and local public health departments were only needed to dispense solid information per their normal education role, not to promulgate orders and sweeping regulatory interventions into every nook and cranny of the nation's economic and social life.

So, the buck stops with Donald Trump because he could have ended this regulatory carnage at any moment, including before it was actually launched. Unfortunately, basic conservative political philosophy and Donald Trump had never chanced to become acquainted.

The Donald is and always has been a raw power seeker aiming to satisfy his own gargantuan ego on the stage of public office. When it comes to policy choices, he's an agnostic who just flies by the seat of his ample britches, with an ear keenly cocked for the sound of applause from the MAGA peanut gallery.

Thus, as late as March 9, when Birx, Fauci, and his feckless son-in-law were pressing hard for the emergency declaration and lockdowns, Trump apparently had not yet heard the roar of the crowds. So, he tweeted that there was nothing to see with respect to the Covid-19:

> So last year 37,000 Americans died from the common Flu. It averages between 27,000 and 70,000 per year. Nothing is shut down, life & the economy go on. At this moment there are 546 confirmed cases of CoronaVirus, with 22 deaths. Think about that!

Apparently, he took his own advice and rethought the entire matter virtually overnight. Two days later, on March 11, he was singing an entirely opposite tune, tweeting that he was prepared to go to war against the virus.

> I am fully prepared to use the **full power** of the Federal Government to deal with our current challenge of the CoronaVirus!

So doing, however, The Donald chose an immensely destructive route that compounded the harm wrought by these sweeping public health interventions. Trump unleashed the Virus Patrol's boot heels on the American public on March 16, and then immediately embraced a fiscal and monetary *compensation strategy* that in essence said, "shut it down, lock them up, pay them off."

In fact, in a tweet on March 18—just two days after he launched sweeping lockdowns across the nation—The Donald made the linkage abundantly clear:

> For the people that are now out of work because of the important and necessary containment policies, for instance the shutting

down of hotels, bars and restaurants, **money will soon be coming to you.** The onslaught of the Chinese Virus is not your fault! Will be stronger than ever!

From that point on it was Katie-bar-the-door when it came to shutting down the economy and social life and curtailing personal freedom and property rights. Yet Trump's public health ukase was belied by the facts on the ground from the very beginning.

The Six Nations of Covid

The figures below reflect "WITH-COVID" fatality rates by age cohort through December 31, 2020. Accordingly, they betray no distortions from vaccination rate differentials which may have impacted the numbers thereafter.

We have labeled these age cohorts the Six Nations of Covid. From practically day one—April 2020—the CDC published these age cohort–based statistics on a weekly basis, and the relative mortality rates per 100,000 among the six groups never really changed.

That is to say, the risk of death was approximately *9,300x* higher for the Great Grandparents Nation during the ten months of the pandemic in 2020 than for the School Age Nation. Likewise, the Grandparents Nation risk of death WITH-COVID was *288x* higher than that of the Socializing Nation (age fifteen to twenty-four) and *15x* higher than that of the Core Working Age Nation (age twenty-five to fifty-four).

These differentials are so flagrantly extreme as to debunk in one fell swoop the "one size fits all" predicate of the Trumpian lockdowns and related universal social control interventions. In effect, Donald Trump's public health version of martial law took the entire population hostage for the ineffectual protection of the few.

Moreover, these same ratios were embedded in the weekly data as early as the second half of April and May 2020. To anyone who bothered to examine "the science," they literally trumpeted that the Trump lockdowns were dead wrong and needed to be abandoned forthwith. The evidence was always there in plain sight, week after week during The Donald's disastrous fourth year.

WITH-COVID Mortality Rate per 100,000 as of December 31, 2020
- School Age Nation (60.9 million age 0–14): *0.2.*
- Socializing Nation (43.0 million age 15–24): 1.4.
- Core Working Age Nation (128.6 million age 25–54): 21.0.
- Near Retirement Nation (42.3 million age 55–64): 105.5.
- Grandparents Nation (45.9 million age 65–84): 402.7.
- Great Grandparents Nation (6.5 million age 85 years+): *1856.1.*

As time went on, the one-size-fits-all strategy fostered by the Trump Administration became increasingly ludicrous in light of the evidence. The idea of closing gyms, malls, movies, bars, sports arenas, restaurants, and other social venues disproportionately frequented by young people was especially mocked by reality.

For instance, from a population of 43.0 million for the fifteen to twenty-four age cohort there had been just *602* deaths WITH-COVID as of December 31, 2020, which was just 12 percent of the *4,912* deaths from homicide alone, which are recorded for this cohort on an annual basis during an ordinary year.

So it was not only not rational but a sign of pure derangement to be closing classrooms and quarantining students in their millions based on WITH-COVID mortality rates that were inconsequential when compared to the ordinary hazards of life. For instance, the WITH-COVID mortality rate of 1.4 per 100,000 was below the rates for notable but rare diseases among this age cohort, such as the 3.2 deaths per 100,000 due to cancer and 2.2 per 100,000 due to heart diseases.

The fact is, the three leading causes of death in the fifteen to twenty-four years old cohort in a typical year are traffic and other accidents, suicides, and homicides. Each of these result in mortality rates vastly higher than the Covid rates of 2020. And for all three categories combined, the normal year-in and year-out mortality rate of *52.7* per 100,000 is *38x higher* than the WITH-COVID figure.

Mortality Rate per 100,000, 15–24 Years Cohort:
- WITH-COVID: *1.4.*
- Homicide: 11.4.
- Suicide: 14.5.
- Auto & other accidents: 31.3.
- Total homicide, suicide & accidents: *52.7.*

To be sure, the proper solution of defaulting to laissez-faire at colleges and universities elicited a shrieked "Killer Campus" charge from the Virus Patrol at the time, but that was always nonsense. Gram and Gramps didn't need to attend homecoming weekend if they believed themselves vulnerable and the grandkids could have taken a Covid test before showing up for Christmas dinner with them. And the same goes for the parents, who were at a fraction of the risk faced by grandparents and great-grandparents.

As to the canard that infected students would have brought Covid home to their parents, despite most likely being asymptomatic, any kind of rational risk assessment said otherwise. Indeed, the risk of death to parents from Covid-19 brought home by students during Thanksgiving weekend was among the least of the risk factors faced by the thirty-five to fifty-four age cohort, ranking only slightly above suicide/homicide.

Mortality Rates for the 35–54 Age Cohort:
- Cancers 60.5 per 100,000.
- Accidents: 57.0 per 100,000.
- Heart disease: 51.9 per 100,000.
- *WITH-COVID: 30.0 per 100,000.*
- Suicide/homicide: 17.8 per 100,000.

Sweden versus Australia Tells It All

We are now forty-two months on from the Donald's foolish empowerment of Dr. Fauci and his Virus Patrol in mid-March 2020, and all doubt has been removed. If there were two countries on planet Earth which had diametrically opposite policy approaches with respect to the Covid, it was Australia, which degenerated into an outright public health tyranny, and Sweden, where officials kept their minds open to the facts and social institutions—schools, churches, shops, theaters, malls, factories, etc.—open to the public.

The graph below, which charts the incidence of confirmed Covid cases on a *cumulative basis,* tell you all you need to know: Namely, that lockdowns and other draconian social control and quarantine measures can temporarily suppress the spread—essentially by extinguishing human social interaction entirely—but cannot keep the genie in the bottle indefinitely.

Thus, as of November 26, 2021, Sweden had recorded 114,000 confirmed "cases" per million people versus just 8,000 per million in Australia, leading the Covidians to say, "We told you so!"

The answer, of course, was not so fast. Either the province of New South Wales and other heavily populated regions of Australia were going to remain outdoor prisons forever, or the lockdowns would eventually be lifted, and the virus would do what respiratory viruses do—spread among most of the population. And fast.

That's exactly what happened, and barely two years later the results were crystal clear. The cumulative rate of cases per million in Australia soared by *55x* to 440,000 during the next six hundred days!

By contrast, the cumulative case rate in both the US and Sweden barely doubled during that period, since the vulnerable population had long since been exposed, infected, and (overwhelmingly) cured.

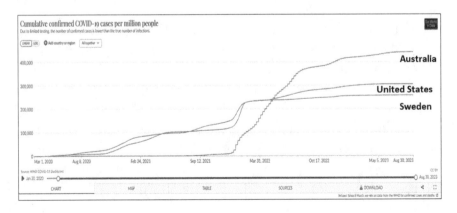

Moreover, it's not as if the late eruption of cases in Australia was owing to the nation being suddenly overrun with anti-vaxxers. That's assuming that the vaccines, as promised, actually stop the spread, which they do not.

Still, the evidence shows that Australia led the vaccination rate parade, as well. As of March 2023, it had administered 250 doses per 100 people or slightly more than the 240 doses per 100 in Sweden and 202 in the US.

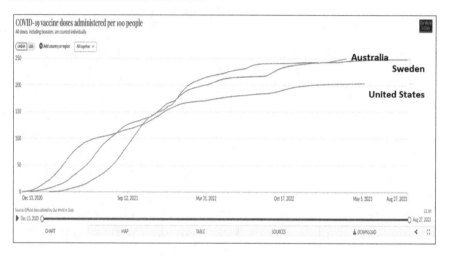

Another perspective is available via the excess death statistics. The chart below tracks deaths from all causes per million population compared to projections based on the most recent pre-Covid years and accumulates the difference or "excess" for the entire period between March 2020 and July 2023.

As it happened, the rate of excess deaths for Sweden at *1,435* per million was just two-fifths of that for the United States (3,740 per million) and also dramatically below that for most other European countries, all of whom had far more draconian public health control regimes than Sweden.

But don't tell Donald Trump. From day one, he loudly denounced Sweden for abjuring lockdowns and allowing personal freedom to reign. On April 30, 2020, The Donald tweeted his culpable state of mind in no uncertain terms:

Despite reports to the contrary, Sweden is paying heavily for its decision not to lockdown. As of today, 2462 people have died there a much higher number than the neighboring countries of Norway (207), Finland (206) or Denmark (443). **The United States made the correct decision!**

Of course, cancelling the liberty and taking the property of the people wasn't the President's decision to make. The authors of the Constitution had settled that 233 years earlier.

Then again, The Donald had never learned anything about the limits of governance under a constitutional republic nor the science that long before April 30th had established that the Covid was no black plague and that suspending the US constitution was utterly unjustified. The chart below leaves no doubt that Donald Trump's foolishness in bringing the lockdowns upon the American people cannot be excused or forgiven.

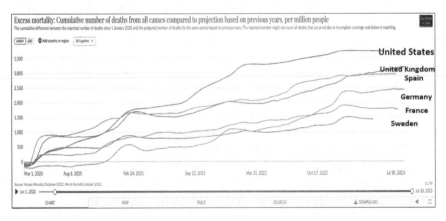

Of course, the flaws in the insane tsunami of numbers about tests, case counts, hospital counts, death counts, and heart-rending anecdotes about individual suffering and loss are now more than evident. But the single most important thing to grasp is that when it comes to the heart of the narrative—the alleged soaring death counts—the narrative is just plain bogus.

The undisputed fact is that the CDC changed rules for causation on death certificates in March 2020, so now we have no idea whatsoever whether the 1.1 million deaths reported to date were deaths *OF* Covid or just incidentally were departures from this mortal coil *WITH* Covid. The extensive well-documented cases of hospital DOAs from heart attacks, gunshot wounds, strangulation, or motorcycle accidents, which had tested positive before the fatal event or by postmortem, are proof enough.

More importantly, what we do know is that not even the power-drunk apparatchiks at the CDC and other wings of the federal public health apparatus found a way to change the total mortality counts from all causes.

That's the smoking gun unless you consider the year 2003 to have been an unbearable year of extraordinary death and societal misery in America, to wit: the age-adjusted death rate from all causes in America during 2020 was actually *1.8 percent lower* than it had been in 2003 and nearly *11 percent lower* than it had been during what has heretofore been understood to be the benign year of 1990!

To be sure, there was a slight elevation of the all-causes mortality rate in 2020 relative to the immediately preceding years. That's because the Covid did disproportionately and in some ghoulish sense harvest the immunologically vulnerable elderly and co-morbid slightly ahead of the Grim Reaper's ordinary schedule.

And far worse, there were also extraordinary deaths in 2020 among the less Covid-vulnerable population owing to hospitals that were in government ordered turmoil; and also due to an undeniable rise in human malfunction among the frightened, isolated, home-bound quarantined population, which resulted in a swelling of homicides, suicides, and a record level of deaths from drug overdoses (94,000).

Still, the commonsense line of sight across the thirty-year chart below tells you one-thousand times more than the context-free case and death counts which scrolled across America's TV and computer screens day in and day out, even as The Donald's Task Force was fanning the flames of hysteria from the White House bully pulpit.

In short, the data below tells that there was no deadly plague; there was no extraordinary public health crisis; and that the Grim Reaper was not stalking the highways and byways of America.

Compared to the pre-Covid norm recorded in 2019, the age-adjusted risk of death in America during 2020 went up from *0.71 percent* to *0.84 percent*. In humanitarian terms, that's unfortunate but it does not even remotely bespeak a mortal threat to societal function and survival and therefore a justification for the sweeping control measures and suspensions of both liberty and common sense that actually happened.

This fundamental mortality fact—the "science" in bolded letters if there is such a thing—totally invalidates the core notion behind the Fauci policy that was sprung upon our deer-in-the-headlights president stumbling around the Oval Office in early March 2020.

In a word, this chart proves that the entire Covid strategy was wrong and unnecessary. Lock, stock, and barrel. And with regard to the Covid-Lockdown disaster, Harry Truman's famous "buck," in fact, stops unequivocally with Donald J. Trump.

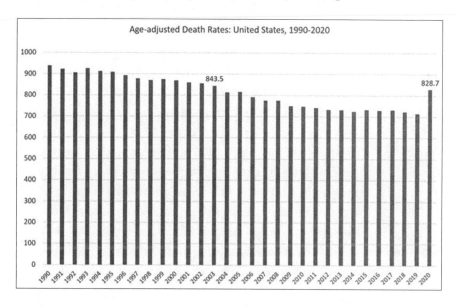

Age-adjusted Death Rates: United States, 1990-2020

There was never any reason for sweeping intervention by the public health apparatus at all. Nor for the coercive one-size-fits all, state-driven mobilization of quarantines, lockdowns, testing, masking, distancing, surveilling, snitching, and ultimately mandated mass vaxxing. In fact, the experimental drugs developed on a reckless pell-mell basis under The Donald's multi-ten-billion-dollar government subsidy scheme called Operation Warp Speed represented what was probably the most insidious statist measure of all. By design the program was intended to stop the disease cold via 100 percent mandatory mass vaccination after a radically foreshortened testing period that could not possibly have proven either the safety or efficacy of the jabs.

Yet there is no mystery as to why The Donald enabled the Fauci-fostered calamity that ensued; he possessed no principles to suggest otherwise and saw it as an opportunity to earn glory and acclaim through muscular generalship of a Washington-led war on the virus.

So yes, at the end of the day, a Caesarist politician is the handmaid of Leviathan. Donald Trump proved that in spades during his first term, and now the nation's rickety economic and fiscal foundation is in no condition to chance another such eruption of statist mayhem in the future.

Indeed, it should never be forgotten that the bully pulpit is a dangerous thing, especially when it is within the grasp of an egomaniacal demagogue who craves the spotlight. That is the real lesson of Donald Trump's anti-Covid crusade.

No Evil Hand

It would not be going too far to say that the eruption of irrationality and hysteria that Trump triggered during his final year in office most resembled not 1954, when Senator McCarthy set the nation looking for communist moles behind every government desk, or 1919, when the notorious raids of Attorney General Mitchell were rounding up purported Reds in their tens of thousands, but the winter of 1691–1692.

That's when two little girls—Elizabeth Parris and Abigail Williams of Salem, Massachusetts—fell into the demonic activity of fortune-telling, which soon found them getting strangely ill, having fits, spouting gibberish, and contorting their bodies into odd positions.

The rest became history, of course, when a local doctor specializing in malpractice claimed to have found no physical cause for the girls' problems and diagnosed them being afflicted by the "Evil Hand," commonly known as witchcraft. Within no time, three witches were famously accused, and as the hysteria spread, hundreds more were tried for witchcraft and two dozen hanged.

Yet there is a lesson in this classic tale that is embarrassing in its verisimilitude. Namely, one of the best academic explanations for the outbreak of seizures and convulsions which fueled the Salem hysteria was a disease called "convulsive ergotism," which is brought on by ingesting rye infected with a fungus that can invade developing kernels of the grain, especially under warm and damp conditions.

During the rye harvest in Salem in 1691, these conditions had existed at a time when one of the Puritans' main diet staples was cereal and breads made of the harvested rye. Convulsive ergotism causes violent fits, a crawling sensation on the skin, vomiting, choking, and hallucinations—meaning that it was Mother Nature in the ordinary course working her episodically unwelcome tricks, not the "Evil Hand" of a spiritual pathogen, which imperiled the community.

The truth is, the witchcraft of Dr. Fauci notwithstanding, it was also Mother Nature in 2020—likely abetted by the Fauci-sponsored gain-of-function researchers at the Wuhan Institute of Virology—which disgorged one of the nastier among ordinary respiratory viruses. Such viruses, of course, have afflicted humankind over the ages, which, in turn, has evolved marvelous adaptive immune systems to cope with and overcome them.

So, as in 1691, there was no Evil Hand or sci-fi pathogen at large, nor a disease that was extraordinarily lethal for 95 percent of the population. The ordinary daily economic and social life of Americans didn't need to be tried and put to the gallows. That was Donald Trump's great mistake and there is no pardon for the crime of it.

In the great scheme of things, however, the Covid-19 pandemic has now already been proven to be merely an unfortunate bump on the road to longer and more pleasant lives for Americans and much of the rest of the world, too.

While the all-cause mortality figure for 2020 shown above did not exist when the CDC published the chart below, the descending line would have depicted it as only a tiny upward blip—of which there have been several during the last 120 years shown below, most notably the Spanish Flu episode of 1918–1919.

Yet even then, the US age-adjusted death rate (lighter, lower line) in 2020 of 828 per 100,000 was actually *67 percent* lower than it had been in 1918 (2,542 per 100,000) because since that time a free capitalist society has gifted the nation with the prosperity and freedom to progress that has ushered in better sanitation, nutrition, shelter, lifestyles, and medical care.

It is those forces which have pushed the age-adjusted mortality rate relentlessly to the lower-right corner of the chart, not the Federales atop their bureaucratic perches in Washington.

It is telling that Donald Trump has never even remotely grasped that basic truth.

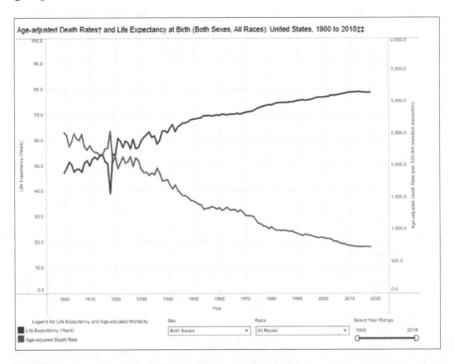

Age-adjusted Death Rates† and Life Expectancy at Birth (Both Sexes, All Races): United States, 1900 to 2018‡‡

Chapter Four

A Big Spender's League All of His Own

A s it happened, the US Congress acted like greased lightning, enacting the $2.2 trillion CARES act virtually sight unseen just eleven days after The Donald's March 16 press conference initiated the Covid lockdowns. The bill was over eight hundred pages long and included a more ostentatious cornucopia of spending authorities and free stuff than had ever before been imagined in even the most profligate quarters of Capitol Hill. This tsunami of money amounted to roughly $6,000 for every man, woman, and child in America, or 45 percent of all federal government expenditures in 2019.

The money was literally shoveled into the US economy in massive dollops with virtually no eligibility standards, qualification processes, and enforcement/accountability procedures. This included:

- $425 billion for the Federal Reserve to support business loans and bailouts.
- $75 billion for direct subsidies to airlines and other industries.
- $350 billion to launch what became the notoriously corrupt SBA-operated Paycheck Protection Program (PPP for small businesses).

- $300 billion to fund checks amounting to $3,400 per family of four, going to approximately 90 percent of the US population.
- $250 billion mainly for the $600 per week unemployment insurance benefit on top of normal state program benefits averaging $355 per week.
- $150 billion in walking-around money for state, local, and tribal governments.
- $140 billion for a sweeping, open-ended array of public health programs.
- Tens of billions more in special interest pork of every kind, shape, and purpose.

Not surprisingly, The Donald did not hesitate to take credit for this grotesque act of fiscal malfeasance:

> We are marshalling the full power of government and society to achieve victory over the virus. Together, we will endure, we will prevail, and we will WIN! #CARESAct

Signing Ceremony for The Most Grotesque Act of Fiscal Malfeasance in American History.

The budgetary outcomes were truly astounding—especially when the second Covid Relief bill signed by The Donald in December 2020 and its extension and companion, Biden's American Rescue Act enacted in March 2021, are added to the total. In all, Washington enacted $6.5 trillion of Covid-relief measures in barely 365 days. This figure was nearly 50 percent larger than the entire federal budget—defense, social security, education, Medicare/Medicaid, interest and all the rest—in the pre-Covid year of 2019.

That's right. Trump ignited a grotesque outbreak of fiscal recklessness far worse than anything GOP orators had inveighed against since the time of FDR. And much of this spending eruption was recorded in the government data series for personal transfer payments. The latter is posted monthly and at annualized rates, thereby capturing in real time the impact of Trump's fiscal cyclone ripping through the US economy.

The annualized run rate of government transfer payments, including the state and local supplemental portions, posted at a normal level of *$3.15 trillion* in February 2020. So that's the pre-Covid baseline. But after the sight-unseen $2.2 trillion CARES act was enthusiastically signed into law by The Donald in late March, it erupted to a *$6.42 trillion* annualized rate in April.

Thereafter a second wave surged the transfer payment rate to *$5.682 trillion* in January 2021 when the second relief act was signed by The Donald in December, followed by a final burst at an annualized rate to *$8.098 trillion* in March 2021 owing to Biden's American Rescue Act.

But even in the case of the latter, the driving force was completion of the $2,000 per person stimmy that The Donald had advocated in the run-up to the election, which had been only partially funded in the December legislation. And this stimmy completion came along with extension of unemployment toppers and other expenditures that had been originated in the two earlier Trump-signed measures.

This was the very worst kind of government spending explosion imaginable. That's because transfer payments are inherently inflationary poison when they are funded by new government debt which, in turn, is monetized (purchased) by the Fed, as these

clearly were. This kind of regime of spend, borrow, and print powerfully gooses demand without adding an iota to supply.

Ironically, therefore, Trump-O-Nomics was the epitome
of anti-supply side. It was a stark repudiation of the theory of
Reaganomics, and far, far worse in its practical impact on federal
spending and deficits than the accidental ballooning of the public
debt on the Gipper's watch.

None of this fiscal madness, of course, would have been even
remotely plausible without the utterly unnecessary lockdowns.
Even then, however, no real Republican would have signed legislation authorizing such massive transfer payments if they were to
be funded exclusively with borrowing and money-printing.

The Donald did so, of course, and there is no mystery as to why.
Trump has no fiscal policy compass at all. So, it was a good way
to quiet what otherwise would have been a fatal political uprising
against the public health martial law that his administration had
imposed during an election year.

That's the real irony of the story. When it comes to the core
matter of fiscal discipline, The Donald was no disrupter at all. He

Annualized Rate of Government Transfer Payments, 2017 to 2021.

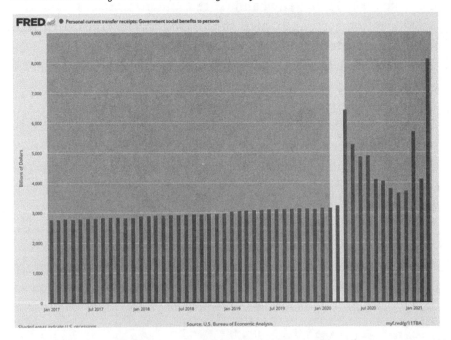

was actually the worst of the lot among the last half-century of Washington spenders, and by a long shot, too.

For avoidance of doubt, here is a longer-term perspective, reflecting the year-over-year rate of change in government transfer payments going back to 1970. That was shortly after the Great Society legislation had kicked off today's $4 trillion per year flood of transfers.

To appreciate the veritable fiscal shock that issued from The Donald's pen, it needs be noted that in the last quarter of 2019 the Y/Y *gain* in government transfer payment spending was about *$150 billion*, which was consistent with the longer-term trend.

However, by Q1 2021 that Y/Y *gain* had soared to *$4.9 trillion*. Again, that was the delta, not the absolute level. That is to say, the year-over-year gain from The Donald's Covid Relief Bacchanalia was *33x* larger than the pre-Covid norm!

And, no, you can't blame this inflationary time-bomb solely on Biden as the MAGA partisans insist, although Biden would surely have signed the two early COVID-bailout measures had he been in The Donald's shoes during 2020.

But that's just the point—The Donald is a paid-up member of the Washington uniparty when it comes to government spending. All of the hideous excesses of the Covid bailouts were launched on his watch, signed into law with his pen, and/or legitimized with the imprimatur of an ostensible Republican president. The American Rescue Act was just the final installment of Trump's unhinged Covid spend-a-thon.

After all, the overwhelming share of the $6.5 trillion of Covid spending consisted of $2,000+ stimmy checks to 90 percent of the public, the $600 per week unemployment toppers, the massive Payroll Protection Program (PPP) giveaways, and the flood of money into the health, education, local government, and non-profit sectors. Every one of these items was blessed by The Donald twice before Sleepy Joe reclaimed these measures as the Dem big spenders' apostasies that they actually were.

Needless to say, the Covid bailouts were not The Donald's only fiscal sin. When you compare the constant dollar growth rate of total federal spending during his four years in the Oval Office

Trump Shoots the Moon: Y/Y Change in Government Transfer Payments, 1970–2021.

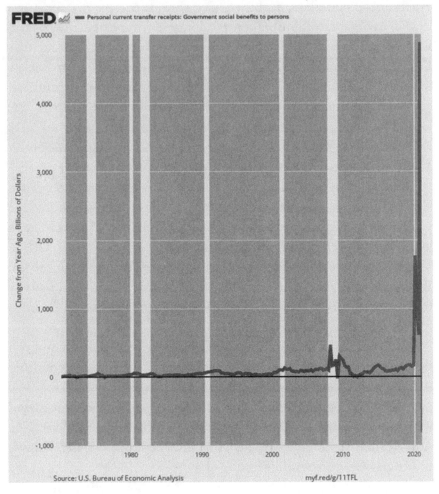

Source: U.S. Bureau of Economic Analysis   myf.red/g/11TFL

with that of his recent predecessors, it is evident that The Donald was in a big spender's league all of his own.

In *constant 2021 dollars*, for instance, the federal budget grew by *$366 billion* per annum on The Donald's watch, a level *quadruple* the big spending years of Barack Obama, and nearly *11x* higher than during the 1993–2000 period under Bill Clinton.

Federal Spending: Constant 2021 Dollar Increase Per Year:

- Trump, 2017–2020: *+$366 billion per annum.*

- Obama, 2009–2016: +$86 billion per annum.
- George Bush the Younger, 2001–2008: +$136 billion per annum.
- Bill Clinton, 1993–2000: +$34 billion per annum.
- George Bush the Elder, 1989–1992: +$97 billion per annum.
- Ronald Reagan, 1981–1988: +$64 billion per annum.
- Jimmy Carter, 1977–1980: +$62 billion per annum.

The same story holds for the annual *growth rate* of inflation-adjusted federal spending. At *6.92 percent* per annum during Trump's sojourn in the Oval Office it was 2x to 4x higher than under all of his recent predecessors.

At the end of the day, the historical litmus test of GOP economic policy was restraint on government spending growth, and therefore curtailment of the relentless expansion of the Leviathan-on-the-Potomac. But when it comes to that standard, The Donald's record stands first among no equals on the wall of shame.

Federal Spending: Annual Real Growth Rate:
- Trump, 2016–2020: *6.92 percent.*
- Obama, 2008–2016: 1.96 percent.
- George Bush the Younger: 3.95 percent.
- Bill Clinton, 1992–2000: 1.19 percent.
- George Bush the Elder: 3.90 percent.
- Ronald Reagan, 1980–1988: 3.15 percent.
- Jimmy Carter, 1976–1980: 3.72 percent.

Likewise, when it comes to ballooning federal deficits and public debt, Donald Trump earned his sobriquet as the King of Debt and then some. Relative to the nation's economic base, the average of The Donald's four deficits at *9.0 percent* of GDP was literally off-the-charts of modern presidential history.

Average Surplus/Deficit as Percent of GDP Under Post-War Presidents (fiscal years):
- Truman (1947–1953): *+0.73 percent.*

- Eisenhower (1954–1961): -0.37 percent.
- Kennedy-Johnson (1962–1969): -0.88 percent.
- Nixon-Ford (1970–1977): -.2.38 percent.
- Carter (1978–1981): -2.33 percent.
- Reagan-Bush (1982–1993): -4.13 percent.
- Clinton (1994–2001): -0.13 percent.
- George W. Bush (2002–2009): -3.31 percent.
- Obama (2010–2017): -4.98 percent.
- Trump (2018–2021)*: -9.00 percent.*

Similarly, in inflation-adjusted terms (constant 2021 dollars), The Donald's ***$2.04 trillion*** per annum add-on to the public debt amounted to double the fiscal profligacy of the Obama years, and orders of magnitude more than the debt additions of earlier occupants of the Oval Office.

Constant 2021 Dollar Additions to the Public Debt per Annum:
- Donald Trump: *$2.043 trillion.*
- Barack Obama: $1.061 trillion.
- George W. Bush: $0.694 trillion.
- Bill Clinton: $0.168 trillion.
- George H. W. Bush: $0.609 trillion.
- Ronald Reagan: $0.384 trillion.
- Jimmy Carter: $0.096 trillion.

Indeed, in the long sweep of things, the real damage was done in the Covid/Lockdowns/Stimmies year of 2020. Federal spending erupted by nearly $2 trillion during that year alone and soared from 22.3 percent of GDP in 2019 to nearly *32 percent* of GDP in 2020. And when state and local outlays are included, The Donald managed to bring government spending in the US to a European social democracy–style 40 percent of GDP.

It might be well and truly asked: With charts like the one below, who needs Republicans of the ilk represented by Donald Trump?

Federal Spending Share of GDP, 2000 to 2021.

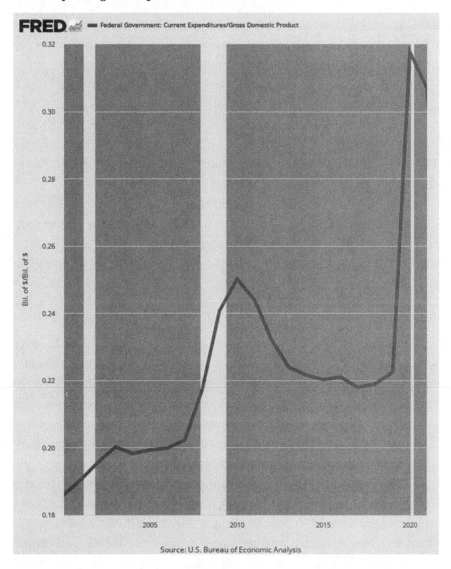

Source: U.S. Bureau of Economic Analysis

There is no secret as to how spending and debt soared like never before during Trump's time in the Oval Office. Trump wanted to wield the biggest defense stick on the planet on the primitive theory that he could bluster his way to foreign policy success just like he claims to have done with the trade unions and subcontractors in New York City.

But to get his big defense stick, he had to accommodate the Congressional porkers on nondefense discretionary spending and leave entitlements untouched. And that he was happy to do because Trump just didn't care about federal spending.

Thus, when big-spending Barack Obama left the White House the national security budget properly measured totaled a staggering *$822 billion*. That included $600 billion for the Pentagon, $46 billion for security assistance and international operations and $177 billion for veterans' compensation and services, which reflect the deferred cost of prior wars.

So much for the "peace candidate" of 2008 and the anti-war democratic party of the Vietnam era and its aftermath. To the contrary, Obama's $822 billion national security budget embodied the cost of global hegemony and the Forever Wars to which it gave rise—notwithstanding that the only real threat to homeland security in the post-war period, the former Soviet Union, had been consigned to the dustbin of history twenty-five years earlier.

Donald Trump came bounding into the Oval Office talking what sounded like a different game—America First. But as his last Attorney General, Bill Barr, recently noted, even if you believe in his policies don't expect him to execute them. His four years in the White House proved he can't organize or lead his way out of a wet paper bag, and his budgetary fiasco in the national security space provides striking confirmation of Barr's observation.

To be sure, Trump did manage to see through the uniparty's demonization of Putin, and the feckless neocon claim that he seeks to recreate the former Soviet Empire. After all, in Washington's theater of the absurd Vlad Putin was simply The Donald's doppelganger when it came to demonization and putting on the beltway hate. So, Trump got that part of the equation right.

But Trump actually had no idea what he meant by "America First" except that the line elicited boisterous cheers from the patriotic throngs at his campaign rallies. The fact is, he was historically ignorant beyond measure; lazy as they come when it involves studying your brief; and a total sucker for military pomp and circumstance and the medal-bedecked uniforms of the generals.

So while Trump talked about bringing the Empire home, he actually fueled its budget like never before. The vastly bloated national security budget left behind by Obama took on *$215 billion* more girth on The Donald's watch. His outgoing broadly measured national security budget (FY 2021) actually broke the trillion-dollar barrier, weighing in at *$1.035 trillion*, or 26 percent more than what Obama and the Congressional uniparty had frittered away in FY 2017.

In short, The Donald was so ill-informed and confused that he ended up with a national security budget which amounted to the Military-Industrial Complex first, not one designed strictly for the defense of the homeland—better termed Fortress America, which was advocated in the early post-war era by Mr. Republican, Senator Robert Taft of Ohio. The latter's views were the very opposite of today's global hegemony views of the neocons who dominate the GOP ranks on the military and foreign affairs committees on Capitol Hill.

Indeed, the truth of the matter is that the present-day GOP was hijacked a few decades ago by a loathsome tribe of born-again Trotskyite statist, who discovered that a perpetual condition of global war was the true passageway to state power and political self-aggrandizement in the Imperial City.

That is more than evident when you compare Trump's resulting trillion-dollar national security budget with the maximum $500 billion spending level that would be needed to fully fund Fortress America. The staggering $500 billion per year difference makes it starkly evident that even on the Pentagon side of the Potomac, The Donald was a thorough-going patsy for the Swamp creatures.

In the first place, a Fortress America–based implementation of The Donald's vague notions about bringing the forces home rests on the truth that in the present world order there are no technologically-advanced industrial powers who have either the capability or intention to attack the American homeland. To do that you need a massive land armada, huge air and sealift capacities, a Navy and Air Force many times the size of current US forces and humongous supply lines and logistics capacities that have never been even dreamed of by any other nation on the planet.

You also need an initial GDP of say $50 trillion per year to sustain what would be the most violent conflagration of weap-onry and material in human history. And that's to say nothing of needing to be ruled by suicidal leaders willing to risk the nuclear destruction of their own countries, allies, and economic commerce in order to accomplish, what? Occupy Denver?

So the entire idea that there is a post–Cold War existential threat to America's security is just plain bogus because, obviously, no alleged foe has the requisite GDP or military heft. Russia's GDP is a scant $1.8 trillion, not the $50 trillion that would be needed for it to put an invasionary force on the New Jersey shores. And its pre-Ukraine defense budget was just $75 billion, which amounts to about four weeks of waste in Washington's trillion-dollar monster.

As for China, let us not forget that even its communist rul-ers sill believe it is the "Middle Kingdom" and therefore that it already occupies the most important territory on the entire planet. So why would Beijing's rulers want to occupy Cleveland OH or Birmingham AL to either extract high-cost production or root out dissenters from Chairman Xi's thought?

More importantly, China doesn't have the GDP heft to even think about landing on the California shores, notwithstanding Wall Street's endless kowtowing to the China Boom. The fact is, China has accumulated in excess of $50 trillion of debt in barely two decades!

Therefore, it didn't grow organically in the historic capitalist mode; it printed, borrowed, spent, and built like there was no tomorrow. But the resulting *façade* of prosperity would not last six months if China's $3.6 trillion global export market—the source of the hard cash that keeps its Ponzi upright—were to crash, which is exactly what would happen if it tried to invade America.

To be sure, its totalitarian leaders are immensely misguided and downright evil from the perspective of their oppressed pop-ulation. But they are not stupid. They stay in power by keeping the people relatively fat and happy and would never risk bringing down what amounts to an economic house of cards.

And the nuclear blackmail card can't be played by either of these foes, either. According to a recent CBO analysis, the annual cost of maintaining and investing America's triad nuclear deterrent—submarine-launched ICBMs, land-based ICBMs, and the strategic nuclear bomber fleet—is just $52 billion per year, or less than 6 percent of the pentagon's current budget and barely 4 percent of overall national security spending.

That triad deterrent is what dissuades both Moscow and Beijing from attempting nuclear blackmail and therefore invasion by nuclear checkmate. That is to say, the lynchpin of America's security lies in the arrangement known as MAD (mutual assured destruction), a mechanism that has worked for seventy years. And it worked even at the peak of the Cold War when the Soviet Union had forty thousand nuclear warheads and leaders far more unstable than either Cool-Hand Vlad or Xi Jinping.

At the end of the day, it is the great ocean moats, the triad nuclear deterrent, and the relative economic diminutiveness of Russia and China that keep the American homeland secure and safe from hostile foreign encroachment. Most of the rest of the massive pentagon budget is based on false predicates, fabricated threats, and the budget-grabbing prowess of its own marketing (i.e., think tanks) and lobbying (i.e., defense contractors) arms.

In this context, Trump did ask the right question, even if he never came up with an actionable answer. Namely, why in the world do we still have costly, obsolete arrangements like NATO thirty-two years after the Soviet Union perished?

The only real answer is that it is a mechanism to sell arms to its thirty-one-member states. Indeed, Europe had long ago proved it did not really fear that Putin would be marching his armies through the Brandenburg Gate in Berlin. That's why Germany previously spent only 1.3 percent of GDP on defense and was more than happy to buy cheap energy via Russian delivered pipeline gas.

Germany's current quasi-warlike posture vis-a-vis Russia doesn't gainsay that history, either. The truth is, the German Green Party—which is what keeps the Scholz social democrat government in power—has gone full-on warmongering for the hideous reason that the Greens live to end the era of fossil fuel. So, what better way to do it than cut off the cheap oil and gas supplies from Russia on which Germany's fossil-fueled economy is based and then blame it on a demonized Putin?

Moreover, even a passing familiarity with European history reminds you that Russians and Poles hate each other and have done so over centuries of wars and bloody altercations. So Vlad Putin may not be a Russian Gandhi, but he is sure as hell way too smart to attempt to occupy Poland. Ditto France, Germany, the Low Countries, Italy, Iberia, and the rest.

In short, Washington doesn't need NATO to protect our allies in Europe because they are not facing any threat that can't be handled by their own ways and means, preferably of the diplomatic variety. In fact, the whole disaster in Ukraine today is rooted in the War Party's mindless expansion of NATO in violation of all of Washington's promises to Gorbachev to not expand an inch to the east in return for the unification of Germany. Yet the double-cross has been so extensive that NATO now includes every one of the old Warsaw Pact nations and has even attempted to extend its reach to two of the former Soviet Republics (i.e., Georgia and Ukraine).

The same holds for Washington's so-called "allies" in East Asia and the massive US military resources committed to the region. The truth is, functioning as the gendarme of the planet is the only possible justification for the extra $500 billion per year cost of the current national security budget.

For example, why does the US still deploy 100,000 US forces and their dependents in Japan and Okinawa and 29,000 in South Korea?

These two counties have a combined GDP of nearly $7 trillion—or 235x more than North Korea, and they are light-years ahead of the latter in technology and military capability. Also, they don't go around the world engaging in regime change, thereby spooking fear on the north side of the DMZ.

Accordingly, Japan and South Korea could more than provide for their own national security in a manner they see fit without any help whatsoever from Imperial Washington. That's especially the case because absent the massive US military threat in the region, North Korea would surely seek a rapprochement and economic help from its neighbors, including China.

Indeed, sixty-five years after the unnecessary war in Korea ended, there is only one reason why the Kim family is still in power in Pyongyang and why periodically they have noisily brandished their incipient nuclear weapons and missiles. Mainly, it's because Washington still occupies the Korean peninsula and surrounds its waters with more lethal firepower than was brought to bear against the industrial might of Nazi Germany during the whole of WWII.

Of course, these massive and costly forces are also justified on the grounds of supporting Washington's commitments to the defense of Taiwan. But that commitment has always been obsolete and unnecessary to America's homeland security.

As it happened, Chiang Kia-Shek lost the Chinese civil war fair and square in 1949, and there was no reason to perpetuate his rag-tag regime when it retreated to the last square miles of Chinese territory—the island province of Taiwan. The latter had been under control of the Chinese Qing Dynasty for two hundred years thru 1895, and after Imperial Japan was expelled from the island in 1945, Taiwan was once again "Chinese."

So today it is separated from the mainland only because Washington arbitrarily made it a protectorate and "ally" when the loser of the Chinese civil war set up shop in a small remnant of China's modern geography, thereby establishing an artificial nation that had no bearing whatsoever on America's homeland security, and in subsequent decades accomplished nothing except bolster the case for a big Navy and for US policing of the Pacific region for no good reason of homeland defense.

That is to say, without Washington's support for the nationalist regime in Taipei, the island would have been long ago absorbed back into the Chinese polity where it had been for centuries. Even now, the Taiwanese would surely prefer peaceful prosperity as the 24th province of China rather than a catastrophic war against Beijing that they would have no hope of surviving.

By the same token, the alternative—US military intervention—would mean WWIII. The only sensible policy, therefore, is for Washington to recant seventy years of folly brought on by the China Lobby and arms manufacturers and green-light a Taiwanese reconciliation with the mainland. Even a few years thereafter, Wall Street bankers peddling M&A deals in Taipei wouldn't know the difference from Shanghai.

In short, there is no need whatsoever for America's massive conventional armada and what is now (FY 2024) its $1.3 trillion annual national security expense. That's the true implication of America First, but The Donald didn't have a clue about its bearing on the actual national security budget.

To the contrary, his support for the massive increases in Pentagon spending was based on the primitive theory that the route to a successful foreign policy was, well, himself!

That is to say, national security would come from a big military stick in his stubby small hands and a lot of eyeball-to-eyeball sit-downs between The Donald and the other ostensible bad guys of the world. But that was sheer nonsense, of course. Implied military threats and dickering at a one-on-one summit of the type Trump had with Vlad Putin, Kim Jong Un, and Xi Jinping were mainly just theater—a global version of *The Apprentice*. What ultimately keeps America safe, however, is its nuclear deterrent. As long as that is intact and effective, there is no conceivable form of nuclear blackmail that could be used to jeopardize the security and liberty of the homeland.

Yet according to the aforementioned CBO study the current annual cost of the strategic deterrent of just *$52 billion* includes $13 billion for the ballistic missile submarine force, $7 billion for the land-based ICBMs, and $6 billion for the strategic bomber force. On top of that there is also $13 billion to maintain the nuclear weapons stockpiles, infrastructure, and supporting services and $11 billion for strategic nuclear command and control, communications, and early warnings systems.

In all, and after allowing for normal inflation and weapons development costs, CBO's ten-year estimate for the strategic nuclear deterrent is just *$756 billion.* That happens to be only 7.0 percent of the $10 trillion baseline for the total cost of defense proper over the next decade and only 5.0 percent of the $15 trillion national security baseline when you include international operations and veterans.

The adoption of a Fortress America national security budget of $500 billion per year over the next decade would save in excess of $5 trillion. And that would surely be more than doable from the $14 trillion CBO baseline for total national security spending excluding the strategic forces.

Under a Fortress America defense strategy, there would be no need for eleven carrier battle groups including their air-wings, escort and support ships, and supporting infrastructure. Those forces are sitting ducks in this day and age anyway but are only necessary for force projection abroad and wars of invasion and occupation. The American coastline and interior, by contrast, can be protected by land-based air.

According to another CBO study, the ten-year baseline cost for the Navy's unnecessary eleven carrier battle groups will approach $1 trillion alone. Likewise, the land forces of the US Army will cost $2 trillion, and that's again mainly for the purpose of force projection abroad.

As Senator Taft and his original Fortress America supporters long ago recognized, overwhelming air superiority over the North American continent is what is actually necessary for homeland security. But even that would require only a small part of the current $1.5 trillion ten-year cost of US Air Force operations, which are heavily driven by global force projection capacities.

At the end of the day, if The Donald had really been committed to an America First foreign policy, he would have done his homework, taken on the national security Swamp Creatures, and put in place a Fortress America budget that could save $5 trillion over the next decade. And from there could have begun the process of putting Washington a sustainable fiscal path.

Then again, when has The Donald ever done his homework, got in real bruising political battles over substantive policy matters rather than tweetstorms, and cared a whit about the nation's fiscal solvency?

How The Donald Threw In the Towel on Domestic Spending

Finally, there is one more element gravitating toward fiscal catastrophe that got a real boost under Trump-O-Nomics. The truth is, the GOP has been thoroughly Trumpified and distracted from its main fiscal mission by The Donald's utterly misguided war on the US borders and demagogic anti-immigrant howling and by his parallel eagerness to embrace big tax cuts without paying for them (see Chapter 6).

Moreover, with The Donald's loud insistence, the contemporary GOP has even taken a powder completely on Medicare, Social Security, and the lesser entitlements. That's $50 trillion of current law spending over the next decade, and yet the GOP recently agreed with Joe Biden and the Dems to cut nary a penny from these monster programs in the last debt ceiling settlement.

But no sooner did they brush themselves off from their shameful surrender on the debt ceiling deal than they were at it again. This time proposing huge tax cuts with no off-setting spending reductions, and again with The Donald's fulsome support.

In total, the recently tabled House GOP tax package encompassed $240 billion of tax cuts such as increasing the standard deduction on income taxes, expanding opportunity zones, rolling back some requirements for reporting transactions to the IRS, and restoring expired Trump-era business expense write-offs.

Thus, under the new GOP tax plan, the standard deduction for singles would increase by $2,000 to $15,850, and for married couples the standard deduction would increase by $4,000 to $30,700. Accordingly, the chief GOP sponsor proclaimed that the day of the proverbial free lunch has truly arrived:

"With this provision in place, an American family of four will **not pay a cent in federal taxes on their first $68,000 of income,**" said House Ways and Means Committee Chairman Jason Smith, Missouri Republican.

And if dogs could whistle, the world would be a chorus! That is to say, has Rep. Smith done the math? Roughly 75 percent of all US workers earn less than $68,000 and yet Republicans are going to exempt them from paying any federal income taxes at all, even as the Washington behemoth is allowed to keep on spending and borrowing like there is no tomorrow?

Of course, there will be a tomorrow, albeit a fiscally disastrous one for which the Trumpified GOP can share fully in the blame. It is supposed to be the party that keeps Washington on the fiscal straight and narrow, but under The Donald's feckless MAGA slogans it has degenerated into the party of gluttonous war spending, unpaid-for tax cuts, and entitlements cowardice.

Once upon a time there was a majority of Republicans led by Senator Robert Taft who believed in fiscal rectitude and small government—and on both sides of the Potomac River. As we have indicated, Taft advocated Fortress America, not global hegemony, as the route to homeland security. His view was right then, and it is still correct now. So the truth is, Donald Trump is the anti-Taft. He's no Mr. Republican at all—just a dangerous poseur.

For avoidance of doubt, just consider what he embraced in order to get his extra national security spending. It might have been supposed, of course, that with control of the veto pen and strong GOP positions in both the House and Senate during these four years that the near quarter-trillion dollars per year of extra largesse for the national security state would have been off-set by some hefty curtailments on the domestic side. The party in power being the fiscally conservative GOP and all.

But not a chance. The nondefense budget of $3.38 trillion left by Obama (FY 2017) weighed in at $6.07 trillion when The Donald finally shuffled out of the Oval Office in FY 2021.

That *$2.69 trillion* nondefense spending increase amounted to a 79 percent gain over the four-year period, averaging nearly *$675 billion* per year. Big spender Obama, by contrast, had increased the non-defense budget by an average of just *$112 billion* per year and Bill Clinton's per annum nondefense increase figure was but *$85 billion*.

Nor can you blame The Donald's domestic spending bonanza entirely on entitlements and interest payments, even though legislative curtailment of these mandatory spending accounts is exactly the job of the GOP in our two-party democracy. As it happened, however, The Donald also presided over a veritable eruption of spending for the third component of nondefense spending—appropriated *domestic* programs.

That's right. We are talking about the very corner of the budget where the presidential veto pen is potentially mightier than the beltway's assembled army of PACs and lobbies or the overflowing pork barrels of hometown goodies. But in round terms, nondefense discretionary spending rose from $600 billion per year to $900 billion during The Donald's four budgets. That's a 50 percent gain, yet there was nary a veto to be hurtled at the appropriations bills and eleventh-hour omnibus spending extravaganzas that came across The Donald's desk.

But here's the thing. Donald Trump has never made any bones about his complete disinterest in curtailing government spending and borrowing. Still, he did not accomplish these monster spending increases by unilaterally defying the will of the GOP congressional delegations, either. These hideous spending and borrowing eruptions represented, instead, the overwhelming consensus of the bipartisan uniparty.

The majority of both parties devoutly desire to feed the Warfare State monster ever greater rations, even as they give a perennial hall pass to entitlement spending and jump at every possible chance, such as the trillions of Covid Lockdown relief spending and the green energy tax credit scams, to open the fiscal spigot wider.

Alas, that gets us to the dirty secret of the nation's now $33 trillion public debt. Mainly that the once and former conservative anti-spending party has been taken over by the MAGA hat "culture warriors" and the neocon warmongers, but most especially by a permanent class of Washington Republican legislators and staff who live for the power and pelf that manning-up the Empire bestows upon them.

Serving on the broad array of national security committees, grazing at the foreign affairs think tanks and NGOs, junketing far and wide across the planet as latter-day pro-consuls, visiting the dozens of occupied countries, and inspecting America's eight hundred military bases—all are far more thrilling than returning to Green Bay to run a car dealership.

So they feed the Empire, and the Empire nourishes their sojourns on the great stage of world affairs. That's the heart of the real Washington Swamp. And the clueless Donald Trump fed it like never before.

The Poison of Relentless Public Borrowing

Ultimately, excessive, relentless public borrowing is the poison that will kill capitalist prosperity and displace limited constitutional government with unchained statist encroachment on the liberties of the people. For that reason alone, The Donald needs be locked-out of the nomination and banished from the Oval Office.

Of course, the great enabler of The Donald's reckless fiscal escapades was the Federal Reserve, which increased its balance sheet by nearly $3 trillion or 66 percent during The Donald's four-year term. That amounted to balance sheet expansion (i.e., money-printing) equal to $750 billion per annum—compared to gains of $300 billion and $150 billion per annum during the Barack Obama and George W. Bush tenures, respectively.

Still, Trump wasn't satisfied with this insane level of monetary expansion. He never did stop hectoring the Fed for being too stingy with the printing press and for keeping interest rates higher than the King of Debt in his wisdom deemed to be the correct level.

In short, given the economic circumstances during his tenure and the unprecedented stimulus emanating from the Keynesian

Balance Sheet of the Federal Reserve, 1960 to 2020.

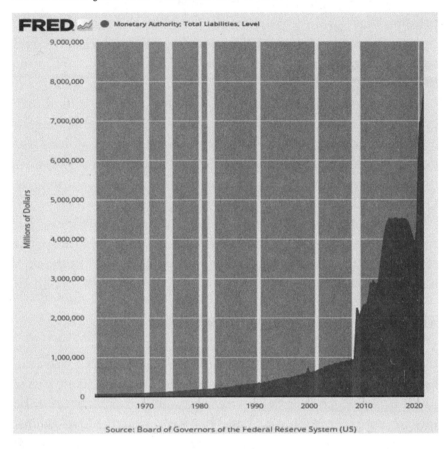

Source: Board of Governors of the Federal Reserve System (US)

Fed, Donald Trump's constant demands for still easier money made even Richard Nixon look like a paragon of financial sobriety. The truth is, no US president has ever been as reckless on monetary matters as Donald Trump. That's why it's especially rich that the die-hard MAGA fans are now gumming loudly for a revival of the great Trump economy. Yet it is the egregious fiscal, monetary, and Lockdown excesses during his tenure that gave rise to the current economic mess.

Then again, the MAGA faithful have been thoroughly Trumpified. After years of The Donald insisting that even more fiat money should be pumped into the economy, the GOP politicians gave the Fed a free pass during the 2022 campaign—and did so during an inflation-besotted election season that was tailor-made for a hammer-and-tongs attack on the inflationary money-printers domiciled in the Eccles Building.

Once upon a time, GOP politicians knew better. Certainly, Ronald Reagan did amidst the double-digit inflation of the early 1980s.

The Gipper did not hesitate to say that Big Government, deficit-spending and monetary profligacy were the cause of the nation's economic ills. He was right, and he won the election in a landslide. Indeed, he was even persuaded to include a gold standard plank in the 1980 GOP platform.

By contrast, consult the videos or transcripts of a score or two or three of MAGA rallies. Did anything remotely resembling the Reagenesque take on inflation ever flow from The Donald's bombastic vocal cords?

Of course not. So to repeat: Donald Trump is not an economic conservative in any way, shape, or form. He's simply a self-promoting demagogue who, during four years in the Oval Office, only managed to compound the nation's ills stemming from bad policy ideas deeply embedded inside the Washington beltway.

Lead among these is runaway federal spending, borrowing, and printing—a terrible policy malfeasance that Donald Trump pushed into a League All of His Own.

Chapter Five

Wreck of the Good Ship MAGA

———

W hen it comes to today's raging stagflation, all roads lead back to Donald Trump's disastrous economic stewardship during 2017 through 2020. That span encompassed the final years of the post-Great Recession recovery and even by the lights of milquetoast Republicanism was supposed to be a time in which monetary and fiscal policy would be resolutely normalized.

Stated differently, The Donald's reckless fiscal and monetary policies were doubly bad. That's because they came at a point in the business cycle when just the opposite was warranted—fiscal consolidation and monetary normalization.

To be sure, we don't cotton much to the idea that financially cleansing recessions like the downturn of 2008–2009 should be aggressively countered with large-scale fiscal deficits and central bank money-pumping. That's just a long-standing Keynesian cover story for incessant expansion of the state by Washington's permanent ruling class of careerist uniparty pols, Deep State apparatchiks, and MSM media shills.

Republicans have usually been on the watered-down "stimulus" bandwagon during recessions, with the brief interlude of 1981–1982 being the only exception. In the latter case, the "stimulus" cure was explicitly rejected by Ronald Reagan's brand of small government Republicanism. He was old fashioned enough to recognize that recessions are needed to purge inflationary excesses of debt, over-spending, malinvestment, and speculation, and therefore must be allowed to run their course, even as unemployed workers and families are temporarily supported by unemployment insurance and the safety net.

Still, even during those years of GOP apostasy before and after Reagan, which culminated in Bush-the-Younger's pathetic anti-recession rebate checks to the American populace in May 2008, Republicans at least insisted that once the so-called "emergency" was over, deficits needed to be sharply reined-in and, ideally, extinguished before the next economic downturn. And it was also assumed that the Fed would do its part to reverse its own anti-recession stimulus policies and bring interest rates and financial conditions back to normalcy.

However, The Donald thought differently. On the fiscal side, the steady march to normalcy during the Obama Administration, when the deficit dropped from $1.4 trillion at the bottom the Great Recession in 2009 to *$580 billion* in FY 2016, was dramatically reversed by Trump-O-Nomics. Even before the egregious fiscal insanity of the 2020 pandemic stimmies, the federal deficit had soared back to *$983 billion* by FY 2019.

Thereafter, of course, it was loony tunes time. The FY 2020 and FY 2021 deficits soared to a combined total of *$5.9 trillion*. Both years were drastically inflated by The Donald's stimmy measures, including their extensions in Biden's American Rescue Plan. As it happens, this two-year total is equal to the entire public debt incurred on the watch of forty-three different presidents over the first 212 years of the Republic!

So let us repeat: The Donald, with a modest boost from his uniparty successor (most of the FY 2021 deficit was due to policies in place on The Donald's watch), added more to the public debt than all the US presidents combined prior to Barack Obama. That's just unforgivable madness under any circumstance, but flat-out beyond the pale for any politician elected on the Republican ticket.

For avoidance of doubt, the federal deficit chart below is the real bill of indictment against The Donald. The deficit was marching downhill in typical cyclical recovery fashion under Obama, and then went bat-shit crazy under Donald Trump.

Federal Deficits, FY 2009 to FY 2021.

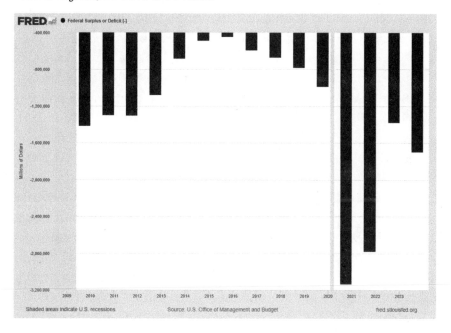

Needless to say, this Trump borrowing spree fostered serious distortions on the main street economy. The only silver lining is that The Donald's storm of red ink–financed stimmies did end up repudiating the Keynesian delusion that artificially goosed consumer spending (PCE) causes sustainable economic growth.

And that was for no lack of trying. The level of total PCE (personal consumption expenditures) was first massively bloated by all the Trump stimmies, including the unpaid-for tax cuts. It was then further fueled by an unprecedented build-up of household cash during the Covid lockdowns, when spending at social venues like restaurants and movies was forbidden by government edict. The subsequent household spend-down of this immense cash accumulation continues to thwart the Fed's belated attempt to bring inflation to heel up to this very day.

At the same time, the usual countervailing impact of monetary policy normalization was nowhere to be seen, either. From the moment in 2017 when the Fed began its tepid moves to get the federal funds rate off the preposterously low zero bound and to shrink its elephantine balance sheet, as Bernanke had promised upon the launch of QE years earlier, The Donald was all over the Fed's back, raging:

> "I'm not thrilled," he said in an interview on CNBC television. "Because we go up and every time you go up they want to raise rates again. . . I am not happy about it. . . I don't like all of this work that we're putting into the economy and then I see rates going up," he said.

Alas, these are the words of a veritable economic dunce. Of course rates were going up—the fools in the Eccles Building had taken them to the zero bound and kept them in that destructive position for years. In fact, here is the inflation-adjusted Fed funds rate in the years before Trump's term, and then the level recorded during 2017–2020 that he insisted should not be going "up and up."

As shown by the chart, during the forty-eight months of The Donald's term, the real federal funds rate was negative in all except for the first seven months of 2019. And even then, the positive rates peeking above the zero line averaged a mere *thirteen basis points*!

Stated differently, those weren't even interest rates in any meaningful sense. They were invitations to government spenders and private speculators alike to scamper into the Devil's Workshop of easy money. It was those utterly falsified rates which fostered massive financial bubbles and the inflationary distortions which have now spilled over onto the main street.

Still, by the fall of 2019—long before the Covid lockdowns—The Donald got his way at the Eccles Building. The short-lived Fed campaign to shrink its balance sheet via QT (quantitative tightening) was over and done. Nothing remotely like Bernanke's promised normalization of the Fed's crisis-bloated balance sheet

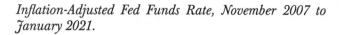

Inflation-Adjusted Fed Funds Rate, November 2007 to January 2021.

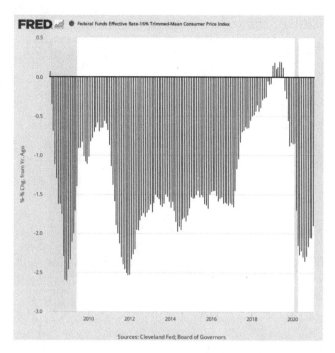

had been accomplished, and, instead, it was soon off to the races with The Donald's enthusiastic blessing.

Between August 2019 and January 2021, the Fed's balance sheet soared by an incredible *$3.6 trillion*. That was nearly *three times* the $1.3 trillion gain that had occurred between November 2007 and December 2008 in response to the Wall Street meltdown and what was alleged to be the worst recession since the 1930s.

At the time of those earlier massive Wall Street bailouts, in fact, the Fed's aggressive monetary actions were considered off the charts of history. They were also completely unnecessary.

As we have seen, the only thing the 2008–2009 Fed bailouts accomplished was to relieve Goldman Sachs and Morgan Stanley from the fate of Lehman Brothers. Yet, had Washington allowed Mr. Market to have his way, the parts and pieces of these and other Wall Street high rollers would have been reorganized in the bankruptcy courts where they belonged, while main street would not have been any worse for the wear.

Needless to say, having thwarted the market's cure for excessive borrowing and speculation once, the Eccles Building was not nearly done. During the present go-round, the Fed nearly tripled-down on its egregious excesses of 2008–2009, yet the Donald didn't say boo. He actually patted Jay Powell on the rear and urged him on for more!

Federal Reserve Balance Sheet, November 2007 to January 2021.

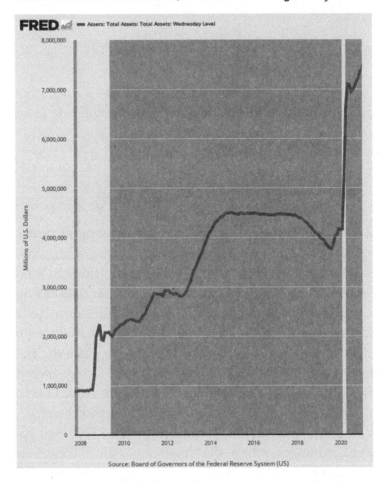

Source: Board of Governors of the Federal Reserve System (US)

Of course, all of this rampant Washington stimulus fostered an unsustainable hot house economy like never before. For want of doubt, we merely need to compare the annual growth of transfer payments between January 2017 and January 2021 with personal income earned from wages, salaries, bonuses, interest, dividends, and profits during the same period.

As it happens, these latter figures encompass all the income generated by the process of production, including even the "output" of government employees. So these sources of private income are the reciprocal of current economic production, while transfer payments reflect the non-production of the Welfare State/entitlements sector.

On The Donald's watch—even after adjustments for inflation—real income growth from non-production exceeded that from production by nearly *eight times*. In our experience of national policy going back to the late 1960s, we are quite certain that Trump was the one and only putative GOP policy-maker who ever embraced such economic folly, let alone had the gall to brag about the results.

Inflation-Adjusted Per Annum Growth, January 2017 to January 2021
- Personal Income Less Govt. Transfer Payments: +2.3 percent.
- Government Transfer Payments: +17.4 percent.

It goes without saying that this flood of Washington money kept the US economy temporarily expanding at a rate far higher than was sustainable on its own steam. Nor was the short-term economic boost from this transfer payment explosion the end of the matter. Owing to involuntary consumption cuts on services during the lockdowns and then the $6.5 trillion flood of stimmies, quarantined households literally could not spend their accumulating piles of cash fast enough.

After rising by about $400 billion to $600 billion per year during the pre-Covid period, household cash balances (currency plus bank deposits and money market funds) erupted by *$3.1 trillion* on a year-over-year basis in Q1 2021. As a result, total cash balances reached $17.4 trillion, representing an incredible $5 trillion gain from the prior historical trend level of $12.5 trillion posted in mid-2019.

What this means, of course, is that the high inflation still rocking the US economy is the bastard son of MAGA. Spending is still out-running production because the utterly artificial and aberrant cash balances spawned by the Donald's lockdowns and stimmies are being steadily drawn down. And it also means that the Fed's rate hiking cycle must necessarily be more brutal—go higher for longer—in order to bring The Donald's roaring inflation to heel.

Ironically, it is the working class that is reaping the whirlwind of the Great Trumpian Inflation. Real hourly wages have been negative on a Y/Y basis for *seventeen straight months*.

In this context, the patently ridiculous claim of MAGA partisans that inflation was only running at 1.5 percent when The Donald left the Oval Office and that today's 5.0 percent Y/Y rate on the trimmed mean CPI is therefore entirely Sleepy Joe's fault needs be thoroughly debunked. The truth is, The Donald lit the inflationary flame—upon which the Biden Dems have poured a goodly amount of additional kerosene.

At the end of the day, Donald Trump is an economic dufus who is a clear and present danger to capitalist prosperity. The GOP would nominate him for an Oval Office reprise only at the risk of an even greater economic calamity than is already unfolding.

Thus, the real Trumpian legacy is not a strong economy or robust investment cycle, but just a further slide into the abyss of profligate monetary and fiscal policies—policies which will eventually bring capitalist prosperity to an abrupt end.

The chart below is the ultimate report card on the Trump years. Given that The Donald inherited an already massively bloated public debt of $19.8 trillion and a bulging Fed balance sheet at $4.5 trillion, his policies should have been focused on balancing the federal budget and supporting the Fed's tepid efforts to normalize its balance sheet and drain the bubble-fueling excess liquidity and credit from the financial system.

Alas, neither of these urgent imperatives materialized on the Donald's watch. By the end of his term, the public debt had risen by $7.8 trillion or nearly 40 percent; and the Fed's balance

Inflation-Adjusted Average Hourly Earnings, January 2022 to June 2023.

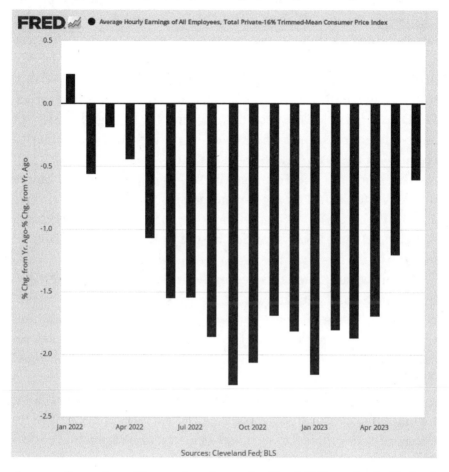

Sources: Cleveland Fed; BLS

sheet—after a lot of hectoring from the Oval Office—had climbed to $7.4 trillion, reflecting an unprecedented gain of 65 percent in just four years. Joe Biden kept on spending, borrowing, and printing where The Donald left off, thereby proving once again that the uniparty is no respecter of elections. At the end of 2022, the public debt was up by another $3.7 trillion and the Fed's balance sheet had further expanded by $1.2 trillion.

But now the long-delayed reckoning begins. The Fed's printing presses have been shut down and will remain idle for a prolonged time to come because a virulent goods and services inflation has been finally released.

Likewise, the built-in public debt is already heading for $55 trillion by the end of the current ten-year budget window, even without another dime of increased spending or tax cuts. Already enacted Trumpian policies did their fair share to fuel that fiscal doomsday scenario. And now his current position against spending cuts for Medicare and Social Security and in favor of a robust DOD appropriations to remediate Sleepy Joe's alleged neglect of national security requirements would only ensure that America remains on the fast track to fiscal disaster.

That's actually the Trumpian legacy—a doubling-down on the uniparty's fiscal and monetary madness.

Meanwhile, the US economy has been twisted, tortured, unbalanced, and booby-trapped by the policy chaos The Donald unleashed during his forty-eight months in office.

As one example of this economic torture, consider the combined effects of the lockdowns in service sector venues like restaurants, bars, gyms, movies, hotels, resorts and sports arenas, and the massive stimmy checks. The effect was to hit the brakes on ordinary spending for services, while causing a doubled-barreled explosion of spending for merchandise goods.

That is, when households couldn't spend their normal allotments at locked-down social congregation venues, they cranked up their Amazon orders for what was believed to be safer front-door-step delivery of merchandise goods.

And not by just a lot. The surge in durable goods consumption spending, in fact, was just plain insane. The chart below tracks the Y/Y change in household spending for durable goods, which fluctuated between +$50 billion and +$100 billion on an annualized basis during the years before the pandemic.

And then, bang! By April 2021, household spending for durables was up by *+$950 billion* versus the prior year or by more than *ten times* the normal gain. That wasn't merely a so-called bullwhip effect; it was an economic cyclone that ripped through the entire economic infrastructure, depleting inventories at all levels and straining a fragile global supply chain to the breaking point.

In turn, however, this drastic supply chain depletion triggered an orgy of replenishment orders among out-of-stock vendors and retailers who became drastically over-stocked when demand abruptly shifted back to services and experiences after mid-2021.

Needless to say, it was the Washington-fueled economic aberration depicted in the chart below that triggered the surging inflation of the last two years. At the insistence of Trump, Congress shoveled out the money and the Fed monetized the resulting explosion of Treasury borrowing. It was a textbook case of state-fueled inflation like never before.

Y/Y Change in PCE for Durable Goods, 1993–2021.

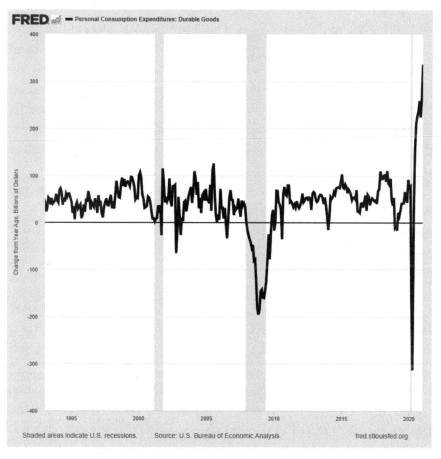

Of course, the opposite disruption occurred in the Leisure & Hospitality sector owing to the government-ordered lockdowns and vastly exaggerated public fears of social contact. In that context, labor hours employed are a pretty good proxy for output levels in the services sector, and the chart below leaves little to the imagination.

In just two months—from February to April 2020—the index of aggregate hours in the Leisure & Hospitality (L&H) sector plunged by a staggering *58 percent*. There is absolutely nothing like it in the archives of labor and economic data. The Donald's lockdowns amounted to a *sui generis* whirlwind of economic destruction.

In fact, in virtually one fell-swoop, The Donald's "two weeks to flatten the curve" campaign rolled back labor utilization in the L&H sector by *forty-one years*—to April 1979 levels!

Truly, you can't make this up or underestimate its significance: Four decades of growth was pulverized in just a few weeks of Trump-initiated madness.

Moreover, hours employed in the L&H sector rebounded strongly after the lockdowns were finally lifted, but even then, the economic mayhem didn't cease. So many millions of workers were driven out of the industry that it took soaring inflationary wage increases to bring them back.

To wit, average hourly earnings had risen by *3.2 percent* per annum between 2012 and February 2020. But that rate of gain more than doubled to *7.5 percent* per annum during the past three years, as the L&H sector was whip-sawed between shutdowns, stimmies and rebounds.

Still, total hours employed in June 2023 remained 4.5 percent *below* February 2020 levels. So the result was the worst of all possible worlds: significantly less output, far more cost-inflation.

Nor was the mayhem limited to ground zero in the L&H sector. For the entire private services sector, which in February 2020 encompassed 108 million jobs in health and education, financial services, retail, wholesale and distribution, transportation, utilities, business services and personal services, too, the impact was calamitous. About *19 million* jobs were lost in just two months.

Index of Aggregate Hours for Leisure & Hospitality Sector, 1979–2023.

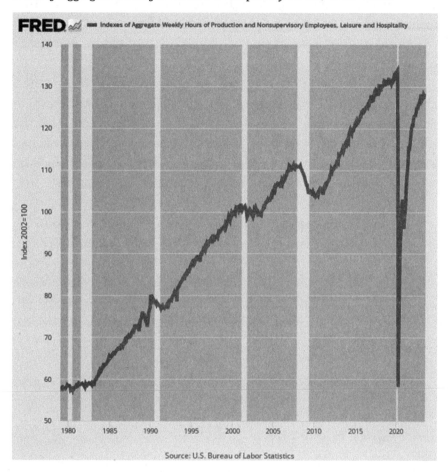

Source: U.S. Bureau of Labor Statistics

Indeed, this abrupt plunge was literally off the charts of history. The normal monthly gain was just one hundred thousand to two hundred thousand jobs, meaning that ten years' worth of new employees in the vast services sector of the US economy were instantly furloughed on The Donald's command. And we do mean The Donald's command. During the above-mentioned March 16 press conference, a reporter professed confusion about whether governors were actually being ordered to shutdown these extensive areas of the economy.

At that point, any conservative worth his salt would have said absolutely not. That's because the government does not have the constitutional right to capriciously "take" what amounted to hundreds of billions in property values from private citizens, whose businesses were being shuttered without due process or compensation.

But not The Donald. He turned the podium over to the insufferable beltway lifer, Deborah Birx, who hemmed and hawed until Dr. Fauci pushed her out of the way. The latter proceeded to read the statement quoted below word for word, and then promptly backed away from the podium beaming from ear-to-ear, as if to proclaim the Almighty had spoken and there was no more to be said.

> ... bars, restaurants, food courts, gyms, and other indoor and out-door venues where groups of people congregate **should be closed.**

As Jeffrey Tucker later succinctly noted, the tone of the press briefing and the handout's instructions amounted to an instantaneous "lights out" order to large swaths of the then $22 trillion US economy:

> Shut it all down. Everything. Everyone. As if the whole economy were a nightclub closing early.

Monthly Change in Private Services Jobs, 1954 to 2021.

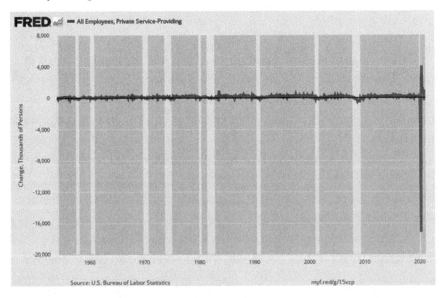

At that point The Donald uttered some weasel words that only confused the matter, even as he left Fauci's ukase to stand. Within hours thereafter, the Lockdown catastrophe was racing like an economic wildfire across the land.

The data on the resulting havoc leave nothing to the imagination. The Donald's Lockdown order triggered instantaneous cliff-dives in economic activity and employment. Thus, during April 2020, nonfarm payroll employment plunged by 20.5 million jobs, while Q2 real GDP contracted at a 35 percent annualized rate.

Self-evidently, there was nothing even remotely comparable in the sixty years of prior history shown below. While the data was not collected in this form during the Great Depression, sudden, violent economic plunges like those depicted by the lines below did not happen even then.

Change in Real GDP and Nonfarm Employment, 1960 to 2020.

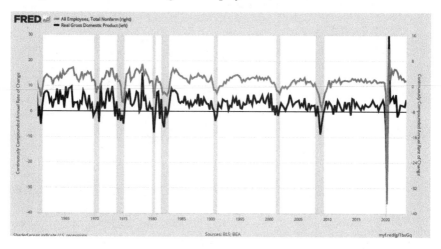

And it didn't end in Q2 2020, either. The imbalances, excesses, distortions, and malinvestments introduced into the US economy owing to the lockdowns, mandates, and Covid hysteria, and then the monstrous monetary and fiscal stimmies designed to relieve these dislocations, plague us to this very day.

The result, of course, is that aggregate measures of economic activity have experienced a yo-yo cycle like never before. As shown in the chart below, the Y/Y rate of spending on durables goods went from +12 percent in Q2 2020 to +58 percent in Q1 2021 to +0 percent in Q1 2022.

By contrast, spending at food service establishments plunged by *-38 percent* during the initial Q2 2020 lockdowns, remained negative through Q1 2021 and then soared by *+68 percent* Y/Y in Q2 2021 when the lockdowns were lifted and the final round of stimmies were distributed.

Needless to say, the wild swings in the chart below were unprecedented and caused massive distortions and inefficiencies throughout the main street economy, as well as capricious windfall gains and losses to the impacted businesses. And it all stemmed from The Donald's two weeks to flatten the curve and the spend-a-thons and print-a-thons which accompanied it.

Y/Y Change in PCE for Food Services & Accommodations versus Durable Goods, Q4 2019 to Q1 2022.

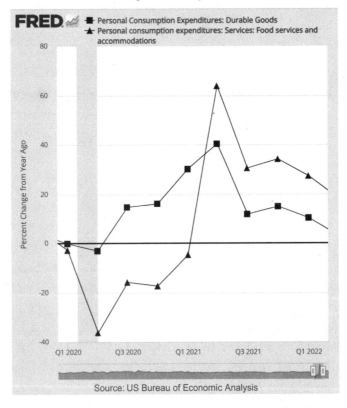

Source: US Bureau of Economic Analysis

For avoidance of doubt, here is the last thirty-two years of Y/Y changes in nominal spending for restaurants, bars, hotels, and resorts. Needless to say, neither American consumers nor businesses had ever previously engaged in the recent burst of drunken yo-yoing on their own accord. To the contrary, the chart depicts the havoc caused by massive state intervention on The Donald's watch.

Y/Y Change in PCE for Food Services and Accommodations, 1991–2022.

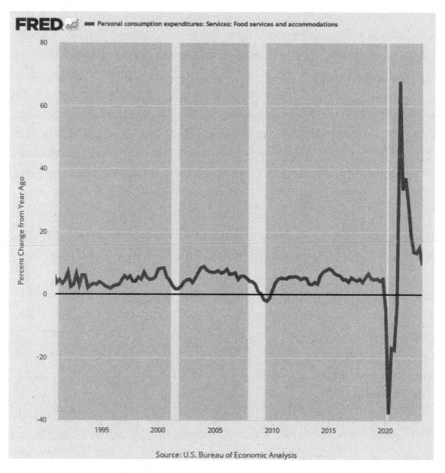

There is endlessly more data where this came from as we amplify it in the chapters to follow. But suffice it here to note that the American economy is more distorted and imbalanced than ever before because during the Trump era Washington had literally gone off the deep-end in its assaults on the free market, fiscal rectitude, and sound money.

Whether the resulting deep impairment to capitalist prosperity and constitutional liberty can ever be ameliorated and reversed is dubious at best. But one thing is sure—Donald J. Trump is not remotely part of the solution going forward.

For crying out loud, the CARES act and its successors were slinging the loot so freely that these so-called emergency handouts often dwarfed normal government distributions. For instance, the $41 billion subvention paid to farmers—who suffered mainly rising prices during the pandemic—was far greater than the entire annual farm subsidy largesse, which itself amounts to a near-criminal heist.

Likewise, the $600 per week unemployment topper payment was offered to one and all among the 60 million workers who drew benefits at one point or another during the pandemic. Yet that add-on amounted to a *169 percent increase* on top of the average regular state benefit of $357 per week which prevailed at the time.

By hook or crook, The Donald was going to have the Greatest Economy Ever—the future fiscal and inflationary consequences be damned. And yet today's MAGA-besotted Republicans still think this fiscal charlatan is the nation's savior.

The Donald's out-of-this-world pandemic spend-a-thons were an important reminder that fiscal profligacy is the handmaid of Leviathan. That is, even in a quasi-free society, citizens resist being regimented, bullied, herded, and commanded. State actions that deeply restrict their freedoms, badly inconvenience their lives, and seriously inflate their cost of living become distinctly unpopular. Very fast.

Unless . . . unless at least a decent share of the populace is paid handsomely to acquiesce. That changes the compliance equation dramatically, as was so starkly evident during 2020–2021 pandemic. And we are not talking merely about the classic free stuff to individuals—the $1.8 trillion of stimmy checks, unemployment toppers, tax credits, and other benefits.

As shown below, the three Covid relief bills amounted to a Noah's Ark of Washington largesse. Everyone, and we mean every organized interest group imaginable, got their fingers deep into the pot. As previously mentioned, for instance, upwards of $835 billion of "loans" went out to upwards of 12 million small businesses, allegedly to encourage employee retention. But the latter was easy as pie to comply with and resulted ultimately in cancellation of nearly 90 percent of the loan repayments.

The real purpose of this tsunami of federal cash, however, was to squelch the political opposition that would otherwise have erupted in the small business sector. By definition the latter is heavily concentrated in the leisure and hospitality space, which was ground zero of the lockdowns and the fear-inspired consumer self-quarantines.

Likewise, upwards of *$2.7 trillion* was showered upon school districts, local governments, the health-care sector, colleges and universities, social service agencies, transportation authorities, the pharmaceutical industry, and every manner of NGO. Even the defense agencies, Postal Service, and subsidized housing authorities garnered more than *$60 billion* of walking around money among them.

To be sure, this torrent of cash was allegedly designed to help communities cope with a total, harsh disruption of their normal modes of daily existence. But there were literally no rules, controls, oversight, or accountability. The hospitals and other medical providers, for example, received upwards of *$200 billion* of extra Medicare/Medicaid payments to test, treat, intubate, and frequently bury patients who expired "with Covid." But the waste and the harm resulting from this money flood has not been even remotely reckoned.

In short, by election season 2020 the American electorate would have been in noisy open rebellion absent the trillions of "compliance" payments which were being showered upon the public on a free-and-easy come-get-it basis. As itemized below, the *$6.5 trillion* authorized by the three Covid relief acts combined amounted to a veritable tsunami of cash from Washington the likes of which had never before even been imagined.

Aid to Individuals and Families:
- Stimmy checks to 100 million households: $817 billion.
- Unemployment toppers and added UI coverage: $678 billion.
- Child tax credits: $93 billion.
- Food stamps and nutrition: $71 billion.
- Childcare: $52 billion.
- Student loan deferrals: $39 billion.
- Other family aid: $50 billion.
- Total aid to individuals/families: ***$1.80 trillion.***

Business Bailouts:
- Payroll Protection Program: $835 billion.
- Economic Injury Disaster Loans: $350 billion.
- Airline bailouts: $80 billion.
- Restaurant subsidies: $29 billion.
- Liberalization of tax loss rules: $193 billion.
- Employer payroll tax deferral: $85 billion.
- Other business aids: $404 billion.
- Total business subsidies and bailouts: ***$1.975 trillion.***

State and Local Aid:
- Elementary and secondary schools: $190 billion.
- Increased federal share of medicaid: $72 billion.
- Transportation aids: $69 billion.
- Direct payments to state and local government: $393 billion.
- Other state and local aid: $141 billion.
- Total state and local aid: ***$865 billion.***

Health-Care Aids:
- Provider grants: $156 billion.
- Vaccine development, treatment, and supplies: $109 billion.
- Testing, monitoring, and research: $46 billion.
- Expanded medicaid and ACA subsidies: $78 billion.

- Medicare subsidies: $56 billion.
- Other health care: $169 billion.
- Total healthcare aids: ***$614 billion.***

Other Spending Programs:
- Disaster relief: $78 billion.
- College and university grants: $59 billion.
- Housing subsidies: $39 billion.
- Farmer aid: $41 billion.
- Defense agencies: $13 billion.
- US Postal Service: $10 billion.
- All other Covid relief: $1,022 billion.
- Total other spending programs: ***$1.262 trillion.***

Unfortunately, the Covid stimmies and bailouts did not function merely to quell the incipient opposition to what amounted to Donald Trump's version of martial law. These massive, extraordinary flows of cash from the state to the main street economy also caused stunning economic distortions, which, in turn, became the motor force of the stagflationary economic disaster now plaguing the nation.

Alas, there never was a good ship MAGA. But surely today's fiscal, monetary, and economic wreckage must be laid at the doorstep of its principal author.

Chapter Six

The Trouble with Trump-O-Nomics

As we have seen, Donald Trump inherited an economy that was tepidly coasting forward on the momentum of the post-crisis cyclical recovery, but he then hammered it into a violent tailspin during his last year in office.

And, yes, the evidence makes clear that the lockdowns and Covid quarantine hysteria were ultimately his doing. Coach Trump sent the Fauci Lockdown play out to the field on March 16, 2020, and stuck with his badly errant pandemic call for the next ten months despite the carnage that ensued on the field of American society.

The net result, as we have also seen, is that the US economy grew at just *1.52 percent* per annum during The Donald's forty-eight months in the Oval Office, representing just half the *3.04 percent* average growth rate under the previous eleven presidents between 1954 and 2016, and the very worst growth score posted among all of them. Moreover, it wasn't just economic growth which scored at the bottom of the presidential league tables. As we have also seen, Trump's jobs, productivity, savings, and investment rates all ended up at or close to the bottom for all presidents since Truman.

So the question recurs: How in the world do the MAGA fans keep insisting that the Trump economy was a time of plentiful economic milk and honey?

As the man said, the transformation of the worst economic record in sixty-six years into a triumph of policy does require some 'splainin'. In that regard, economic ignorance and partisan willfulness probably go a long way toward the answer, but there are also some specific factors that shed light on the question as well. These include—

- The GOP's catechismic assumption that the economy was good just because Trump cut taxes.
- The failure to acknowledge that policy actions have a considerable lag and that much of what presidents implement during their time in the Oval Office shows up on the doorstep of their successor.
- The (deserved) partisan loathing of Joe Biden, which enables the Donald's tenure to be cast in a favorable light retrospectively—at least relative to the stagflationary blow-off now underway, much of which Sleepy Joe inherited from Trump, his predecessors, and most especially the Fed.

Stated differently, the record during Trump's tenure was punk and its legacy during the subsequent years was worse, as we amplify further below. The only thing that gives it a glow in hindsight is Joe Biden bashing. But that's partisan hectoring, not analysis.

In any event, consider what is held to be the supreme economic achievement during Trump's tenure—the sweeping 2017 tax cuts. Yet mere passage of a revenue bill that was officially estimated to add *$1.46 trillion* to the public debt over ten years (2018–2027) is hardly proof of anything—except the GOP's latter-day axiom that red ink–financed tax cuts are inherently good and that deficits don't matter.

That's dangerous nonsense, of course, but it is worth noting that the Trump tax cut legislation was heavily focused on the reduction of the corporate rate from 28 percent to 21 percent and the parallel pass-thru provision for non-corporate payers that provided a 20 percent deduction for qualified business income. The estimated ten-year revenue loss from these two provisions alone was $1.76 trillion, meaning that the balance of the act actually raised taxes by about $300 billion.

So, it would be fair to say that the Trump/GOP tax cut did pack a fair wallop in the direction of incentivizing business to invest. But the fact is, you can't find a trace of evidence for that in the investment data. During the five years ending in 2017, the real growth rate of business fixed investment was *3.72 percent* per annum. By contrast, during the five years after the Trump tax cut became effective (2018–2022) real business investment growth slipped to *2.98 percent* per annum.

Moreover, when you reach back to the heyday of American prosperity, the robust investment rates during those times cause the ballyhooed Trump tax cut impact to pale by comparison. To wit, real gross nonresidential investment grew by *5.32 percent* per annum between 1954 and 2000 or nearly two times faster than during the five years after the Trump tax cut.

Even then, the above figures are unduly flattering because they represent the gross level of real investment before deduction for capital stock consumed in production during the current year. What matters in terms of investment for future growth and productivity gains, however, is the net investment figure after capital consumption.

And on that score the data leaves nothing to the imagination. Between 1954 and 2000, real net non-residential (i.e., "business") investment grew by *6.20 percent* per annum. That figure was nearly *11x* larger than the anemic *0.57 percent* per annum growth rate of real net business investment during 2016 through 2021.

To be sure, historic comparisons are always tricky because all things are never equal and many other factors beyond tax policy impact investment rates—including stage of the business cycle, interest rates, inflation rates, foreign competition, and more. Still, to claim a sterling policy success there should be at least a tad of evidence in the data—especially when on the margin the US treasury borrowed $1.7 trillion to make it happen.

But even factoring in the business cycle swings in private domestic investment and taking the long view of economic history, it is hard to see how the Trump business tax cuts levitated what was a falling cyclically adjusted long-term trend. Thus, two years on from the Trump tax cut at the pre-Covid cyclical peak in 2019, domestic private investment was just 17.8 percent of GDP—well below the 19 percent to 20 percent of GDP levels achieved at the top of previous business cycles.

Private Domestic Investment as Percent of GDP, 1978 to 2020.

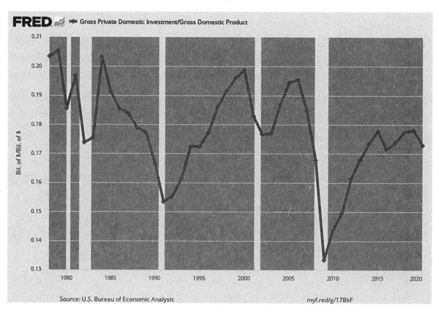

Nevertheless, the truth of the matter is that these huge tax cuts did massively increase the after-tax cash flows of US businesses, albeit cash flows which were funded by Uncle Sam's credit card. Yet there is no mystery as to where the overwhelming share of the increased after-tax cash flow from the Trump/GOP tax cuts went: namely, to monumental levels of stock buybacks and dividend payments.

In the case of stock buybacks, there was an immediate surge during the first quarter after the business cuts became effective

(Q1 2018), which persisted through the end of 2019. The Covid-induced economic crash in the first half of 2020 did temporarily curtail buyback activity, as shown by the chart below, but by Q3 2021 the dollar volume of S&P 500 stock buybacks hit nearly $235 billion, representing a 70 percent gain from the 2017 pre-tax cut level.

Likewise, the sum of S&P 500 stock buybacks and dividends rose from $960 billion in the last year before the cut (2017) to $1.51 trillion by 2022. That amounts to a *$550 billion* annualized increase or *56 percent gain* in shareholder distributions. Either way, the benefit of the business tax cuts didn't get downstreamed to the main street economy; it got upstreamed to the top 10 percent of households which own 89 percent of all US stocks.

Indeed, the distributional aspect of the shareholder returns depicted below is nothing short of flabbergasting. Between Q4 2016 and Q4 2021, the value of stocks held by the top 1 percent of households rose from $10.8 trillion to $22.8 trillion. That $12 trillion gain compares to just a $117 billion rise in the value of stocks held by the bottom 50 percent of households during the same period.

When viewed on a per household basis the results border on the hideous. According to the Fed's own data, the stock portfolios of the top 1 percent of households gained $9 million *each* versus $1,800 *each* for the bottom 50 percent.

That's right. The stock market bonanza fueled by the combination of the Fed money-printing and the Trump tax cut resulted in the 1.3 million wealthiest households in American each gaining *5,000x* more stock wealth than the average household among the bottom 66 million.

These mega-distributions to shareholders at the tippy top of the economic ladder, in turn, were a function of a bubble-bloated and speculation-ridden equity market that was fueled by the Fed's relentless money printing. That is to say, The Donald's insistence on ultra-low interest rates and a continuation of the Fed's massive bond-buying program was surely a reinforcement to that folly, if any was needed, and resulted in cancellation of

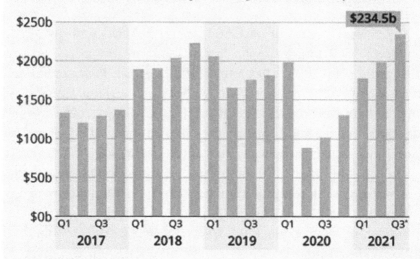

S&P 500 Buybacks Hit Record After Covid Pullback

Total volume of stock buybacks by S&P 500 companies

* Q3 2021 data is preliminary
Sources: S&P Dow Jones Indices, The Wall Street Journal

statista

any incentive effect the tax cuts might have otherwise had on productive investment.

Under the rules of the free market, of course, businesses are entitled to do what they deem best with their cash flows, and we do not question that axiom for a moment. But corporate executives should not be artificially induced to distribute rather than reinvest by baldly inflationary monetary policies. And Uncle Sam should never borrow trillions in order to indirectly fund stock buybacks and dividends that mainly accrue to the top 1 percent and 10 percent of US households.

However, these precise features—easy money, rampant stock market speculation, and immense public debt increases—were the very essence of Trump-O-Nomics.

Infrastructure Boondoggles

The Donald's propensity for borrow-and-spend was also evident in his endless promotion of a large-scale national infrastructure program. This incepted during the 2016 campaign when he called for at least $1 trillion in new infrastructure spending over ten years—a theme that the Trump White House resurrected multiple times during The Donald's tenure. As *Bloomberg* later described it shortly after the 2020 election:

> Donald Trump campaigned on a $1 trillion infrastructure plan. "We are going to fix our inner cities and rebuild our highways, bridges, tunnels, airports, schools, hospitals," he said in his 2016 election night victory speech. "And we will put millions of our people to work as we rebuild it."
>
> A real estate developer who once referred to himself as "the builder president", Trump held multiple "Infrastructure Weeks" calling for investments in transportation, electricity and water systems during his presidency. . .

Large-scale federal infrastructure spending and conservative economics, however, mix no better than oil and water. The former is based on the shopworn beltway proposition that the nation's infrastructure is in a dilapidated state and that a river of new cash from Washington is needed for its repair and rehabilitation, and that these so-called "public investments" will goose the GDP and jobs in the process.

Well, no. The dilapidated infrastructure canard is essentially the hobby horse of lobbies for the construction, building supply and architecture/engineering industries, as well as state and local officials who are always pleased to spruce-up the hometown with projects paid for with other peoples' taxes.

Indeed, the failing infrastructure story is nearly as old as the hills. We heard it when we first came to Washington in 1970 and the only thing that ever changes is that the purported "deficit" of infrastructure "investment" just keeps getting larger and larger with every passing decade.

When the beltway bandits run low on excuses to spend, they trot out florid tales of crumbling infrastructure, pothole ridden roads, collapsing bridges, failing water and sewer systems, electric power grid deficiencies, inadequate rail and public transit and the rest. This is variously alleged to represent a national disgrace, an impediment to economic growth and a sensible opportunity for fiscal "stimulus."

Needless to say, The Donald and his Steve Bannon–style politicos fell for these shibboleths lock, stock, and barrel. And they did not hesitate to embrace the companion fable that infrastructure presents a swell opportunity for Washington to create millions of new "jobs."

In fact, at the time of The Donald's inauguration there was no deficiency in infrastructure spending at all, and there hadn't been for decades. Total national infrastructure spending in constant dollars stood at $425 billion in 2016. That was *three times* the $140 billion (2017 $) level that prevailed in 1956 when the Eisenhower Administration had famously enacted the Interstate Highway program.

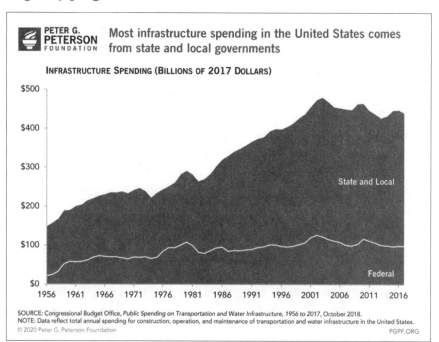

PETER G. PETERSON FOUNDATION

Most infrastructure spending in the United States comes from state and local governments

INFRASTRUCTURE SPENDING (BILLIONS OF 2017 DOLLARS)

SOURCE: Congressional Budget Office, *Public Spending on Transportation and Water Infrastructure, 1956 to 2017*, October 2018.
NOTE: Data reflect total annual spending for construction, operation, and maintenance of transportation and water infrastructure in the United States.
© 2020 Peter G. Peterson Foundation   PGPF.ORG

Likewise, had the Trumpites bothered to do their homework they might not have also fallen for the false notion that roads, bridges, tunnels, transit lines, buses, waterworks, sewer systems, ports, etc. are the job of Washington to fund and oversee at the national level. Actually, except for the core interstate highway system, even a goodly share of spending in the federal area in the graph above properly belongs at state and local levels.

These are inherently local functions, conferring local benefits and costs. And if they are escalated to the national level, the very essence of pork-barrel politics comes to the fore with local politicians promoting ever bigger and more wasteful projects in order to boast about delivering benefits to their constituents, while diffusing the costs among 160 million national taxpayers who never know what hits them.

To be sure, the Trump Administration didn't actually get around to implementing a serious add-on infrastructure program on top of the copious steady-state spending levels it inherited. But the Bloomberg post-election assessment cited above, perhaps inadvertently, exposed the Achilles heel of the whole misguided campaign:

> . . . "We believe this will create a great return on taxpayer dollars," stated a 2018 White House press release, which cited a $5.4 billion light-rail referendum in Nashville as the kind of locally funded project the administration hoped to encourage. **Nashville voters rejected the rail measure three months later.** And the president's building vows never came to pass.

The bolded sentence tells you all you need to know. If local voters won't pony up the taxes for projects of overwhelmingly local benefit, then they shouldn't be undertaken at all. Federal funding in part or whole severs the nexus between costs and benefits, opening the door to the proverbial pork barrel that Washington politicians have feasted upon since the time of Henry Clay.

In truth, a large-scale national infrastructure program is the very essence of Big Government and a breeding ground for Swamp Creatures of every size and shape. A real conservative Republican, therefore, needs be ever vigilant in opposition, not beating the drums for $1 trillion of new pork barrel spending, as Trump did continuously during his sojourn in the Oval Office.

As it happened, we were witness to the crumbling infrastructure myth up close and personal more than forty years ago when even Ronald Reagan got bamboozled by the Washington spending lobbies. Indeed, they literally talked the Gipper out of his firm anti-spending, pro-private sector, pro-local government principles as they loaded up the legislative wagon with pork.

Donald Trump, of course, had no economic policy principles at all when he stumbled into the Oval Office in pursuit of his own power and glory. Accordingly, he was the "mark" of a lifetime for Washington's public sector investment porkers.

In this context, the "crumbling bridges falling down" story is a useful and revealing template for the entire perennial campaign on behalf of massive federal infrastructure spending and borrowing. In fact, the stark distinction between myth and reality with respect to the so-called "deficient and obsolete bridges" is powerfully illustrative of the disinformation on which the entire infrastructure gambit is based.

To hear the K Street lobbies tell it, motorists all across America are at risk of plunging into the drink at any time owing to defective bridges. And they have been saying exactly the same thing ever since even Ronald Reagan fell for that canard four decades ago.

As it happened, during the long trauma of the 1981–1982 recession, the Reagan Administration had stoutly resisted the temptation to implement a Keynesian-style fiscal-stimulus and jobs program—notwithstanding an unemployment rate that peaked in double digits. But within just a few months of the bottom in late 1982, along came a Republican secretary of transportation, Drew Lewis, with a presidential briefing on the alleged disrepair of the nation's highways and bridges. The briefing was accompanied by a Cabinet Room full of easels bearing pictures of dilapidated bridges and pot-hole fractured roads, accompanied by a plan to dramatically increase federal highway spending.

Not surprisingly, DOT Secretary Drew Lewis was a former Pennsylvania governor and the top GOP fundraiser of the era. So the Cabinet Room was soon figuratively surrounded by a muscular coalition of road builders, construction machinery suppliers, asphalt and concrete vendors, governors, mayors, and legislators and the AFL-CIO building-trades department. And if that wasn't enough, Lewis had also made deals to line up the highway safety and beautification lobbies, bicycle enthusiasts, and all the motley array of mass transit interest groups. They were all singing from the same crumbling infrastructure songbook.

As Lewis summarized at the time and Donald Trump was apparently channeling forty years later, "We have highways and bridges that are falling down around our ears— that's really the thrust of the program." And the Gipper quickly added his own refrain:

> "No, we are opposed to wasteful borrow and spend," Reagan recalled. "That's how we got into this mess. But these projects are different. Roads and bridges are a proper responsibility of government, and they have already been paid for by the gas tax."

Well, they hadn't been, and by the time a pork-laden highway bill was rammed through a lame duck session of Congress at year-end, the president's speechwriters had gone all-in for the crumbling infrastructure gambit. Explaining why he signed the bill, the scourge of Big Government was scripted to claim:

> We have 23,000 bridges in need of replacement or rehabilitation; 40 percent of our bridges are over forty years old.

Needless to say, thirty-five years later Donald Trump averred that those very same bridges—presumably fixed by Reagan's infrastructure spending program—were purportedly still falling down!

But they weren't. What the data actually showed can best be described as "The Tale of Madison County Bridges to Nowhere" as per the one-horse bridges memorialized by Clint Eastwood's memorable movie set in an Iowa county of the same name. In fact, there could not be a more striking illustration of why Donald Trump was way off the deep-end with his trillion-dollar infrastructure boondoggle; and also, why the principle that local users and taxpayers should fund 100 percent of local infrastructure is such a crucial tenet of both fiscal solvency and honest, minimal government.

The crumbling-bridges myth starts with the claim by DOT and the industry lobbies that there are sixty-three thousand bridges across the nation that are "structurally deficient." This suggests that the nation's highway grid is dotted with waterway spanning hazards.

It is not. Roughly one-third, or nineteen thousand, of these purportedly hazardous bridges are located in just six rural states located in America's midsection: Iowa, Oklahoma, Missouri, Kansas, Nebraska, and South Dakota. The fact that these states account for only 5.9 percent of the nation's population seems more than a little incongruous but that isn't even half the puzzle.

It seems that these thinly populated town-and-country states have a grand total of *118,000 bridges*. That is, one bridge for every 160 citizens—men, women, and children included. And the biggest bridge state among them is, yes, Iowa.

The state has 3 million souls and nearly twenty-five thousand bridges—one for every 125 people. So suddenly the picture is crystal clear. These are not the kind of bridges that thousands of cars and heavy-duty trucks pass over each day. To the contrary, they are mainly the kind Clint Eastwood needed Meryl Streep (playing a local farmwife) to locate— so he could take pictures for a National Geographic spread on "covered bridges."

Stated differently, the overwhelming bulk of the six hundred thousand so-called "bridges" in America are so little used that they are more often crossed by dogs, cows, skunks, and tractors than they are by passenger motorists. These country bridges are essentially no different than local playgrounds and municipal parks.

They have nothing to do with interstate commerce, GDP growth, or national public infrastructure.

If they are structurally deficient as measured by DOT engineering standards, that is not exactly startling news to the host village, township and county governments that choose not to upgrade them. So, if Iowa is content to live with five thousand bridges—one in five of its twenty-five thousand bridges—that are deemed structurally deficient by the DOT, so what?

Self-evidently, the electorate and officialdom of Iowa do not consider these bridges to be a public-safety hazard. If they actually were, something would have been done about them long ago. Local officials are not the dunces the Washington political class deems them to be.

Compared to the nineteen thousand so-called "structurally deficient" bridges in the six rural states cited above, there are also nineteen thousand such deficient bridges in another group of thirty-five states—including Texas, Maryland, Massachusetts, Virginia, Washington, Oregon, Michigan, Arizona, Colorado, Florida, New Jersey, and Wisconsin, among others.

But these states have a combined population of 175 million, not 19 million as in the six rural states; and more than six hundred citizens per bridge, not 125 as in Iowa. Moreover, only 7 percent of the bridges in these thirty-five states are considered to be structurally deficient, rather than 21 percent as in Iowa.

So, the long and short of it is self-evident: Iowa still has a lot of one-horse bridges, and Massachusetts— with 1,300 citizens per bridge— does not. None of this is remotely relevant to a purported national-infrastructure crisis today—any more than it was in 1982 when even Ronald Reagan fell for "23,000 bridges in need of replacement or rehabilitation."

Stated differently, Ronald Reagan failed to drain the swamp despite his best intentions. Donald Trump, by contrast, was well on the way to filling it deeper no sooner than he had taken the oath of office.

In fact, within days of the inauguration in January 2017, the Trump White House was promoting a list of fifty priority infrastructure projects purportedly worth $140 billion. In truth, however, this list was actually a fifty-state Noah's Ark of long-languishing public works projects that the National Governors Association (NGA) had forwarded to the Trump transition team after the election.

It comprised a dog's breakfast of boondoggles and white elephants that the nation's governors sincerely hoped *taxpayers from states other than their own would fund*. But the inexperienced and ill-informed Trump and his lackeys didn't even know they were being served warmed-over rancid pork. Nor did they possess the policy principles to discern that a large-scale infrastructure program has nothing whatsoever to do with making the American economy great again.

To the contrary, any new administration genuinely bent on restoring capitalist prosperity and draining the Washington Swamp would have deposited the NGA list in the round file forthwith. For example, one such project was a multi-billion-dollar high speed rail line between Houston and Dallas. It was a truly wondrous example of how federal taxes were to be extracted from the ailing rust belt counties of Michigan and Wisconsin in order to gift the flush precincts of the shale belt with public amenities they would never tax themselves to obtain. And it was especially rich coming from the state of Texas, which doesn't tax its own residents' income at all.

As it happened, the untutored White House staff thought the NGA list was just swell, and soon incorporated nearly all the NGA projects in a "working draft" of Trump's $1 trillion infrastructure stimulus plan. While the latter never did really see the legislative light of day, the relevant point is that right out of the starting gate Trump was peddling big-time economic policy actions straight from FDR's playbook.

That's right. A core element of Donald Trump's plan to make the American economy great again amounted to a dog-eared list of public works pork that had been passed around the beltway for years, if not decades. But a mid-July 2017 piece in the *New York Times* left no doubt that the Donald stood four-square behind it:

> In the White House, Mr. Trump has continued to dangle the possibility of "a great national infrastructure program" that would create "millions" of new jobs as part of a public-private partnership to rival the public works achievements of Franklin Delano Roosevelt and Dwight D. Eisenhower. **He chastises anyone who forgets to include it near the top of his to-do list**, telling one recent visitor to the Oval Office, "Don't forget about infrastructure!"

Needless to say, the contents of the always imminent but never delivered plan tells you all you need to know about The Donald's propensity for Big Government conducted out of the very swamps of Washington DC that he professed to be draining. The fact is, the whole scheme was belied by its faulty predicate. In fact, the bridges of America were not falling down, and roads, streets, subways, sewers, waterworks, and power lines didn't need dollars from Uncle Sam's over-extended credit card.

Actually, Washington's primary, if not sole, public infrastructure job is maintenance of the core Interstate Highway System. And the latter was in pretty good shape then, including its heavily trafficked bridges, as it still is now.

More importantly, if additional "investment" is required on the interstate highway grid, no Trump-style, debt-financed "infrastructure" extravaganza is needed to secure it. To the contrary, highway users should pay for it in the normal course with a modest increase in the federal gasoline tax. Indeed, the 18 cents per gallon levy hasn't been increased since 1992 despite a 120 percent increase in the CPI since then. So, it now brings in less than half of its 1992 value in purchasing power terms.

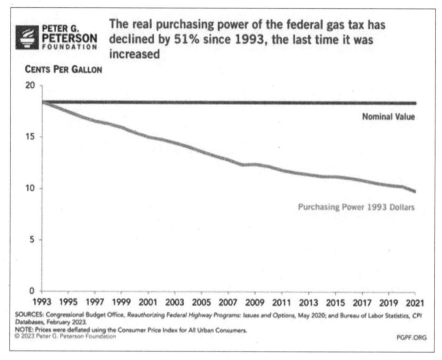

Better still, Washington merely needs to rescind the earmarks that *divert more than half* of the existing *$40 billion* per year of federal fuel tax revenues to state and local roads, mass transit, bike trails, walking paths, weed removal, transportation museums, wildlife crossings, electric vehicle charging infrastructure, intelligent transportation technologies, cybersecurity protections, rural barge landings, waterfront infrastructure projects, privately-owned ferry terminals, and countless other diversions. Absent these earmarks, the pavement and bridges of the Interstate Highway system would be in tip-top shape from the current fuel tax levies, and in short order.

So did the Trumpites make any effort to re-prioritize the use of highway trust fund revenues to the original purpose as envisioned by Ike in 1956?

They did not. In good part that's because the GOP Public Works Committee members in the House and Senate are all-in on the current smorgasbord of "highway" pork. And The Donald was not about to rock the boat where it needed disruption the most because in his mind the bigger the federal spending monuments to his leadership the better.

Beyond the core Interstate Highway system, moreover, upwards of 95 percent of what passes for infrastructure investment — state and county roads, city streets, local bridges, airports, seaports, mass transit, water and sewer, the power grid, parks and recreation, etc.—are the responsibility of the private sector and should be paid for by users or, arguably, constitute local "public goods" and amenities.

In turn, the latter should be managed by state and local governments and be funded by local users and/or taxpayers. But give the beltway lobbies and infrastructure racketeers an inch and they will take a mile. After decades of federal mission creep, there is virtually no aspect of local "infrastructure" spending that has not wormed its way into the federal budget.

That's just another reason why the nation has $33 trillion of public debt already. And that's why Trump's abortive infrastructure program amounted to little more than political sanction for the massive waste already embedded in the Washington Swamp. That is, the Donald spent four years squandering the GOP's fiscal sobriety brand by endlessly promoting the quintessence of Big Government.

Back in the day, of course, Republicans were intrepid defenders of Federalism and the notion that the domestic functions of government should be conducted as close to the local level as possible. After all, what's the point of some eighty-nine thousand units of state, county, city, township, village, and special district government if these taxpayer-funded agencies can't even provide for-fare box revenues on local bus routes, maintenance of secondary highways and city streets, or water and sewer services to local residents?

When all of this gets federalized on an ad hoc basis as proposed by the Trump infrastructure extravaganza, however, you end up with the worst of all possible worlds. That is, random redistribution of resources among localities; wasteful projects and inefficient pork barrel allocation of funding; and a centralization of politics where Washington's permanent governing class always wins, and the working taxpayers of Flyover America are left out in the cold.

Of course, no one ever explained this to Trump because he wasn't much interested in conservative policy and philosophy anyway. To the contrary, The Donald chooses issue positions based on little more than his own ill-informed prejudices, half-baked theories, and momentary impulses about how to make the American economy "great again."

And that's the heart of the matter. Donald Trump is a clear and present danger to capitalist prosperity and constitutional liberty in America because his mind is a hairball of crackpottery, ad hocery, and can-do statism in the economic policy realm. MAGA economics, in fact, is just Washington business-as-usual decorated with Trumpian bombast.

That's why debunking Trump's abortive $1 trillion infrastructural program is so important. Everything in the whole grab-bag of infrastructure promotion is at odds with core principles of pro-market, pro-liberty economics.

Thus, in just the narrow area of highways, the extent of mission creep and pork barrel politics is stunning. The *forty-seven thousand miles* of interstate highways constitute only *1.1 percent* of the *4 million miles* of streets, roads and highways in the entire nation.

Indeed, one of the reasons we have state and local governments in the United States is precisely to take care of 99 percent of road surfaces that the great Dwight D. Eisenhower said should remain a non-federal responsibility. And that was in fact his position, even as he pioneered the Interstate highway system and trust fund.

Yet less than $15 billion, or one-third, of the annual federal highway program goes to the forty-seven thousand-mile Interstate Highway System that President Eisenhower fathered. The rest gets auctioned off by the congressional politicians to state, county, and local roads and to the far-flung array of mass transit and other of non-highway purposes and earmarks itemized above.

Of course, if The Donald had chosen to fund his $1 trillion infrastructure extravaganza with new taxes it would have at least been fiscally neutral, even as it undermined economic growth by reallocating resources from the productive private sector to the inefficiency-ridden public sector.

But his Wall Street advisers in the White House had an even worse idea. They proposed to issue tax-exempt public works bonds to fund these massive boondoggles. The dubious theory, of course, was that such "green ink" national infrastructure bonds would somehow be more economically benign than the "red ink" bonds issued to fund the regular US Treasury deficits. That is, the borrowings incurred to repair the nation's allegedly "collapsing" infrastructure would be a form of "self-liquidating" debt, which would eventually pay for itself via enhanced national economic growth and efficiency.

Needless to say, that's what the hapless government of Japan has been saying for the last fifty years. With its public debt ballooned by massive infrastructure spending to 235 percent of GDP and its economy barely growing at all, what is being liquidated, in fact, is the nation's taxpayers, not its "construction" bonds.

Indeed, we do not need any more federal subsidies for any category of infrastructure. For instance, airport modernization and operations are already being funded at $20 billion per year mainly from ticket taxes, general aviation user fees, and the like.

If that isn't enough, as indicated by air-traffic congestion and crowded airports, there is a simple solution. The 10 percent of the population that accounts for 90 percent of air travel should pay for higher spending via increased user charges on their tickets or landing fees on their G-5s.

Likewise, if the $65 billion currently being spent to subsidize the capital and operating costs of local mass transit systems is not enough, then let local taxpayers absorb the burden, not unborn generations that will inherent the nation's $33 trillion public debt.

And when it comes to enhancing real economic productivity and growth, nothing could be more inimical than to pour tens of billions into hopeless white elephants like Amtrak and the high-speed rail boondoggles.

In short, the infrastructure boosters have it exactly upside-down. The economic crisis confronting the nation is owing to the state getting way too big, not because public spending on infra-structure or anything else has been too small.

Besides that, the overwhelming thrust of large-scale national infrastructure programs is not the repair and rehabilitation of supposedly dilapidated existing infrastructure, but the funding of new projects, facilities, and capacities that the nation flat-out doesn't need, such as mass transit and windfarms. Such economic white elephants are driven by green energy and other ideological agendas that are harmful to capitalist prosperity, not supportive.

For instance, one feature of the Trump infrastructure pro-gram was tens of billions for investments in the utility power grid, including a boost to solar and wind capacity. But the actual truth is that there was no shortfall of productive investment in the utility sector whatsoever. The so-called shortfall in green utility capacity was owing to it not being economically competitive, not because capital investment was being starved.

In fact, funding had been bountiful. Construction investment by private and public utilities combined had grown from a $35 billion annual rate in Q4 2002 to nearly $110 billion by Q4 2016. That amounted to a robust 8.3 percent per annum growth rate, and a clear signal that the utility sector didn't need any infrastruc-ture pork from Washington.

Indeed, green energy investment in the utility sector through the backdoor of federally subsidized infrastructure programs was the last thing the Trump administration should have embraced. After all, to his credit The Donald did cancel the Paris Accord and his administration generally did not embrace the Climate Crisis hysteria.

Moreover, to borrow a phrase, the Trump infrastructure shills were actually bringing coals to Newcastle in the case of the power grid. That is to say, thanks to the Fed's misguided interest rate repression policies, long-term utility financing had never been cheaper in real terms, nor more plentiful in quantity, as the chart below makes abundantly clear.

Still, the basis for the misbegotten notion that there is a financing shortage for the single largest category of infrastructure spending—utilities and power—is just plain ridiculous, as

Annualized Rate of Construction Spending for Utility Power, 2002 to 2016.

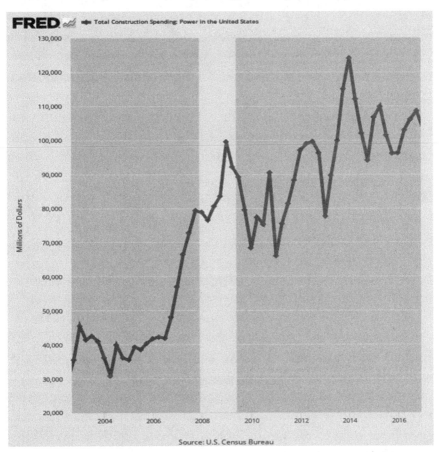

is the infrastructure cheerleaders' hoary claim that $30 billion is "wasted" each year due to inefficient power transmission. That is, the 8–15 percent of power output at the generation station that does not make it to end consumers owing to losses at step-up transformers, high voltage transmission lines, step-down transformers, and distribution transformers and cables.

So, yes, there is inherent frictional power loss in the process by which central-station bulk power is distributed through high voltage power lines and then across the local distribution grid. But it's a matter of physics and economic trade-offs. If you invest a lot more in high performance transmission systems, you will absolutely get less power loss but at far higher capital cost.

In any event, that's a pricing issue and could readily be alleviated—to the extent that it's a real problem—by intelligent rate reform. Dig deep enough, however, and it becomes obvious that a whole wing of the infrastructure lobby—apparently unbeknownst to the Trumpites—is really composed of radical Climate Change Howlers.

The infrastructure they want to replace is not crumbling and an impediment to economic growth; it's actually a low-cost contributor to growth and jobs which happens to generate carbon dioxide emissions attributable to the 15 percent of central station fuel that is lost on the grid. In fact, this completely ulterior—and false—agenda against CO2 emissions was actually admitted to by a typical spokesman:

> The wasted electricity from the obsolete power grid is the same as the output of **200** average coal-burning power plants—causing an extra 280 million tons of carbon to spew into the air each year.

Right. Replace perfectly good conventional transmission capacity with ultra-high-cost advanced transmission capital and for what purpose? Why, to force the uneconomic substitution of expensive transmission line capital for low-cost fossil fuel, even as you add even more debt to the nation's balance sheet and destroy existing capital long before is useful life has been reached.

Another category of alleged infrastructure starvation targeted by the Trump program was wastewater and sewage treatment, and here the story is even worse. The EPA started making multi-billion-dollar grants for sewer plants during the early 1970s, and since then more than $120 billion in grants and loans have been dispersed to upwards of 15,000 local treatment plants and facilities across the nation.

Unfortunately, owing to the disconnect between local benefits and federally funded costs, municipalities have wasted massive amounts of resources building over-sized plants, and then under-charging their business and residential customers for their use. The ridiculous amounts of spending on waste treatment plants at the national level caused an immense waste of resources that would not have occurred if local users had to pay the full cost of services, or if local taxpayers had been obliged to cover any fiscal shortfalls.

So the truth in this category was not prolonged fiscal starvation but chronic economic obesity! Under a regime of full economic pricing for waste treatment services, the nation's infrastructure budget could be sharply reduced at the local level, while the multi-billion annual federal aid program could be eliminated entirely.

That's because higher, unsubsidized prices at the municipal system intake pipe would cause an outpouring of technological innovation and practice changes among users and waste generators. Such economically-driven innovation and user conservation investments, in turn, would dramatically reduce the capacity requirements and cost of building and operating end-system treatment plants.

Moreover, even under the current system of waste treatment socialism, there were no facts whatsoever that support the starvation argument. Annual US spending for waste treatment was $24 billion in 2016—a figure 50 percent higher than the $16 billion level in 2002.

To be sure, it is absolutely true that in selective localities in the US there are obsolete sewage-treatment plants, water supply systems, and much else, just as in the case of pothole ridden roads and streets. But you can't blame that on inadequate spending—something that even more federal funding would only make worse.

That's because the real problem is local government corruption, inefficiency, pork barrel politics, and the excessive power of the municipal unions and the construction trades. That's true in spades, even for the local transportation sector. The disgraceful condition of roads and streets in places like New York City and Philadelphia, for example, is owing to the fact that billions have been siphoned off by drastically overpaid union labor and deeply corrupted contract award processes.

Needless to say, waste and corruption are the very opposite of a funding shortfall. For instance, Trump inherited nationwide highway spending of $94 billion in 2016—a level which was 24 percent higher in constant dollars than the $75 billion (2016$) spent in 2002.

So the solution was never more dollars from Washington per an extravagant Trumpian infrastructure program. What was actually needed was drastically fewer federal infrastructure dollars and more local funding and accountability, and therefore a tighter cost and benefit nexus.

For instance, if the voters really wanted better roads and streets throughout the localities of the nation there was one simple solution that had everything to do with conservative economic principles and nothing to do with Trumpian grandeur. To wit, governors, legislators, mayors, and city fathers need to raise state and local gas taxes and/or user fees and tolls to fund such improvements.

Stated differently, the proof is ultimately in the pudding. There is apparently nothing that Americans treasure more than their autos and the freedom to motor far and wide. If they can't be persuaded to pay higher road taxes and tolls, then by definition there isn't a "shortage" of highway investment.

At the end of the day, what was "crumbling" in January 2017— when the Donald stumbled into the Oval Office with essentially no economic program at all, nor even any discernable economic policy principles—was not the nation's infrastructure, but the case for a bloated Washington pork barrel. In the end, the Trump trillion-dollar infrastructure brouhaha was just another variation of the misbegotten Keynesian notion that the state can command economic growth via borrowing or printing money in order to fuel "aggregate demand."

For want of doubt, just recall this *Wall Street Journal* headline from April 2019 after a White House meeting with the congressional leadership: "Democrats, Trump Agree to Aim for $2 trillion Infrastructure Package." The story made clear that the Donald was enthusiastically going about the business of making Big Government even bigger:

> "I like the number you've been using, Nancy," Mr. Trump told House Speaker Nancy Pelosi (D., Calif.), according to a Democratic aide. **"Two trillion."**
>
> In unusually positive comments about negotiations with the president, Mrs. Pelosi and Senate Minority Leader Chuck Schumer (D., N.Y.) said that the meeting was productive, and that they had agreed to return in three weeks to hear Mr. Trump's ideas about how to pay for an infrastructure bill.
>
> "There was goodwill in this meeting, and that was different than some of the other meetings that we've had," Mr. Schumer said.
>
> Mrs. Pelosi said the two sides had "come to one agreement: **that the agreement would be big and bold."**

The bolded phrase in praise of bold tells you all you need to know. The Donald's economics are about a politician's state that's "big and bold," not a republican one that's minimal, unobtrusive, and solvent. In fact, for good measure The Donald explained to the gathered Congressional leaders the essence of his enthusiasm for Big Infrastructure:

> Mr. Trump told lawmakers he wanted the infrastructure money to be well spent, telling them he was impressed by the "beautiful

walls" he had seen in China—**"not a dent, no paint was chipped,"** according to a person familiar with the discussion. Mr. Trump said U.S. highways, in contrast, were an embarrassment, and criticized the company that he said sells "dented walls."

At the end of the day the Donald's infrastructure boondoggle was no different economically than *building debt-funded pyramids in every state of the union.* The economic waste represented by federal borrowing to build over-sized sewage plants or unused local roads or to upgrade one-horse bridges or to build inefficient mass transit lines, or to construct uneconomic super-conducting power lines or to repair "dented walls" is exactly the same.

In fact, however, true economic growth and wealth generation stems from the supply side of the economy. That is, from the exertions and productivity of labor and the efficiencies, innovations and investments generated by entrepreneurs.

And that leads to the real reason for our present debilitated economy. Over the last two decades there has been a 10 percent decline in real net business investment (after depreciation of the existing capital stock), while labor hours utilized by the business economy have inched forward by barely 0.6 percent per annum during the same period. That is to say, there has been a yawning shortage in the supply of both labor and productive capital.

Moreover, there has also been a stunning decline in net business formation and entrepreneurial activity. If Trump had really wanted to deal with faltering economic growth, he would have worked on removing the regulatory, tax, monetary, and welfare state barriers behind these ominous supply side trends, not the economic will-o-wisp of Big Infrastructure.

In a word, the real Trumpian legacy is not a strong economy or robust investment cycle, but just a further slide into the abyss of profligate monetary and fiscal policies—policies which will eventually bring capitalist prosperity to an abrupt end.

The Donald's Deregulation Puffery

Finally, it needs be noted that all of the Trumpite ballyhoo about The Donald's putative war on government regulation doesn't make up for his Big Government fiscal and monetary policy sins, either. That's because most of what was advertised by the White House as stirring successes on this front amounted to paint-by-the-numbers trivia, as measured by minor regulations rescinded; or did not extend much beyond cancelling a handful of eleventh-hour over-the-top Obama regulations, such as the Clean Power Plan, that had never been implemented and would have likely been cut back substantially by the courts anyway.

The truth is, outgoing administrations of the liberal ilk tend to load the wagon high with far-reaching rulemakings during their last days in office, which the next "conservative" administration dutifully puts on hold or modifies drastically. Cancelling the outgoing Carter Administration's eleventh-hour regulatory overreach, for example, was a good part of the Reagan deregulation success story as well.

But that doesn't roll back or even nick Washington's destructive regulatory juggernaut; it just temporarily slows it down or tempers it. What the Trump Administration actually did was to basically *validate* the existing sweeping federal regulatory structure by tinkering with existing regulations to allegedly make them less onerous, leaving the door wide open for the next "liberal" administration to reverse these tweaks via a subsequent rulemaking.

That's exactly what has happened, in fact, with Trump Administration's tweaks on efficiency standards for shower heads, washers and dryers, furnaces, auto fuel efficiency standards, light bulbs and countless more. The Biden Administration has either already reversed these measures or is in the process of doing so— or the courts have done the job for them.

For instance, the Trumpites did a fair amount of crowing about a rule modification that cut the year-over-year improvements schedule needed to reach an auto fleet average of nearly 55 mpg by 2025. Instead, the Trump rule brought that number down to about 40 mpg by 2026.

So what? Mandating 40 mpg is just a minor difference of degree and timing and is essentially just as bad as the Obama rule. And now Biden's Climate Crisis Howlers have already withdrawn the Trump tweak, anyway.

But the point is, this wasn't "deregulation" in any meaningful sense. The latter actually would have meant legislatively challenging the whole destructive CAFE (corporate average fuel economy) apparatus. It would have also meant using the White House bully pulpit to denounce CAFE as a costly infringement on motorists' right to do their own trade-offs between mileage and auto purchase price—since fuel efficiency just involves an engineering trade-off between capital and operating costs.

And, most importantly, it would have involved backing up The Donald's Paris Accord withdrawal with a campaign against the real reason for rising CAFE standards. Namely, to further the globalist war on fossil fuels and the main street liberty and prosperity that it enables.

That approach would have been real deregulation, and it could have been furthered by an executive order telling the DOE to not write or enforce any CAFE standards while the battle was being waged.

Likewise, the fake deregulators in the White House beat the tom-toms loudly about a tweak of the federal efficiency standard that sets a 2.5 gallon-per-minute maximum flow rate for showerheads. That's right! There is such a thing from a 1993 statute, and it presented with an Obama administration tweak to ensure that 2.5 gallons per minute applied to the *total* water output of a showerhead, regardless of how many nozzles were featured on a single device.

So, what the Trump folks did was not use the bully pulpit to ridicule this utterly ludicrous Nanny State intrusion into people's shower stalls; instead, they just tried to open up a loophole to allow each nozzle on a multi-nozzle device to be counted separately for purposes of compliance with the 2.5 gallons-per-minute standard.

For crying out loud! That's not deregulation—it's just beltway trivial pursuits. If a so-called conservative government is unwilling to attempt to eliminate entirely something as stupid and intrusive as showerhead regulation, it should simply throw in the towel and drop the pretense of being pro-free market. After all, if we can't trust the free market to offer consumers products with a range of cost and performance trade-offs on this mundane matter, what the hell is even the point of pretending we have a free market?

Then there was the matter of utterly unnecessary appliance efficiency standards for washers and dryers. We actually took that one on way back in 1978 as a member of the House Energy Committee, when this nonsense was first being promoted by the Carter Administration. Yet nothing has changed in forty-five years: Consumers still don't need a Washington Nanny to design the cost-performance trade-offs of their laundry equipment. That's what the vast retail marketplace is designed to facilitate.

Yet did the Trump Administration propose to repeal the under-lying 1974 statute and stay the implementation of existing appli-ance efficiency standards in the interim? It did not, but instead proposed to invent a new category of "quick cycle" laundry prod-ucts that would be exempt from the standards.

Specifically, top loading washing machines with normal cycle times of less than thirty minutes, front-loading washing machines with normal cycles less than forty-five minutes, and dryers with normal cycles less than thirty minutes were to constitute a new class of appliances. And the existing efficiency standards wouldn't apply to these quickies.

Yet how long did that cop-out last? Well, about as long as it took Biden's energy efficiency nannies to find their new offices and liberal lawfare outfits to file suit.

Indeed, the story is the same in one after another of the exist-ing federal regulatory domains. In the case of light bulbs, autos, showerheads, washer-dryers, furnaces, toasters and the rest, the matter is straightforward. There is no case for federal regulation of any way, shape, or form—whether tweaked by so-called conser-vatives or pushed to the full monte by liberals. The litmus test of true "deregulation," therefore, is an all-out drive to abolish the utterly unneeded, counter-productive, and wasteful Devil's work-shop known as the Department of Energy (DOE).

Fighting hammer and tongs to abolish wasteful organiza-tions like the DOE is what constitutes deregulation; all else is Washington gamesmanship.

The same is true of the smattering of small-time rules changes the Trumpites made at OSHA. In fact, health and safety regu-lation in the workplace is strictly a state and local police func-tion. And one in which blue state ideologues in New York and California might well push to costly extremes, thereby enabling more and more of America's business activity to migrate to Texas, South Dakota, and Florida, among others.

So real deregulation involves the abolition of OSHA, too. And the same is true of "efficacy" regulation of new drugs by the FDA and wage rate regulation under Davis-Bacon and the Fair Labor Standards Act by the Labor Department. The only way to con-strain the state's regulatory intrusions and costs in these areas is to devolve the authority to the states and localities. That would enable enlightened local officials to welcome new businesses and jobs into their jurisdictions—even as liberal ideologues in other states sent businesses fleeing from the reach of their regulatory dragnets.

Even in the case of EPA's necessary protection of collective air and water resources owing to the valid matter of "externalities" there is a productive approach to deregulation that the Trump Administration did not remotely consider. To wit, any major air and water pollution rule involving a cost abatement curve that rises very steeply as the last increments of smokestack or tailpipe emissions are eliminated should be flat-out cancelled.

Trade-offs like these are inherently a legislative function for the people to decide through their elected representatives, not a matter to be delegated to EPA civil service apparatchiks building their own regulatory empires. That is to say, any rule with a cost of more than $100 million should be subject to prior approval by a majority of both houses of Congress. Full stop.

So, did The Donald at least carry the torch of conservative eco-nomics on the regulatory front?

He most definitely did not.

At the end of the day, the real trouble with Trump-O-Nomics is that it had no overall redeeming merit—its ballyhooed deregulation campaign included.

Chapter Seven

The Upside-Down Economics of The Donald's Border Wars

O n everything that matters for prosperity and liberty—fiscal rectitude, sound money, free markets, and small government—Donald Trump has been on the wrong side of the policy fence.

He is simply an opportunistic, self-promoting demagogue who chanced to stumble upon the migrant menace theme (murderers and rapists) on his way down the elevator to the announcement of his presidential candidacy in June 2015, a theme he then paired with his lifelong adherence to a primitive form of trade protectionism.

Accordingly, the essence of this couplet was the misbegotten notion that America's problems are caused by foreigners lurking off-shore, making it incumbent upon Washington to stop the alleged hordes of illegal aliens at the border and to staunch the flow of foreign goods into US ports. And also, that what America needed, therefore, was a tough-as-nails and smart-as-a-whip business negotiator who would cause the nation to start winning against these nefarious foreign foes.

That was ill-informed juvenile nonsense, of course, yet it remains the heart of Trump's domestic program. In fact, foreigner-bashing and "winning again" is nearly all there is to it.

And it's not surprising. The Donald is the furthest thing from a thinker or idea advocate. His whole checkered business career was built on attempting to bash and bully his opponents—a *modus operandi* that he simply escalated to the national and world stage after he entered the political arena.

Still, it is hard to think of any proposition that could be so wrong-headed, so lacking in factual foundation, so confused as to cause and effect and so utterly irrelevant to the underlying ills that actually plague the US economy.

To be sure, we do have too many imports and there are millions of immigrants piled up chaotically at the southern border. But for crying out loud, those conditions are not evidence that America is being assaulted by evil forces emanating from outside our borders. Instead, they are the spoiled fruit of policy mistakes originating in Washington from the very Swamp that The Donald decries.

In a word, the flood of imported goods is due to the Fed's wildly inflationary monetary policies. And the teeming hordes at the border are the result of utterly stupid and obsolete federal laws which prohibit millions of work-seekers from legally entering US territory in a safe and orderly manner.

Washington's perverse and outmoded immigration quota regime and the so-called War on Drugs are the real underlying causes of the bedlam, human deprivation, family separations, and lawlessness rampant on the Mexican border. And the basis for that proposition is evident in a simple thought experiment.

What would happen if these counter-productive projects of state aggrandizement and political opportunism were eliminated completely? That is, if the Donald's wall were symbolically sold for the scrap heap that it is and replaced with forty or fifty "welcome stations" for job seekers located approximately every fifty miles along the US/Mexican border.

At these facilities, employers or their agents would vet and recruit potential employees and be free to make offers without regard to the existing immigration system's convoluted quota categories to anyone meeting their own needs and qualifying standards. In other words, a system embodying a purely economic basis for entry.

So long as the resulting employers punched a monthly federal form verifying that such workers were still on their payroll or that of a new employer, these portable Guest Worker permits would be extended for up to ten years. At that point, guest workers would be deemed American citizens, perhaps after paying a modest initiation fee of a few thousand dollars, as well.

The fact is, the overwhelming share of migrants now being hounded on the border would accept that deal every day of the week and twice on Sunday. After all, they come here to engage in honest work and peaceful commerce. Harsh, sometimes violent law enforcement is just a perverse artifact of a border enforcement policy based on politics and lies, not the basic principles of a free society and the needs of a productive capitalist economy.

Indeed, a large-scale Guest Worker program in lieu of today's crazy quilt labyrinth of family, occupational, and "asylum" based immigration quotas would end the so-called undocumented migrant crisis in one fell swoop. And it would also enable the American economy to boom again by alleviating the inflationary shortage of workers that is currently holding it back, as we amplify below.

It would also mean that rather than being greeted by the hobnail boots of the DEA and Border Patrol officials and shunted off to what are essentially concentration camps, immigrants seeking work and a better life would be welcomed by job fairs, where employers or recruitment agencies would be prepared to offer them signing stipends and transit to jobs at work sites all over the country.

The truth is, the overwhelming share of immigrants come to the border looking for work but find no employers or their agents offering jobs because, well, it is illegal to hire illegals! And that's downright perverse in a country that has a huge and growing demographic deficit and a rapidly shrinking native-born work force, as we document below. But among the numerous things that The Donald and his MAGA followers don't understand is the law of supply and demand. Yet when it comes to the lower-skill, lower-pay class of workers there is a dire shortage in the US, a teeming surplus in Central America and elsewhere, and no legal intake channel in the convoluted US immigration system to allow the marketplace to flexibly and freely match-up supply and demand.

Accordingly, all of the stupid statistics paraded daily on *Fox News* about the millions of "encounters" with illegals at the border and the hundreds of thousands of deportations each year are representative of nothing more than a vast, unnecessary human pile-up. And one which is owing to the fact that politicians in Washington won't let the market clear, while having turned the legal immigration system into a lawyers' racket and bureaucratic puzzle palace.

Of course, The Donald would have you ignore the fact that upwards of 95 percent of the "illegals" pressing upon the border are job-seekers and families seeking a better life. Instead, he and his minions brandish false claims that these migrant populations are teeming with criminals, drug dealers, welfare cheats, and jobs stealers.

But those are all truly red herrings that fuel Trumpian demagoguery and misdirected public fears and resentments. That is to say, they are an extension of The Donald's deeply deformed personality, which oozes anger and resentment.

The facts, however, tell a wholly different story. America has an immigration crisis, but it has precious little to do with "open borders" and Fox News' nightly cavalcade of alleged "illegals" flooding across the Rio Grande.

In fact, the chart below is far more informative than a posse of Trumpite operatives braying about the border crisis or Fox journalists equipped with night vision tracking "illegals" through the Arizona bush in the pitch darkness.

In a word, America's prime age civilian population and active labor force (age twenty-five to fifty-four years) *stopped growing fifteen years ago.* Furthermore, the underlying demographics show that the purely native-born component of the prime age labor force is now actually shrinking and will do so for the indefinite future.

To wit, the total population of the twenty-five to fifty-four years age cohort grew from 70 million in 1970 to nearly 126 million in 2008, or by 1.55 percent per annum. By contrast, between 2008 and 2022 the population of this age cohort barely inched up to 127 million. The resulting negligible growth rate of only *0.1 percent* per annum represented a 94 percent plunge from the pre-2008 growth rate of prime age workers.

On top of that, there was a huge one-time increase in the female participation rate between 1970 and 2008, causing the overall participation rate to rise from 72.1 percent in 1970 to 83.1 percent in 2008. As a result of rising participation, the so-called active "civilian labor force" as defined by the BLS more than doubled in size—from 50 million in 1970 to 104 million in 2008, nearly a *2.0 percent* annual growth rate.

By contrast, since the Great Recession the participation rate has fallen slightly, causing the BLS-defined prime age "labor force" to remain nearly flat at 105 million. In a word, what has happened is that the motor force of America's growth machine—prime age workers—has been stranded on the flat line for the last decade and a half.

Nevertheless, it needs be recalled that upwards of 50 percent of America's GDP growth has been accounted for by increased labor hours, with the balance consisting of productivity gains. So when the growth rate of the prime age labor force crashes from *2.00 percent* per annum during 1970 to 2008 to just *0.01 percent* per annum since then, you don't need a PhD in economics to figure out the implications. Actually, you barely need arithmetic.

Moreover, when it comes to the single most experienced and productive portion of the labor force—pre-retirement workers aged fifty-five to sixty-four years—the shift from worker abundance to drought is downright startling.

Between 2000 and 2018 the number of combined male and female labor force participants aged fifty-five to sixty-four years

US Prime Age Labor Force 25–54 Years, 1970 to 2022.

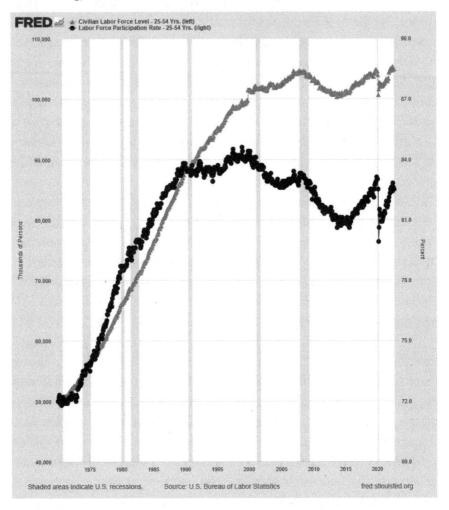

old nearly doubled, rising from 14.6 million to 27.7 million. That's a *3.62 percent* per annum growth rate. Since 2018, however, not so much. This key labor force cohort experienced outright shrinkage of -0.21 percent per year through 2022.

The abrupt leveling of the graph below during the last few years is just the pig-thru-the-python phenomena of baby boomers trekking toward retirement at a goodly clip as the calendar of aging marches on. This template will extend inexorably to increasingly larger shares of the labor force; it's the compelling reason why US economic growth will grind to a snail's pace unless the borders remain open to willing workers wishing to immigrate to America.

Needless to say, the demographics of this abrupt supply-side stagnation are baked into the cake. Even a sweeping swing toward Welfare State benefit curtailments designed to flush potential workers back into the labor force and restore the prime age participation rate to the turn-of-the-century peak (84.1 percent) would have only raised the post-2008 labor force growth rate to *0.18 percent*. But that would still be only one-tenth of the pre-2008 growth trend.

That's made further evident by the figures for the population as a whole, regardless of whether or not the Bureau of Labor Statistics deems them to be "labor force participants." Thus, during the half century between 1965 and 2015, the post-college population (twenty-five to sixty-four years) doubled, growing from 86 million to 173 million. That 87 million population gain represented a *1.41 percent* per annum growth rate over the fifty-year period.

During the two decades between 2015 and 2035, however, this twenty-five to sixty-four years cohort will grow by only 10 million or just *0.28 percent* per annum. And even that is due entirely to an assumed 18 million new immigrant workers. By contrast, the American-born cohort of twenty-five to sixty-four-year-old potential workers will actually shrink by 7 million over that two-decade period. We are talking here about nearly the entire working age population. As the saying goes, that's all there is, there ain't no more. So even with continued modest levels of immigration, the current and projected growth rate of labor hours would represent barely *15 percent* of its pre-2008 average.

And that's why The Donald's border closure policies are dead wrong. What America actually needs during the years ahead is a dramatic step-up in the level of working-age immigrants, not their arrest and deportation.

Moreover, the falling dotted line after 2015 in the below chart would have been even worse absent prior decades of immigration. Although not broken out in the chart above,, the sub-population of twenty-five- to sixty-four-year-old persons born here to American-born parents since 1965 would drop from 128 million in 2015 to just 120 million by 2035. That's a *6.5 percent* shrinkage.

Working Age Population 25–64 Years, 1965 to 2035.

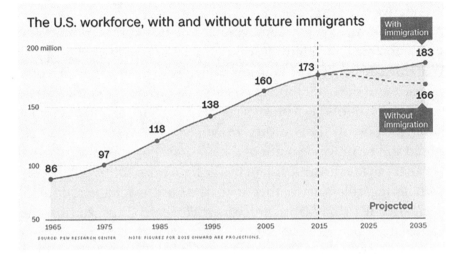

In short, two generations of immigrants, past and prospective, account for the difference between a projected 2035 US workforce of 183 million per the graph above versus the 120 million that would have resulted from American-born workers born to American-born parents. That 63 million difference accounted for by recent past and current immigrants amounts to fully *one-third* of the projected 2035 labor force.

So had the Trumpite immigrant bashers gotten their way since the 1960s, the American economy would already be rapidly sliding down the slippery slope.

Indeed, the nation's utter reliance on imported workers for growth is owing to the fact that long-ago the fertility rate for native born women had dropped below the replacement rate (2.0). As a consequence, here is the gain in working age population from native born parents by decade since 1965. The numbers leave no room for debate.

Change In Working-Age Population 25–64 Years for Workers Born To US-Born Parents By Decade:

- 1965–1975: +13.3 million.
- 1975–1985: +20.0 million.

- 1985–1995: +15.1 million.
- 1995–2005: +10.6 million.
- 2005–2015: +4.8 million.
- 2015–2025: *-4.3 million.*
- 2025–2035: *-3.9 million.*

Since the overwhelming share of the 11 million so-called "illegals" in the US are of working age or younger (i.e., future workers), it cannot be denied that America's desperate need for imported workers is being overridden by claims of societal harm that purportedly exceed the obvious benefits.

That is to say, the hue and cry about "illegals" pouring over the border and living in our midst is really a claim that they are a clear and present societal danger, fixing to inflict injury on innocent law-abiding taxpayers unless they are apprehended and deported.

The rest of the Trumpite rhetoric about the "sanctity of borders," the civic duty to obey the law, etc. is just political window-dressing and humbug. It is dispensed in order to add a patriotic sheen to the real reasons—pure politics—for Washington's counter-productive crackdown on borders and immigrants.

And when we use the term "pure politics" we are indeed talking about the elephant in the room. Namely, the thinly disguised view of the GOP's close-the-border crowd that immigration is bad despite its pro-market roots because these new arrivals vote heavily for the Democrats!

To obfuscate this grossly political angle, therefore, the Trumpite wing of the GOP alleges that illegal immigrants are:

- *fiscal parasites* who gobble-up welfare and unfairly burden law-abiding taxpayers;
- *job-stealers* who deprive the native orn of employment or higher wage rates; or
- *incipient criminals* who threaten the security and safety of America's neighborhoods.

The purpose at hand, therefore, is to debunk these canards, myths, and often deliberate lies and expose the statist (Big Government) predicate behind the Donald's Border Wars and why they are actually MAGA's worst enemy.

The Welfare Parasites Narrative Is a Washington-Made Concoction

The first of these, the welfare parasite meme, is risible nonsense. The 11 million undocumented immigrants, 2 million visitors on temporary visas, and even most of the 13 million green card holders and refugees are flat-out *ineligible* for federal welfare benefits. Indeed, to gain eligibility for federal welfare benefits the 26 million non-citizen immigrants in these categories must be resident in the US for five years.

Moreover, this ban on welfare eligibility is sweeping in its coverage. It encompasses thirty-one different programs which will dispense about $650 billion of the $700 billion of current means-tested federal outlays.

These ring-fenced programs encompass Temporary Assistance for Needy Families (TANF), Food Stamps, Supplemental Security Income (SSI), and most federal health programs including non-emergency Medicaid, the Children's Health Insurance Program (CHIP), and the Medicare program.

The ban also covers Foster Care, Adoption Assistance, the Child Care and Adoption Fund, and low-income energy assistance. Undocumented immigrants are likewise not eligible to receive insurance subsidies under the Affordable Care Act or to participate in the ACA insurance exchanges.

As it happens, therefore, the much-ballyhooed welfare abuse is not the nefarious doings of illegal immigrants but is actually the handiwork of Washington politicians and policy bureaucrats who have confected seven-ways-to-Sunday around these sweeping eligibility restrictions.

So, there is need for a Trumpian Wall alright, but rather than one made of cement and steel on the Mexican border, what is actually needed is a sturdy legal wall around federal welfare that the Washington lobbies and bag-carrying pols of the beltway cannot vault over, tunnel under, or shimmy through.

And we are not speaking just metaphorically. There is actually no better example of a cynical, loophole-ridden mockery of a putative policy rule than the immigrant welfare ban.

For instance, the school lunch and breakfast programs have been excluded from the ban. Likewise, pursuant to federal guidelines, every single state has elected an option to provide all immigrants—legal and otherwise—with access to the Special Supplemental Nutrition Program for Women, Infants and Children (WIC).

Similarly, short-term noncash emergency disaster assistance remains available without regard to immigration status. Also exempted from the welfare ban are other in-kind services necessary to "protect life or safety," including child and adult protective services, programs addressing weather emergencies and homelessness, shelters, soup kitchens, and meals-on-wheels.

Also exempted by the "life and safety" loophole are medical, public health, mental health, disability, and substance abuse services—along with "emergency" Medicaid services. And these Medicaid emergency services alone amount to something like $2 billion per year of expenditures for illegal immigrant medical care.

Finally, in the case of the 14 million *legal* permanent resident immigrants, there is a whole laundry list of categories which have been exempted from the five-year eligibility rule by Congressional legislation or administrative rule-making. These include refugees, people granted asylum, Cuban/Haitian entrants, certain Amerasian immigrants, Iraqi and Afghan Special Immigrants, and survivors of human trafficking—along with qualified immigrant veterans, active-duty military and their families, and also children who receive federal foster care delivered by US citizens.

This massive labyrinth of exceptions, loopholes, and emergency provisions, of course, provides fodder to demagogic proponents of what might be termed the "welfare queen 2.0" thesis. It enables them to cite data showing large amounts of "welfare" going to immigrant families, thereby purporting to validate the fiscal burden argument for Trumpian-style crack-downs at the border and deportation raids throughout the country.

For instance, one major study showed that immigrant families with three or more children received an average of $14,500 of welfare benefits in a recent year. But $10,000 of this was due to the Medicaid exception for "emergency" care—a discretionary loophole that makes the underlying statutory ban on Medicaid services for routine, chronic, and even non-emergency but life-threatening conditions non-operative in many, if not, most cases.

Likewise, another $1,000 was for exempted school lunch and WIC benefits and $2,600 (most of the balance) was due to the Food Stamp ban's exception for children of immigrants.

Indeed, the oft-made claim that 60 percent of immigrant households are on federal welfare is essentially a statistical trick. It results from the fact the kids of immigrant households are required by law to attend public school, where they are automatically enrolled in the federal school lunch program; and where social workers often make their parents aware of the food stamps loophole for low-income immigrant children.

Accordingly, in one fell swoop, these school lunch and food stamps enrollments result in a statistical count of millions of illegals on "welfare." Never mind that a few thousand dollars per year per recipient is not likely to break the bank. Nor is it plausible to think that millions of working-age adults bring their families to the US illegally just to get their kids on school lunches and food stamps.

Still, even that statistical reason for illegal immigrant welfare could be erased with a stroke of the pen by canceling the food stamps and school lunch loopholes. And the same is true for the other major source of welfare spending—the emergency Medicaid loophole.

Needless to say, the hard-pressed, unorganized, and shadowy community of so-called illegal aliens in the US did not hire slick K-Street lobbyists to turn the immigrant welfare ban into statutory Swiss cheese. The fact of high welfare costs and elevated participation rates is not the fault of immigrants themselves, and is no justification for keeping willing workers out of America or deporting the millions already here.

To the contrary, the vast loopholes described above are the product of Washington do-gooders and liberal lobbyists and legislators seeking to promote humanitarian objectives or pro-Hispanic lobbies claiming to promote social justice. So if the Trumpites wish to stop welfare abuse by immigrant populations they should repeal every single one of these welfare ban loopholes.

At the same time, if working families with children want to come to America, give them a work permit at the aforementioned border stations. And also, a clear explanation that until they work and pay federal taxes for ten years they will not be eligible for a dime of public welfare. No exceptions!

In short, Washington needs to build a sturdy statutory wall around federal welfare in lieu of The Donald's useless $40 billion physical wall. The former statutory wall would actually save billions per year in welfare costs and remove any semblance of incentives for immigrants to come to America for welfare rather than work.

Immigrants Don't Steal American Jobs—They Add to Total Employment

The second false argument for The Donald's Border Wars—that immigrants take American jobs—is complete nonsense. For crying out loud. Immigrants are filling, not stealing, lower paying domestic jobs since, for reasons of culture and welfare inducements, the native-born simply won't take them.

Indeed, the now surging wage rates in the leisure and hospitality (L&H) sector actually knock the whole jobs theft canard into a cocked hat. That is to say, if immigrants were actually taking entry level jobs in bars, restaurants, hotels, theme parks, sports venues, movie theaters, etc., from American workers, the rate of pay increases in the L&H sector would be sharply depressed relative to gains in the higher pay sectors of the economy dominated by native-born workers.

But the opposite is true. During the last decade, average hourly wages in the Leisure and Hospitality sector have risen by

60 percent compared to just *34 percent* in the high-pay manufacturing sector and *41 percent* for private sector workers overall.

Thus, there is no depression of wages at the bottom of the jobs ladder due to immigrant workers (legal and illegal). To the contrary, there is a severe labor supply shortage in this sector—the very condition that a large-scale Guest Worker program would help ameliorate. And it would also be just what the economic doctors at the Fed have ordered: namely, reduced wage push pressures in the domestic services industries that since December 2020 have seen L&H wages rise at a *11.0 percent* annual rate.

To be sure, in the absence of even today's limited immigrant labor supply, the robust rise of L&H wages would likely have been even steeper. But in a market economy, cost inflation does not happen in a vacuum or go unanswered by off-setting adjustments elsewhere. What needs examination, therefore, is the cascading second and third order consequences of the current labor shortage.

Since the American economy is largely open to global trade and financial flows, it is continuously assaulted by numerous wage-depressing and jobs-displacing forces from all around the planet, and the most important of these is actually self-inflicted by Washington policymakers. That is, the domestic wage-price-cost structure generally has been grossly inflated by knuckle-headed Fed policy for so many decades that what might have remained solid domestic jobs and worker incomes under sensible monetary policies have been massively off-shored.

There is no mystery, of course, as to why this has happened. It is the result of unfavorable domestic labor and other *cost premiums* compared to the China Price for goods, the India Price for services, the Mexico Price for assembly labor and the Technology Substitution Price for jobs vulnerable to displacement by robots and automation. These large cost gaps make for profitable labor arbitrage, even when you allow for the off-setting costs of extended global supply chains or labor-saving capital investment.

Left to its own devices, of course, the free market under a regime of sound money would function to minimize these gaps via deflation of prices, costs, and wages. But the Fed's foolish pro-inflation policy functioned in the opposite manner, causing the cost gap to be sharply and unnecessarily widened.

Needless to say, American businesses did not take the Fed's inflationary hits sitting down. The latter has caused the institutionalization in American business of a relentless search for least-cost solutions to high wage bills. This has included not only massive off-shoring but also the aggressive substitution of technology-based automation for labor whenever it is cost-effective.

For instance, a recent *Los Angeles Times* piece on "Flippy" the robotic fast food kitchen worker makes starkly clear that even a 100 percent ban on low-wage immigration would not protect domestic service jobs for very long:

> In a test kitchen in a corner building in downtown Pasadena, Flippy the robot grabbed a fryer basket full of chicken fingers, plunged it into hot oil—its sensors told it exactly how hot—then lifted, drained and dumped maximally tender tenders into a waiting hopper. . . .
>
> The product of decades of research in robotics and machine learning, Flippy represents a synthesis of motors, sensors, chips and processing power that wasn't possible until recently. . . .
>
> Off-the-shelf robot arms have plunged in price in recent years, from more than $100,000 in 2016, when Miso Robotics first launched, to less than $10,000 today, with cheaper models coming in the near future.
>
> As a result, Miso can offer Flippy's to fast-food restaurant owners for an estimated $2,000 per month on a subscription basis, breaking down to about $3 per hour. A human doing the same job costs $4,000 to $10,000 or more a month . . . And robots never call in sick.

To be sure, capital and technology substitution is a natural and vital feature of dynamic, wealth-generating capitalist markets and ordinarily should be allowed to run unimpeded. That's the ultimate source of prosperity and rising living standards.

But when such substitutions result from artificial and unnecessarily high labor costs, they do not actually result in improved economic welfare. Instead, either domestic production and wage incomes are lost to foreign vendors as production is off-shored, or overall domestic production cost are higher, even if such inflated costs are recorded in the capital rather than labor cost column of the ledger.

The better approach, therefore, is to keep the playing field level and permit domestic businesses to do their own economics-driven math as between labor and capital inputs. And also, for policy-makers to recognize that the US economy has become a coiled spring of labor-cost substitution capabilities.

The latter means, of course, that artificially restricting immigrant labor to putatively protect American jobs and wages will surely backfire. It demonstrably only triggers more off-shoring of production or capital substitution for labor, meaning that the jobs allegedly shielded from immigrant worker competition end up going to foreigners or robots.

Of course, you can seek to "solve" that problem with a further extension of Trumpian economics. That is to say, attempt to stop off-shoring with high tariffs and quotas on imported goods and regulatory restrictions on such things as off-shoring customer service operations to India. And when those impediments to free market commerce led to ballooning domestic production costs and therefore even higher levels of automation and robots, you would next need to regulate business CapEx to reduce investment in robots. And so on.

But then you wouldn't have anything that resembled market capitalism or the resulting domestic prosperity it brings, at all. Instead, you'd have an increasingly impoverished economy battered by inflationary cost spirals. That is, you would soon be at the inherent dead-end of Trump-O-Nomics.

On the other hand, the opposite effect would ensue from substantially increased supplies of low-wage immigrant labor via a large-scale Guest Worker program. On the margin, it would reduce wage levels in impacted sectors, and therefore the rate at which low-skill domestic jobs give way to automation or off-shore labor. That's because lower wage rates would at least partially dilute the payback for off-shoring or labor-saving technology investments.

To be sure, there is no free lunch. Some workers currently holding low-paying jobs that can't be easily off-shored or automated immediately might realize slightly higher incomes under a regime of enforced labor shortage via The Donald's Great Mexican Wall. But, overall, the effect would likely be temporary and would definitely be reductive to overall societal welfare.

Sharply restricting immigrant labor supply as so vociferously advocated by The Donald would ultimately be no different than the impact of, say, raising the minimum wage to $40 per hour. That is, if you force low-skill wage rates high enough, someone will invent self-trimming lawn grass or robotic burger-flippers. It's all just a matter of the market's genius for uncovering new least-cost routes to goods and services sought by consumers.

In any event, the adverse effects of higher minimum wages and restrictive immigration policies are the same. Both stimulate substitution effects on the free market and eventually result in decreased low-skill employment, higher domestic production costs, and lower US output and wealth.

So the place to fix the problem of too much inflation and too little growth in real wages is not with a wall at the Mexican border or via an asinine program to deport willing workers. The real culprits dwell in the Eccles Building and could be summarily replaced if someone actually wanted to address the underlying problem.

That "someone," of course, is most definitely not Donald Trump.

The Red Herrings of the Drugs and Crime Narrative

The question thus recurs: Why do we continue *deporting* willing foreign workers when we should be aggressively *importing* them?

As we have seen, the real answer cannot be admitted to by the Trumpite GOP. Even they would be reluctant to acknowledge they wish to deploy the Border Patrol and other law-enforcement arms of the state for the purpose of keeping potential Democrat voters out of the country.

Unfortunately, the "drugs and crime" cover story involves more than just erroneous facts with respect to cross-border drug traffic and crime rates among immigrants. The truths here easily dispatch these smokescreens.

The larger nasty is that the once and former party of fiscal austerity, free market economics and constitutional liberty has gone off the deep-end of statism and cultural chauvinism on the matter of immigration. As a result, the workingman's party built in modern times on President William McKinley's "full lunch pail" economics and the vast ranks of immigrant labor in America's Midwestern industrial belt has gone restrictionist, nativist, xenophobic and blindly intolerant.

Needless to say, the GOP's descent into the dark side was only made worse by the Donald's harsh law and order demagoguery ala the campaign launch imagery of June 2015 that has now become embedded in the Trumpite catechism:

> . . . They're sending people that have lots of problems, and they're bringing those problems with them. They're bringing drugs. They're bringing crime. They're rapists. And some, I assume, are good people.

That was not remotely correct. There's not a shred of truth to the immigrant crime meme beyond cherry-picked anecdotes about horrendous murders and assaults by illegals, whichprove exactly nothing. That's because there is a small fraction of every sub-population which consists of thugs, criminals and misanthropes.

What is relevant, however, is the statistical incidence of these anti-social behaviors among native born versus immigrant populations, not sensationalized anecdotes.

And on that score, it is also crucial to start with a fact long known to students of crime, if not to demagogic politician like Donald Trump. Namely, violent crimes and property theft are overwhelmingly attributable to young men.

So when you standardize the crime statistics by age for the native-born versus immigrant population the data is crystal clear.

Native-born young men ages eighteen to thirty-nine years commit crimes at *two to three times higher rates* than immigrants, as measured by incarceration rates. And that gap has not diminished during the last three decades—even as incarceration rates for both groups having risen moderately, mainly owing to the War on Drugs.

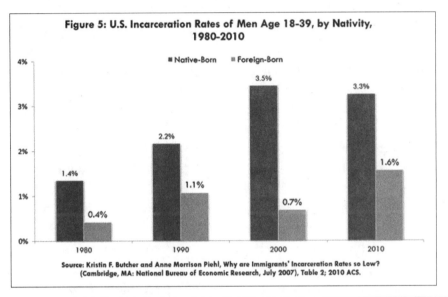

Figure 5: U.S. Incarceration Rates of Men Age 18-39, by Nativity, 1980-2010

Source: Kristin F. Butcher and Anne Morrison Piehl, Why are Immigrants' Incarceration Rates so Low? (Cambridge, MA: National Bureau of Economic Research, July 2007), Table 2; 2010 ACS.

In point of fact, the only time that "illegals" and immigrants are statistically involved in a high incidence of "crime" is when they are engaged in the violent, law-of-the-jungle business of selling and distributing illegal drugs.

But drug crime is not a border-crasher. It is a home-grown scourge fostered by the state because "prohibition" invariably drives distribution underground. That is, when you make something contraband that is strongly desired by consumers, it becomes scarce, and the price goes up. A lot.

In turn, the resulting surplus margin in the supply chain provides a powerful incentive for violent behavior and also generates the financial wherewithal to support the extensive criminal organizations and lower-level gangs which feed off the trade. In effect, artificially high prices provide an economic umbrella for black market operators to absorb the high costs of illicitly moving the merchandise from producers to users, as well as foot the vast product shrinkage costs due to government interdiction of goods, and even the cost of armed contingents needed to enforce contracts and protect territories and markets.

Stated differently, the so-called illicit drug problem isn't due to borders open to potential wage workers but reflects the historically proven fact that state-enforced "prohibition" everywhere and always fails because it is defeated by the primal forces of economics. Consequently, you do not need a border wall, more ICE agents, or additional hobnailed boots in the DEA (Drug Enforcement Agency) to stop these needless scourges.

To the contrary, if an end to the drug problem is desired—then get these now illegal drugs out of the black market and into open, legal commerce. Prices would fall, drug-related crime would disappear, and Phillip Morris and the teamsters union would have new businesses and jobs.

The often brutal violence that does occasionally occur along the US-Mexico border is most definitely not perpetrated by desperate parents willing to kill and maim in order to find work on the US side of the border. It is the result of drug syndicate warfare over territory and trade, and the heavy-handed—often militarized—efforts of the DEA, Border Patrol, and local law enforcement to accomplish the impossible. That is, the interdiction and extinguishing of the ultra-lucrative commerce in illicit drugs, even as these futile efforts at restricting supply, ironically, make it yet more lucrative.

Moreover, notwithstanding the illegal drug trade noise in the data, the immigrant crime story still doesn't wash. The fact is, at the very time that the inflow of immigrants has surged, violent crime rates in the US had fallen dramatically. During the twenty-eight-year interval between 1960 and 1988, total immigration was just 12.3 million or about *440,000* persons per year. After that, immigration rates surged by 2.3x. The inflow thus averaged *1.01 million* per year during 1989–2016 and totaled 28.5 million over the period.

Accordingly, the foreign-born share of the US population climbed sharply after the 1970 low, rising from *4.7 percent* to *13.4 percent* by 2016.

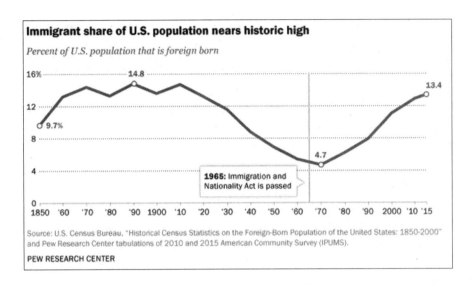

Immigrant share of U.S. population nears historic high

Percent of U.S. population that is foreign born

1965: Immigration and Nationality Act is passed

Source: U.S. Census Bureau, "Historical Census Statistics on the Foreign-Born Population of the United States: 1850-2000" and Pew Research Center tabulations of 2010 and 2015 American Community Survey (IPUMS).

PEW RESEARCH CENTER

At the same time, however, the rate of violent crime in the US fell from *750* per 100,000 residents in 1991 to just 388 per 100,000 in 2012 or by nearly 50 percent. Since then (not shown), the rate has more or less plateaued, hitting a low of 362 per 100,000 in 2014 and rising slightly since then. In fact, notwithstanding highly publicized flare-ups in a few aberrant big cities like Baltimore, Chicago, Los Angeles, San Fransisco, Portland, Seattle, New York City, and Philadelphia, the violent crime rate was *396* per 100,000 in 2021. That's still *47 percent below* the 1991 rate.

Source: Pew Research

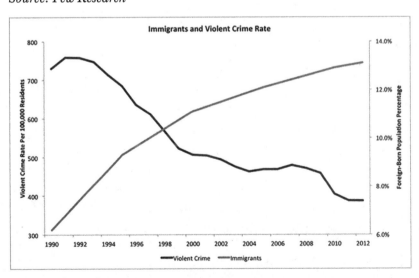

Immigrants and Violent Crime Rate

The "X" pattern in the chart above thus powerfully refutes the "immigration fosters crime" narrative, but that is not surprising. The underlying issue has always been not immigrant crime in the abstract, but whether undocumented populations have disproportionately higher rates of criminal conduct than native born populations. In this regard, a study based on uniquely comprehensive arrest data for 2012 through 2018 from the Texas Department of Public Safety is especially dispositive. After all, Texas is ground zero for the alleged flood of border crime.

This definitive study found that undocumented immigrants have substantially lower crime rates than both native-born citizens and legal immigrants across a range of felony offenses. Relative to undocumented immigrants, US-born citizens are:

- Over 2 times more likely to be arrested for violent crimes,
- 2.5 times more likely to be arrested for drug crimes, and
- Over 4 times more likely to be arrested for property crimes.

In addition, the proportion of arrests involving undocumented immigrants in Texas was relatively stable or decreasing over the 2012 to 2018 period. That was the very time The Donald was waving the bloody shirt of a purported floodtide of immigrant crime.

Given the above, it follows that US citizens shown in the long bars below account for 90 percent to 98 percent of all major crime categories. The only exception is drug trafficking, and the latter is largely definitional because the mules who bring "illegal" drugs across the border originate elsewhere.

Equally notable is the fact that as of 2015 the estimated 11 million illegal immigrants committed a slightly smaller share of violent crimes, property crimes, and traffic infractions than their 3.4 percent share of the US population. And the same is true of the 14 million immigrants who had legal status.

So, the hard-core Trumpite/GOP has essentially misappropriated the machinery of the state to help it win elections by conducting Border Wars. Self-evidently, the illicit purpose of these actions has been to keep unwanted voters, not criminals, out of America and to propagate fear and xenophobic reactions among the citizens.

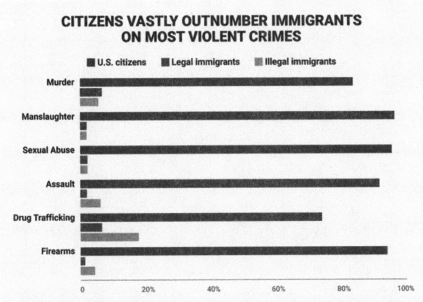

CITIZENS VASTLY OUTNUMBER IMMIGRANTS ON MOST VIOLENT CRIMES

■ U.S. citizens   ■ Legal immigrants   ▨ Illegal immigrants

- Murder
- Manslaughter
- Sexual Abuse
- Assault
- Drug Trafficking
- Firearms

0   20%   40%   60%   80%   100%

NOTE: Data is based on 71,003 defendants sentenced under the Sentencing Reform Act between Oct. 2014 and Sept. 2015. The SRA only collects information on cases sentenced under their guidelines. Crimes outside of these guidelines are not included.

SOURCE: United States Sentencing Commission   BUSINESS INSIDER

At the end of the day, most of the "crimes" committed by border crossers result from a 1929 law which, for the first time after 140 years of essentially "open borders," made unlawful entry into the US a federal misdemeanor on the first offense, and a felony on the second. Not incidentally, this law was authored by Senator Coleman Livingston Blease of South Carolina, a white supremacist who had not inconsiderable support from the Klu Klux Klan and other nativist forces.

Yet this "crime" is essentially victimless, thoroughly un-American, and capable of being eliminated by the stroke of a simple statute. Namely, the aforementioned law authorizing the issuance of guest worker papers at the border to any worker and his family members who want to come to the US to take a job.

Self-evidently, a large-scale Guest Worker program would eliminate 99 percent of the so-called crimes authored by Senator

Blease. No matter how you slice it, therefore, the immigrant crime story is a red herring. The underlying motivation is a faulty zero-sum economic theory, rank political opportunism by the GOP, and the rise of a nativist chauvinism that glorifies a mythical American "nation" that never really existed.

Chapter Eight

The Trumpian Immigration Fallacy and Bedtime for the Boomers

Unlike most other more homogeneous nation-states on the planet, America was never rooted in a tribe, folk, people, or nationality. To the contrary, it was a vast melting pot of diverse ethnicities and nationalities bound together by the ideas of personal liberty, constitutional democracy, and free market opportunity and prosperity. America's greatest period of growth and wealth creation from 1870 to 1914, in fact, was built on exactly those principles.

During that halcyon era the only document work-seeking immigrants needed was to sign in at Ellis Island. No passports were required to enter the US until May 1918, and even that was the result of the anti-German hysteria elicited by Woodrow Wilson's phony patriotism and crusade to make the world safe for his foggy brand of "democracy."

Thus, in 1870 the population of the US was just 39 million. During the next forty-four years more than 25 million immigrants entered the country. Accordingly, these new arrivals represented nearly *two-thirds* of the entire 1870 population!

Yet notwithstanding a half dozen short-lived recessions or "panics" during that interval, real GDP growth averaged *3.8 percent* per year for more than four decades running. That rate of continuous growth had not been achieved before, nor has it since.

During 1907, for example, 1.3 million immigrants entered the US, adding more than 1.5 percent to the existing US population (85 million) in a single year. Overall, during 1900–1910 nearly 9 million immigrants were admitted to the US, which amounted to about *12 percent* of the nation's entire population of 76 million in 1900.

By contrast, a century later the 13 million immigrants arriving during 2000–2010 represented just *4.6 percent* of the 282 million population in the year 2000. The net immigrant inflow in 2016 peaked at 1.2 million and amounted to just 0.4 percent of the nation's 325 million population, while by 2021 the net immigration figure of 247,000 was just 0.07 percent of the US population. These figures thoroughly debunk the hysterical Trumpite claim that America is being overrun with immigrants.

Accordingly, the 1.5 percent ratio of new immigrants to the total US population during the heyday of 1907 was 4x to 21x higher than the low and high ratios of recent years. Likewise, immigrants during the pre-1914 golden age of economic growth and rising middle class prosperity represented a far larger share of the work force. Without them, the booming industrial belt from Pittsburgh through Youngstown, Cleveland, Toledo, Detroit, Gary, Chicago, Milwaukee, Rockford, Quad Cities, and St. Louis simply would have never happened.

In any event, the foreign-born population peaked at just under 15 percent of the total US population during 1890 to 1914, and then began a long descent. This interim decline was triggered initially by the interruption of global commerce and labor mobility during WWI and then by the restrictive immigration act of 1924. The latter established immigration quotas based on national origin for Europeans, although it did not restrict immigration from the western hemisphere, including what Trump had referred to as the "shithole countries."

So while total immigration was cut by 70 percent from the pre-1914 peak levels, it still exceeded 4 million during the economic boom of the 1920s. What caused the annual inflow to collapse to barely forty thousand persons per year during the 1930s was the Great Depression. Foreigners stopped coming when there was no work or economic opportunity—even when the new quotas would have permitted far larger numbers.

Number of US Immigrants by Decade, 1820 to 2010. Source: Cairco.org

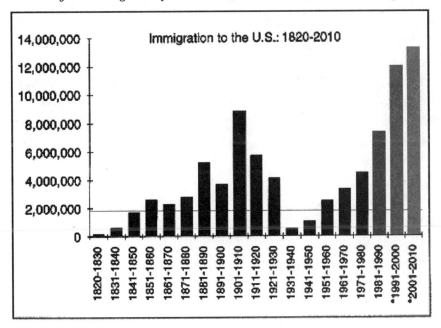

The historic truth that immigrants came to America overwhelmingly for jobs and opportunity couldn't be more obvious. Not surprisingly, therefore, when prosperity returned in the mid-1950s, annual inflows rebounded to the three hundred thousand per year level as permitted by the national origin quotas based on 1890 country-by-country levels. At length, however, the national origin system became unworkable, unfair, and increasingly obsolete so it was abolished in 1965. But its replacement was hardly any better, since it too was not governed by economics and work-seeking.

Instead, the overwhelming share of the new quota system was allocated to family reunification. This included unlimited slots for direct minor children and parents of US citizens and 226,000 slots per year for family members of green card holders. Beyond that were 140,000 annual slots for professionals, scientists, artists, and skilled workers in short supply, to be later defined by bureaucrats and business lobbyists. In the case of political refugees, the annual limit is determined by the President—with new annual arrivals varying between twenty thousand and eighty thousand annually since the year 2000.

Stated differently, the economically based, work-driven, quota-free system that prevailed prior to 1914, and which had worked so brilliantly to fuel America's industrial might, has been replaced by a politics driven system. The latter shifted the determinants of the flow and composition of immigration from the free market to the legislative and bureaucratic arenas of Washington, and to the vast networks of influence peddling and lobbying which drive action inside the beltway.

Not surprisingly, this evolution has increasingly turned immigration into a matter of pure partisanship. The Democrats now seek a route to electoral dominance through an immigration-fueled increase in the non-white population, while the GOP fights a nativist rearguard action to preserve the electoral dominance of its Red State coalitions.

Still, notwithstanding the rigidities and anti-market nature of the current immigration control system, the dramatic rebound in the foreign-born share of the US population in recent decades was materially driven by economics and work-seeking. The agricultural industries, hotel and restaurant sectors, lawn and home care, domestic service, and countless other lower-skilled sectors are testament to that truth.

Unfortunately, the Trumpites have obfuscated this true immigration history beneath the veneer of The Donald's anti-market attacks on capitalism. After all, free *labor markets* have been just as crucial to capitalist prosperity as were free markets for goods, capital, technology, and enterprise. Trumpian walls, border patrols, and ICE raids, in fact, amount to statist Big Government writ large.

At the end of the day, the Trumpite effort to close the borders is a denial of history and negation of the very force that created the largest and most prosperous economy and middle class in world history. In this context, the chart below is a reminder of the stunning ignorance that underlies the Trumpian attack on immigrants. It shows that the 194 million US population of 1965 would have grown to just *251 million* at present absent post-1965 immigrants and their descendants. So, without the addition of immigrants to the post-Baby Boom population, existing American families would have only had enough babies to keep the US population more or less constant as far as the demographer's eye could see, but at least through 2060.

As it has happened, of course, the US population has grown to about *335 million* at present due to post-1965 immigrants and their children and grandchildren. And under policies extant before The Donald and his wall-building mania arrived on the scene in 2017 that figure would have grown to 404 million by 2060, thereby accommodating at least modest growth in the future labor force.

But under the Trumpian close-the-borders ukase, much of that growth could vanish. The graph shows that nearly *three-fourths* of projected population growth from the present level thru 2060 would be eliminated if the number of immigrants were to be cut by 50 percent from pre-2015 levels.

These numbers show that the only way to give the US economy a fighting chance to shoulder the tsunami of public debt expense and Welfare State retirement spending that is coming down the pike at an accelerating pace is to import millions of new workers. This is due to potential native-born American parents saying "no" to having kids. And now, the GOP in its Trumpian stupor have become the anti-supply side party, as well as the political battering ram for a guaranteed fiscal calamity in the decades ahead.

And it will be a calamity. The public debt is already baked into the cake at $50 trillion by the early 2030s and will exceed $100

Source: NumbersUSA.org

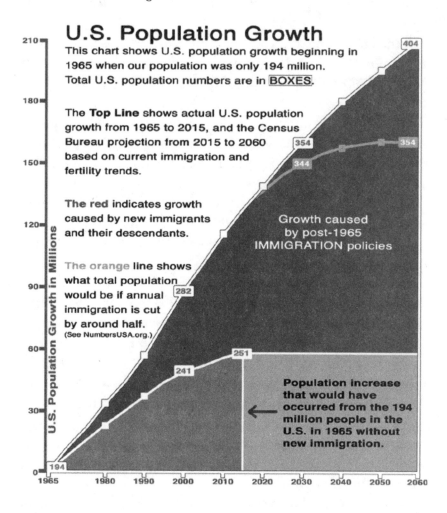

trillion by mid-century. At the same time, the Baby Boom is flooding onto the retirement rolls, where it will be collecting lavish levels of benefits that were never earned in an insurance sense, but simply granted by legislative fiat as a transfer from future workers to present retirees.

In fact, the number of Baby Boomers over sixty-five years of age will have grown from 21 million in 2016 to nearly 78 million by 2030. That's nearly 50 million more retirees in just fifteen years—a stunning testimony to the aforementioned pig-through-the-python nature of the nation's demographics.

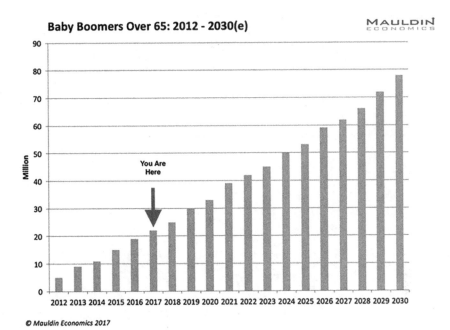

© Mauldin Economics 2017

In all, the retirement rolls in the US are climbing incxorably higher and the rate of gain will actually accelerate after 2030, climbing to 82 million by 2040 and nearly 100 million by 2060.

Accordingly, in the absence of robust immigration the declining number of native-born workers wouldn't stand a chance. They would literally be crushed by the never before imagined level of payroll taxes needed to keep Social Security, Medicare, and the rest of the retirement complex minimally funded.

So if today's younger cohorts vote for Donald Trump in 2024 to keep immigrants out of America, they will surely rue the day.

More importantly, the bracing retirement growth curve shown in the graph below means that America really has no time for Donald Trump's juvenile anti-immigrant antics and wall-building charades. The very idea of locking down the borders in the face of a screaming demographic deficit and shrinking labor force when the nation's social insurance burden is climbing skyward is just plain nuts.

Consider the crucial fiscal math shown in the graph below. Whether we get the current demographic projection of weak labor

Source: US Census Bureau

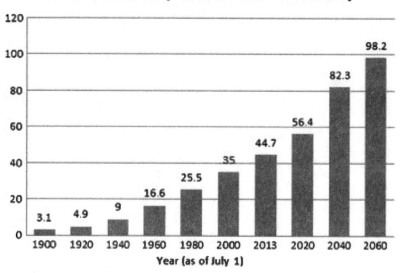

**Number of Persons 65+,
1900 to 2060 (numbers in millions)**

force growth, or no growth at all if the Trumpite border closers prevail in Washington, the ratio of workers to retirees is fixing to plummet from the 5:1 ratio at the turn of the century to just 2.5:1 by 2040 and continue to fall thereafter.

Needless to say, under Trumpian immigration policies the nation would reach in the not-too-distant future the point where every two workers will be carrying one retiree on their backs in terms of payroll taxes. And that's to say nothing of the onerous income and other general taxes that will be needed to pay multi-trillion-dollar annual interest charges on the mushrooming public debt and to fund the exorbitant costs of the Warfare State and Welfare State outside of social insurance.

Either that or there will be thundering political carnage if the current built-in 30 percent benefit cuts are triggered when the OASDHI trust funds become insolvent early in the next decade. That is to say, the very last thing that the American Republic can afford under this circumstance is four more years of Trumpian bombast about closing the borders and complacency about the

The U.S. Working-Aged Population Will Halve by 2040

Workers   Workers
5.0   4.9   5.0

Number of Working-Aged
Persons Per Retired Person

4.5   4.5

4.0   4.2   4.0

3.5   3.5

3.0   3.0   3.0

2.5   2.5

2.0   2.0

99   04   09   14   19   24   29   34   39

Source: United Nations and Citi Research.

ballooning public debt. No more toxic combinations of policies are actually imaginable.

Moreover, it also needs be understood that the implied tax burden increases are even more severe than suggested by just the plummeting worker-to-retiree ratio. That's because Social Security is ultimately a Ponzi Scheme in which all retirees receive substantially more in lifetime benefits than they paid in payroll taxes during their working years.

That's partially due to the progressive wage replacement formulas in the benefits schedule and also due to the fact that lifetime wages are indexed for both inflation and productivity during the period in which workers were paying into the system.

The latter is problematic in its own right because wages earned by twenty-year-olds are escalated for both inflation and all productivity gains during the next forty-seven years of their working lifetime. For instance, if a hypothetical worker had earned $5,000 in 1975 and retired in 2022, those wages would be indexed by

7.01x, or to $35,000 for purposes of calculating the monthly Social Security benefit.

And if this worker had been a low-wage worker his entire life, the benefit replacement rate for these indexed wages (AIME or average indexed monthly earnings), would be 90 percent.

Not surprisingly, this structure of wage indexing and progressive benefit formulas results in a vast disconnect between the *present value* of payroll taxes paid and benefits received. Based on 2021 dollars, here are the taxes-to-benefits ratios for seven typical beneficiary types.

Constant Dollar (2021 $) Lifetime Taxes versus Benefits=Ratio

- Single Low Wage Worker: $195,000 Taxes/$481,000 Benefits=**2.46x.**
- Single Average Wage Worker: $434,000 Taxes/$615,000 Benefits=*1.41x.*
- Single High Wage Worker: $694,000 Taxes/$725,000 Benefits=*1.04x.*
- Married Couple, One Low Wage Worker: $195,000 Taxes/$934,000 Benefits=*4.79x.*
- Married Couple, One Ave. Wage Worker: $434,000 Taxes/$1,162,000 Benefits=*2.68x.*
- Married Couple, One High Wage Worker: $694,000 Taxes/$1,348,000 Benefits=*1.94x.*
- Married Couple, Two Ave. Wage Workers: $867,000 Taxes/$1,303,000 Benefits=*1.50x.*

In short, under steady-state population conditions, the Social Security/Medicare trust funds would inherently go tilt because virtually the entire population gets far higher benefits than they pay in taxes. And there are no working period returns on accumulated "pension" assets, either, because the system has been pay-as-you go since the 1960s.

Accordingly, the only way the system can remain even remotely solvent is under conditions of strong, sustained growth in both productivity *and the number of workers employed.* Alas, the data show that both factors have been dramatically fading since the turn of the century.

In this context, the bottom-line metric for labor supply is the index of aggregate hours worked by the US labor force. However, the latter has been heading south for the last two decades. Between 1964 and 2000, for instance, the index rose by a robust 2.0 percent per annum, but since the turn of the century the growth rate has dropped by nearly three-fifths to just *0.8 percent.*

And that's just the backward-looking trend. Without a large-scale Guest Worker program, the growth rate during the next several decades would be lucky to average even *0.2 percent* per annum, just one-tenth of the historic trend—a rounding error in the scheme of prior history.

Index of Aggregate Hours Worked by Private Sector Employees, 1964 to 2023.

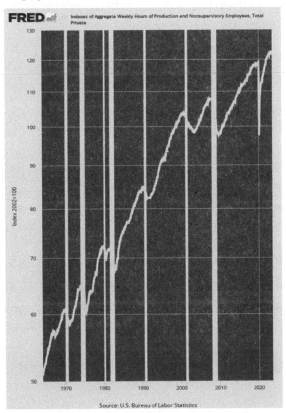

Source: U.S. Bureau of Labor Statistics

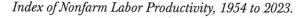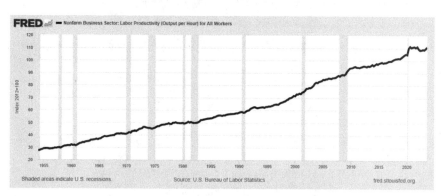

Likewise, you don't even need a magnifying glass to see that something ominous is happening to the seven-decade long productivity trend shown below. Productivity growth peaked ten quarters ago and now stands 2 percent *below* its Q3 2020 level.

Needless to say, the recent downward hook depicted in the graph has never before even remotely happened. And even when you credit the artificial productivity surge in early 2020, which was ironically caused by the massive lockdown furloughs (i.e., output fell far less than payroll counts), productivity growth has slowed dramatically.

The historic productivity growth trend was *2.80 percent* per annum between 1954 and 1973 and *2.11 percent* during the entire half century through the year 2000. But the growth rate has now slumped to just *1.05 percent* since Q1 2012. That's just two-fifths of its pre-1973 trend and half of the per annum gain recorded during the entire second half of the twentieth century—and even those tepid figures assume that the current negative growth rate will right itself forthwith.

Index of Nonfarm Labor Productivity, 1954 to 2023.

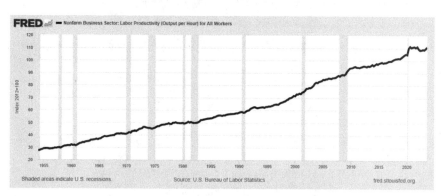

The collapse of productivity growth since 2012 is not just a statistical curiosity, however. Even the *New York Times* dyed-in-the-wool Keynesian economics commentator, Paul Krugman, once noted that—

*Productivity isn't everything, but in the long run, it's **almost** everything.*

The reason productivity is nose-diving, of course, is the succession of money-printers at the Fed, most of whom—Greenspan, Bernanke, Powell—were first appointed Chairman by Republican presidents.

But the verdict of their monetary apostasy is now clear as a bell. During the last two decades the capital markets have been mangled by relentless financial repression and ultra-low interest rates. That is to say, the sustained negative real cost of short-term funds on Wall Street has been a carry-cost bonanza for leveraged speculators.

Moreover, the Fed's belated pivot to inflation-fighting has not nearly undone the damage. As of June 2023, the real Fed Funds rate was still -0.5 percent. and had been in negative territory for *96 percent* of the last 184 months.

This speaks of damage to productivity growth that is nearly beyond measure. The Fed has fostered immense levels of malinvestment and unproductive speculation that would never occur in a free market operating with honest money.

As we have seen, the negative real cost of long-term debt has caused PE ratios to soar, thereby incentivizing the C-suites of corporate America to seek stock-option wealth via Wall Street–based financial engineering schemes rather than old-fashioned internal investment in the business.

Needless to say, the capital market distortions from years of financial repression are not close to being reversed, either. As of Q2 2023, the real ten-year UST yield was still *-1.2 percent*, and that's after a decade in which real yields have been negative (or only slightly positive) virtually all of the time.

Indeed, the chart below is the real smoking gun. The ten-year UST is the reference value for the entire financial asset market—stocks, bonds, and real estate. Yet owing to Fed policy, those asset classes have been drastically mispriced for years on end.

The result has been a sweeping re-allocation of capital market flows from productive investment in plant, equipment, technology and work force upgrades to rampant financial engineering.

Inflation-Adjusted Yield on 10-Year UST, 2011 to 2023.

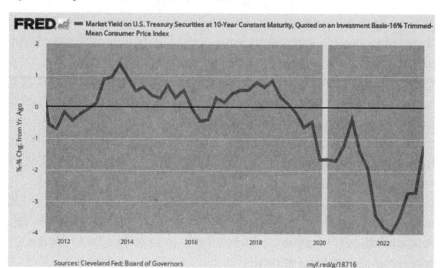

Sources: Cleveland Fed; Board of Governors   myf.red/g/18716

The latter has totaled *$25 trillion* in stock buybacks and largely unproductive M&A deals over the last two decades.

The result has been flat-lining business investment after inflation and depreciation since the turn of the century. And that's about as anti-supply side as it comes.

At the end of the day, the US economy desperately needs a huge increase in the number of workers and a dramatically stepped-up level of investment in productive assets in order to re-accelerate economic growth, and thereby handle the tsunami of 100 million retirees coming down the pike. These requirements, in turn, necessitate a revival of supply-side policies appropriate to current conditions.

To be sure, reduction of marginal income tax rates is always welcome—if compensating spending cuts are also made to eliminate current massive deficits and to compensate for the inherent revenue loss from lower tax rates. And, no, Art Laffer, marginal rate cuts from current levels do not pay for themselves. Not even remotely.

Instead, the supply-side policies actually needed today are a large-scale Guest Worker program and the abolition of the FOMC and return to the market-based discount window upon which the

Fed was originally based. That would put the free market in charge of the Fed's printing press as its original architect, Congressman Carter Glass (see Chapter 11), intended.

So, the question recurs. Does Donald Trump have any clue whatsoever with respect to these crucial supply-side requirements?

The essence of the matter, of course, is more labor and less money, even as The Donald loudly and militantly demonstrated during his four years in the Oval Office that he stands for less labor and more money.

So, as the man said, "nuff said!"

Chapter Nine

The Trumpian Canard of Global Grand Theft

———

Donald Trump's approach to economics was downright primitive from the get-go. He essentially held that America was falling from greatness due to trade policy stupidity in Washington and especially owing to a penchant for bad deals by past presidents. The undeniable economic decline of Flyover America, therefore, amounted to a kind of Global Grand Theft from America.

As The Donald told it, what rightly belonged to America was being stolen by immigrants, imports, and the nefarious doings of foreign governments. Accordingly, what was needed to Make America Great Again (MAGA) was a Washington-erected moat around the nation's borders to hold back the tide of bad people and unfair foreign economic assaults.

Even more crucially, the key to MAGA was a new sheriff in the Oval Office with the "smarts"—with which he believed himself to be amply endowed—to start "winning" again. As he averred in one tweet storm from the Oval Office:

> The United States has an $800 Billion Dollar Yearly Trade Deficit because of our **"very stupid"** trade deals and policies. Our jobs and wealth are being **given to other countries** that have taken

advantage of us for years. They laugh at what fools our leaders have been. No more!

We are on the losing side of almost all trade deals. Our friends and enemies have taken advantage of the US for many years. Our Steel and Aluminum industries are dead.

So a return to good policies—as in sound money, fiscal rectitude, and free markets, about which The Donald was ill-informed and could have cared less—wasn't even on his agenda. Instead, Trump's solution was, again, himself!

Accordingly, as he settled into the Oval Office Donald Trump boasted that he was the greatest negotiator and deal-maker to ever come down the pike and pledged to put a hard stop on any further theft of American jobs and wealth by the rest of the world. All of his crazy foreign trade bashing and over-the-top tariff raising flowed from that simple proposition.

Of course, he was dead wrong. Bad trade deals had nothing to do with what ailed America's economy and trade protectionism was only guaranteed to make it worse. Unfortunately, however, the takeover of his campaign in August 2016 by Steve Bannon, a belligerent nationalist and protectionist, only served to give the Donald's disheveled basket of bromides, braggadocio, and bile a rightist political veneer and proto-intellectual rationalization.

The real problem, of course, was not the evil flowing into the American homeland from abroad—whether imports, illegals, or terrorists. Rather, it was the outward flow of Washington's monetary and military imperialism that was gutting capitalist prosperity at home and generating terrorist blowback abroad.

Accordingly, Trump-O-Nomics never identified the real culprits behind America's economic decline. These actual causes of the nation's economic setback included—

- The cheap money policies of the Fed, which induced foreign central banks to buy dollars and thereby weaken their own currencies to keep their exports "competitive" and their trade surpluses with the US expanding.

- The military-industrial-intelligence-foreign aid complex of the Warfare State, which massively drained America's fiscal and moral resources.
- The hugely insolvent institutions of the Welfare State social insurance system (Social Security and Medicare), which entombed the federal budget in deep and permanent red ink.
- The prodigious level of federal spending on means-tested entitlements (Medicaid, food stamps, EITC, etc.), which became an anti-supply side drain on the nation's labor market.

Most especially, Trump did not grasp in the slightest that the root cause of Flyover America's distress was the Fed's multi-decade regime of interest rate repression and stock market coddling and bailouts. This egregious manipulation and falsification of the core financial signaling system of market capitalism had manifold adverse effects on main street America, even as it showered leveraged speculators on Wall Street with unspeakable windfalls of ill-gotten wealth.

In fact, the most deleterious symptoms of distress on main street could be laid exactly at the Fed's doorstep. Yet the Donald's policy was to incessantly demand even more monetary excesses from the Fed, not a return to sound money and honest interest rates. Consequently, his recurrent "easy money" expostulations exacerbated every one of the long-term trends that were eroding middle class living standards, including—

- Depletion of the real pay of workers and the massive off-shoring of good jobs owing to the FOMC's misguided 2 percent inflation target.
- Savaging the bank balances of savers and retirees via ZIRP (zero interest rate policy).
- Gutting jobs, investment, and real pay in the domestic business sector via the C-suites' strip-mining of corporate balance sheets and cash flows to fund Wall Street-pleasing

> stock buybacks, fatter dividends and M&A empire
> building.
> - Impaling the bottom 80 percent of households on an
>   unrepayable treadmill of (temporarily) cheap debt in
>   order to sustain a simulacrum of middle-class living
>   standards.

Given these adverse fundamental economic trends, the left-be-hind working classes rallied to Trump's cause, notwithstanding his flawed candidacy and pastiche of pugnacious pettifoggery. His Grand Theft from America theme appealed especially to blue collar constituencies in the burned-out industrial belts of western Pennsylvania, Ohio, Michigan, Wisconsin, and Iowa, as well as to the retirees of Florida and Arizona and culturally-threatened main streeters domiciled in the small towns and countryside of Red State America.

In these beleaguered precincts, the 2016 election was not espe-cially won by Trump. Rather, the electoral college was defaulted to him by a snarky denizen of Imperial Washington. After a twen-ty-five-year sojourn on the banks of the Potomac, Hilary Clinton simply had no clue that war, welfare, and windfalls to the wealthy were no longer selling in Flyover America.

The Donald thus won the 2016 election by a hairline finish in the Electoral College, but like the proverbial car-chasing dog which finally caught its prey, Trump had no idea what to do when he arrived at 1600 Pennsylvania Avenue. Bannon's raw nation-alism and The Donald's walls and crooked trade expostulations were not remotely up to the task of ameliorating America's eco-nomic, fiscal, and financial ailments. Thieving foreigners simply didn't account for the post-2000 stagnation of median household incomes, the huge loss of middle-income jobs to Mexico, China, India and elsewhere, and the actual decline of real net investment by the business sector.

To the contrary, the heart of the problem—the vast off-shor-ing of US production and breadwinner jobs—was due to wage arbitrage, which, in turn, was fueled and exacerbated by the Fed's

chronic and increasingly profligate pro-inflation monetary policies. This ultra-low interest rate regime consequently fostered an
explosion of household borrowing that sucked in inexpensive foreign goods and fed the continuous inflation of domestic costs,
wages and prices, thereby curtailing US exports and encouraging
massive import substitution.

To clarify, consider the trends in household debt, CPI inflation, and aggregate wage and salaries from the time of Nixon's
destruction of the gold-convertible dollar in August 1971 to the
Donald's arrival at the White House forty-six years later. To wit,
the purchasing power of the 1971 dollar had plunged to just 17
cents, while household debt had soared by an incredible *29x,* from
$500 billion to $14.5 trillion.

At the same time, however, household wage and salary incomes
did not remotely keep up, rising by just 14x during the same
period. In essence, the household sector's leverage ratio doubled
during that period, even as the Fed's fiat dollars had fueled rampant inflation of the domestic economy.

So, The Donald did truly inherit an economic mess. The problem
is he thought it was caused by malefactors of trade all around the
planet when the culprits were actually domiciled ten blocks from
the White House at the Fed's Mariner Eccles Building headquarters.

In this context, the three charts below are worth a thousand words and nullify all the econometric equations they have
been stuffed into the Fed's computers, as well as The Donald's
fire-breathing rhetoric about nefarious foreigners. The first one
shows that between Greenspan's arrival at the Fed shortly after
June 1987 and The Donald's White House premier in January
2017, *nominal* hourly wages for the private sector overall had
risen by *136 percent* while *real* weekly earnings had changed by,
well, *0.0 percent*!

That juxtaposition was a flat-out, screaming indictment of
Keynesian central banking. It had put workers on a long-running
inflationary treadmill with serious untoward consequences as we
amplify below. It was therefore the very thing that Trump should
have been attacking hammer and tongs.

That was especially the case because this inflationary tread-mill, which more than doubled nominal wages but generated zero gains in real earnings over three decades, was far from economi-cally neutral. Its highly uneven impact on the main street econ-omy refuted entirely the money-printers' implicit presumption that domestic inflation is benign and symmetrical. But the truth is, over any meaningful period of time wages and prices do not march in lockstep to the beat of the 2.00 percent inflation drum-mer at the central bank. That is to say, not everybody gets the same trophy as the price level steadily rises.

That's because all workers face the same CPI on the cost-of-living side, but experience highly differentiated wage inflation on their incomes. The latter depends upon whether their employer competes with the China Price for goods, the India Price for ser-vices, the Mexico Price for assembly, the Pilates Instructor Price for personal care, the Civil Service Price for government output or numerous other differentiating factors in the globally exposed domestic labor market.

Thus, compared to the aforementioned 136 percent average hourly wage gain between 1987 and 2016 for all private produc-tion and non-supervisory workers, the increase for manufacturing workers during that same period was only *109 percent,* while for health and education workers it was *163 percent.*

Obviously, manufacturing wages got hammered by the China Price in world trade whereas health and education sector wages were more or less shielded by government monopolies and pro-vider cartels. So while the average private sector wage gain was just enough to compensate for three decades of inflationary mon-ey-printing at the Fed, that was of cold comfort to actual work-ers because it was merely a statistical average. Within the various segments of the domestic work force there were actually big-time winners and losers, defying completely the Fed's gospel of 2.0 per-cent inflation for all.

But what is worse is that the PhD's domiciled in the Eccles Building implicitly held that persistent domestic inflation was also neutral internationally. But it wasn't. Not even remotely so.

Nominal versus Real Wages, 1987 to 2016.

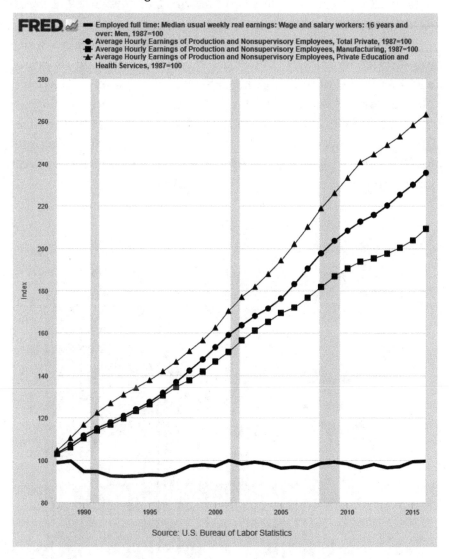

Source: U.S. Bureau of Labor Statistics

The fact is, in the face of low-wage competition arising from China and elsewhere after the mid-1990s, the inflation-swollen US wage and price levels needed to be thoroughly deflated in order to preserve at least a semblance of America's competitive position in global markets. As of 1995, for example, the bloat in US unit labor costs owing to a quarter century of dollar inflation after the end of Breton Woods was enormous. Private sector unit labor costs—that is, wage costs less productivity gains—were *193 percent* higher than they had been in 1970.

The US tradable goods and services sector was therefore a sitting duck economically. But rather than shutting down its printing presses and permitting the old-fashioned sound money cure of deflation, the Fed relentlessly pursued a pro-inflation policy at +2.00 percent per annum compounded, meaning that by the time The Donald arrived in the White House, US unit labor costs were now *275 percent* higher than they had been during the last days of quasi-sound money.

US Unit Labor Costs Index, 1970 to 2016.

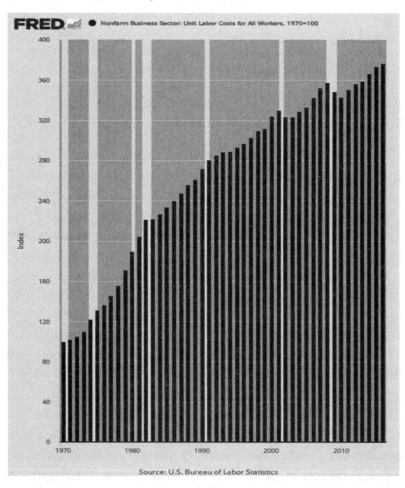

Of course, according to the reigning Keynesian theories none of this history was supposed to matter owing to presumed foreign exchange adjustments. That is, if the CPI and nominal wages went up too much, the dollar's exchange value would fall. In turn, that would make foreign goods more expensive in dollar terms, thereby braking what would otherwise be a runaway increases in the nation's trade deficit.

Unfortunately, the supposed downward FX adjustment in response to high domestic inflation and excessive monetary ease only works in Keynesian textbooks and in the imagination of the late professor Milton Friedman. The latter more than anyone else convinced Nixon to trash the Breton Woods gold-anchored dollar in favor of fiat money and free market-based FX rates.

It is plain as day, however, that since August 1971 there has never been a free market in currencies. To the contrary, what has materialized instead are massive, continuous "dirty floats," representing central bank manipulation of exchange rates in the service of mercantilist trade policies all around the world, but especially in Asia.

Consequently, when US manufacturing wages rose by 109 percent in virtual lock-step with the CPI over 1987–2016, the dollar's exchange rate didn't drop relative to the currencies of low wage competitors like China, India, and South Korea, which were building up huge trade surpluses with the US. A weaker dollar, of course, would have made the dollar cost of their goods more expensive, but the very opposite actually happened.

In response to the Fed's massive export of unwanted dollars, these countries retaliated with red-hot printing presses at their own central banks. That is, they bought in dollars and sold their own currencies hand-over-fist in order to keep their exchange rates from appreciating and their exports competitive in dollar terms.

That was the Dirty Float in action. What it meant under a condition of chronically rising nominal wages in US tradable goods and services industries, therefore, was just more wage arbitrage and even greater off-shoring of US production. In a word, the

Fed's idiotic 2.00 percent inflation policy was the greatest destroyer of American job and real wages ever imagined.

Of course, the Keynesian economists at the Fed and on Wall Street alike have convinced the world that "deflation" is a terrible economic plague. But it is not. Contrary to their evidence-free deflation-howling, people don't stop buying things they need or want when prices are falling; they just get more mileage out of the incomes and savings they have available.

So due to the super-inflation of the 1970s and early 1980s, what the US actually needed after the rise of global supply chains in the early 1990s was an inflation target of, say, -2.00 percent, not the relentlessly rising pro-inflation "goal" the Fed actually pursued. A falling CPI and static or falling nominal wage rates would have erased at least some of the catastrophic unit labor cost increase shown in the chart above, and thereby kept America's industrial base in the ball game as China and other low-cost suppliers flourished in world commerce after the turn of the century.

A sound money regime on the free market, in fact, would have enabled deflation. It would have permitted interest rates to rise sharply to premium levels after the early 1990s when Mr. Deng's gleaming new export factories began to fill the rice paddies across the length and breadth of China. Sharply higher US interest rates, in turn, would have triggered a systematic contraction of domestic credit and the deflation of prices, wages, and costs, thereby minimizing the gap between the domestic production price and the China Price for consumer goods, the South Korea Price for cars, chips, and electronics, the Mexican Price for assembled manufactures and the India Price for back-office services.

In short, had Greenspan stuck to his former sound money principles, the US would have experienced a persistent but benign deflationary trend rather than the actual *+111 percent increase* in the CPI price level between 1987 and 2016. This three-decade period, therefore, would have been much like the salubrious, inflation-free super-growth era of the later nineteenth century—an environment that was hardly conducive to the rise of Trumpian protectionist demagoguery.

Moreover, when it comes to labor arbitrage-based off-shoring, we are not talking about a one-way street. There are some serious residual advantages to domestic production including far lower transportation and insurance costs, smaller inventory investment levels, much simpler, speedier, and more flexible supply chains, and generally higher labor productivity per hour in the US. Accordingly, in the context of a disinflationary domestic economy and falling nominal wage rates (but rising purchasing power) these considerable deterrents to off-shoring would have weighed much more heavily on corporate production and sourcing decisions.

Worse still, once the global central banking system had essentially been transformed into a beggar-thy-neighbor FX management and manipulation racket, it didn't take long for many foreign central banks to basically adopt a "see and raise" posture. That is, not only did their pegging operations aim to match the Fed's prodigious money-printing and thereby keep their exchange rates from appreciating against the dollar, but they also attempted to push their FX rates lower.

In a sense, the post-1971 Fed had declared open season for bad central bank money. Its reckless expansion of dollar liabilities was bound to be followed by aggressive money-printing in the rest of the world because the short-run consequences of not doing so were too unpleasant.

The result is illustrated by the chart below, which indexes the South Korean won, the Chinese yuan, and the Indian rupee to a 1982 value of 100. During the next thirty-four years through 2016, the US CPI rose by a blistering 123 percent. So according to the textbooks the USD should have weakened and bought fewer and fewer won, yuan, and rupee over time—meaning that the indexed lines in the chart should have been trending downward from the starting point of 100.

As is evident, just the opposite happened. By the eve of The Donald's arrival at the White House, the US dollar was buying 1.6x more won, 3.5x more yuan, and 7.1x more rupees than it had in 1982. And, in turn, that meant even more off-shoring of US jobs and production to these low-wage economies.

After all, with a *stronger* won, yuan, or rupee, the dollar cost of goods or services from these countries would have been a lot higher. In turn, that would have narrowed the gap with US-based production costs, which reflected the 150 percent rise in the CPI and 170 percent rise in average hourly US wages during that period. However, it didn't turn out that way, and the considerably *weaker* exchange rates in the export currencies shown in the graph below actually widened the competitive gap.

Transmission of the Fed's Bad Money Disease, 1981 to 2016.

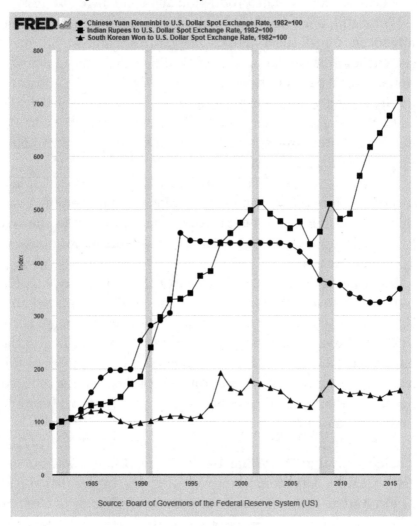

In the case of what we have called the Mexican Assembly Price, the widening of the dollar cost gap owing to Mexico's rampant money-printing and exchange rate depreciation had been even more dramatic. When Greenspan launched what amounted to Keynesian monetary policy after mid-1987, Mexican workers were earning pesos worth 74 cents, but by the time the Donald took office their peso earnings were worth only 5 cents.

In short, Greenspan and his heirs and assigns had unleashed a global monetary monster. They had exported the bad money disease to central bank printing presses all over the world, thereby essentially making bad money contagious owing to the overwhelming role of the greenback in global trade and finance.

So doing, they turned Flyover America into a wasteland economically and into Trump World politically. But the very last thing The Donald was about to do was to fix the underlying easy money problem that made his fluke victory possible.

What MAGA really required was a president wielding a monetary cattle prod aimed at getting the Fed to aggressively jack-up its zero-bound interest rates and to shut-down its massive bond buying program in favor of a sweeping liquidation of its Brobdingnagian balance sheet. After years of essentially zero-cost money, the US economy needed high nominal rates, not virtually invisible ones. In turn, those actions would have sharply curtailed growth of the nation's mountains of cheap debt and triggered a thorough-going recession/deflation of domestic wages, prices, and costs—the essential steps to actually make America's economy great again.

Moreover, that literally became imperative once Mr. Deng pronounced it glorious to be rich and opened up gleaming new export factories in east China on the back of a red-hot communist-style printing press. At that point, the clock was literally ticking on the future of America's industrial economy.

But the Greenspan Fed didn't have the gumption to tell the public the truth or to face down the vicious uprising that would have instantly incepted on Wall Street had it reverted to sound money policies. Instead, the Fed kept nominal interest rates lashed to the zero bound, when even an economic blind man could see that this had touched off a rampant household borrowing spree. Just in the period after 1987, it took household debt from $2.7 trillion and 80 percent of wage and salary income to $15.5 trillion and 180 percent of wage and salary income by 2018.

To be sure, this temporarily enabled the middle class to live high on the hog by leveraging their balance sheets to buy shoes, shirts, toys, video games, laptops, iPhones, etc. from the cheap labor factories of China's Red Ponzi. But it was a phony prosperity, and it could not last.

Moreover, we are talking here not merely about the loss of domestic production capacity for labor intensive products like shoes and toys. The real economic crime of the Fed's pro-inflation policies and +2.00 percent target happened throughout the globally traded economic space, which is a lot larger than is often recognized. That's because internet-enabled services, such as call centers and financial processing operations, can now be off-shored too, and therefore face what amounts to the India Price for services.

For example, as IBM transitioned from a hardware company to a technology services provider its employment in India had grown from zero in 1993 to 130,000 by 2018. By contrast, its domestic payroll had shrunk from 150,000 to less than 90,000 during the same twenty-five-year period. That is to say, its traditional hardware manufacturing business got off-shored to foreign competitors, while its new-style services business got potted abroad too, in India. Either way, American jobs and incomes got the short end of the stick.

Indeed, you cannot emphasize enough the monetary cause of America's massive trade deficits and hollowed-out production sector. During the Greenspan and subsequent era America's #1 export had been a tsunami of Fed created excess dollar liabilities. And, as we have indicated, this flood essentially house-trained the other central banks of the world—but especially those of the so-called emerging markets and resource economies—to run their monetary policies based on exchange rate targeting and export mercantilism, not on old-fashioned criteria of sound money.

In fact, in the context of a dollar-based global monetary system the post-1987 Fed had turned worldwide central banks into a convoy of money printing machines. Foreign central banks accomplished this by virtue of the aforementioned constant and heavy-handed intervention in FX markets. Buying trillions of dollars, they sold (printed) like amounts of their own currencies in order to keep their exchange rates down and their export factories humming.

As a consequence, the ballyhooed macroeconomic saving/investment identity got bollixed big time. Of course, Keynesian economists averred that large, chronic US trade deficits didn't matter much precisely because of this accounting identity. That is, the giant US trade deficits would be matched by a surfeit of foreign savings.

But that was academic pettifoggery promulgated especially by Ben Bernanke to justify his egregious money-printing. The truth of the matter, however, was that nineteen-year-olds working in Foxconn's sweatshops twelve hours per day in Shenzhen (China) were not saving too much, thereby generating the financial wherewithal to loan American consumers the money to live high on the hog. To the contrary, the international "savings" which were allegedly funding the massive US current account deficits were actually the fiat money emissions of foreign central banks.

That's right. These massive purchases of US debt amounted to crooked international finance because they occurred at far higher prices (lower yields) than would have transpired on an honest free market. Stated differently, this meant that a goodly part of the "investment" which funded the US current account deficits was nothing more than "asset" accumulation by fiat credit-emitting central banks.

Just in the sixteen years up to Trump's election, foreign central bank holdings of US Treasury debt had soared by 8x—from $500 billion to $4 trillion. And the impact of the latter was further amplified by private speculators front-running this artificial central bank fueled bull market in US Treasury bonds.

Source: US Bureau of Economic Analysis

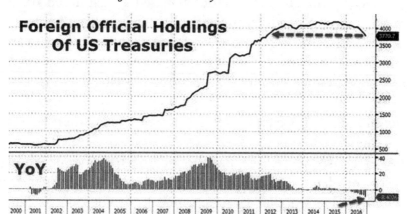

Needless to say, the fraudulent financing of the US current account in this manner enabled America's chronic trade deficits to remain uncorrected. That's undoubtedly why Trump thought he had an overwhelming case against cheating foreigners. Almost to the year that the Trade Act of 1974 was put on the books, in fact, the US experienced its last annual trade surplus in goods in 1975.

Since then, there had been a continuous and deepening plunge into the red on the US trade account. By the peak of The Donald's tariff-raising frenzy in 2018, in fact, it had accumulated to nearly *$15 trillion* more of stuff America bought versus what it sold to the rest of the world.

Needless to say, that doesn't happen on a level playing field. Under a regime of sound money, the rise of significant, recurring trade deficits causes an outflow of monetary reserves and a result-ing contraction of credit, domestic demand, imports, and deficits.

In the absence of such a settlement mechanism and discipline, however, the free trade theory of comparative advantage and uni-versal societal welfare gains doesn't work very well. It permits trade deficits to swell and endure indefinitely, thereby enabling the Fed's regime of domestic inflation and subsidized debt-financed consumption to progressively hollow-out the domestic economy; and to also foster an alienated electorate in Flyover America that understandably had no use for the nostrums of the patronizing beltway cut-out who was The Donald's 2016 opponent.

As it happened, Trump's so-called free trade critics had their heads buried deeper in the sand than even the orange comb-over. That's because most of the academics who reflexively champion free trade are either Saltwater Keynesians of the Harvard/IMF/ Brookings school or Freshwater Keynesians of the Friedman/ Chicago/AEI persuasion.

Either way, these academic free-traders seemed to think that America could run larger and larger trade deficits forever and ever, world without end; and that the mangled state of the US economy after four decades of this kind of trade mayhem was a natural outcome of relatively free markets at work.

No, it wasn't!

Even when you throw in the $4 trillion surplus on the services account (tourism, transportation, insurance, royalties and business services) during the same forty-three-year period prior to Trump's election, the deficit on the goods and services account with the rest of the world was still $11 trillion, and that's in then-year dollars. Inflated to 2017 purchasing power, the balance with the rest of the world since 1975 had amounted to upwards of *$19 trillion* or 100 percent of the then current GDP of the United States.

So notwithstanding his rhetorical bombast and primitive mercantilism, The Donald was on to the underlying problem, even if he was clueless about why it had happened or how to fix it. Ironically, that's also why his candidacy rallied large swaths of voters in Flyover America, and it is also ultimately why he won the electoral college, effectively, in a few score of trade-hammered industrial precincts in Pennsylvania, Ohio, Michigan, Wisconsin, and Iowa.

But The Donald was dead wrong about the reasons for the *$11 trillion* economic enema depicted between the upper and lower lines of the graph above. It was not the work of fools, knaves, or traitors in the trade departments of the US government. In fact, the US trade Representative (USTR), the Commerce Department and the State Department trade apparatchiks had comparatively little to do with these desultory outcomes. Nor can they be pinned

43-Year Cumulative Current Account Deficit—$11 Trillion.

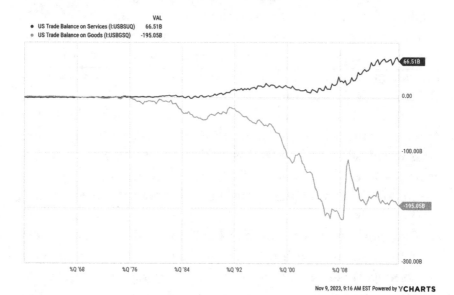

on NAFTA, the WTO (World Trade Organization), or even the globalist minions at the IMF, World Bank, and WEF, either.

Instead, the names of the malefactors were Alan Greenspan, Ben Bernanke, Janet Yellen, and Jay Powell. America was losing its shirt in trade owing to bad money, not bad deals.

So to repeat: Keynesian monetary central planning had its economics upside down. It sought to inflate domestic prices, wages, and costs at *+2 percent* per year (or more if correctly measured) in a world teeming with cheap labor, whereas a regime of honest money would have generated deflationary adjustments designed to keep American industry competitive.

Likewise, its rampant money-printing had resulted in drastic financial repression, ultra-low interest rates and debt fueled consumption and financialization, while sound money would have caused the opposite. The latter would have entailed high interest rates, subdued consumption, enhanced levels of savings and productive investments in plant, equipment, technology, and staff—not Wall Street financial engineering—in order to maintain sustainable competitive equilibrium with the rest of the world.

Above all, America's historical economic strength was not merely embodied in the healthy and nearly continuous trade balances racked-up every single year between 1893 and 1971, but actually was rooted in the ideas and institutions of free enterprise, sound money and capitalist innovation and invention. Yet it had all gone wrong after Tricky Dick's disastrous lurch into 100 percent state-controlled money at Camp David in August 1971.

America's Leading Post-1971 Export—Monetary Inflation

By unleashing the world's leading central bank to print money at will, Richard Nixon paved the way for the Eccles Building to become a massive exporter of monetary inflation. As we have indicated, these floods of unwanted dollars mightily encouraged the mercantilism-prone nations of East Asia, the petro-states, much of the EM, and sometimes Europe, too, to buy dollars and thereby inflate their own currencies. As we have seen, they did this in order to forestall exchange rate appreciation and the consequent short-run dislocations in their own heavily subsidized export sectors.

Needless to say, in the pre-Keynesian world there would have been no such thing as *$15 trillion* of continuous US merchandise trade deficits over forty-three years running. That's because the aforementioned monetary settlement system anchored in gold governed the flow of trade and international finance. The drain of such reserve assets from chronic deficit nations triggered automatic compensating adjustment of domestic economic conditions.

Accordingly, the large US trade deficits caused by the mobilization of cheap labor from the Asian rice paddies and cheap energy from the sands of Arabia would have generated their own correction. To wit, the resulting outsized US current account deficits (largely from consumer goods and oil) would have triggered a painful outflow of the settlement asset (gold or gold-convertible currency), which, in turn, would have caused domestic interest rates to rise, domestic credit to shrink and prices, wages, and costs to deflate.

At length, imports would have declined, exports would have increased, and the US current account would have returned to sustainable equilibrium, thereby bringing about a reflow of the settlement asset back to the US.

As it happened, however, the Fed's destructive monetary inflation spread like an infectious disease, and nowhere is that more evident than in the case of what became Donald's favorite whipping boy—NAFTA. The latter was an arrangement that Trump did not even vaguely understand, as attested to by the fact that his ballyhooed NAFTA "deal" after months of huffing and puffing and "negotiating to win" amounted to little more than a name change.

As to the underlying substance, however, the new "United States/Mexico/Canada Agreement" changed nothing because the central banking source of the problem had not been addressed in the slightest.

The real source of America's drastic trade imbalance with Mexico, as we have seen, was that the latter had gone whole hog printing its own currency in response to dollar inflation after the inception of NAFTA and the peso crisis in the early 1990s. After that, the peso's exchange rate against the dollar had plunged from about *3:1 to 20:1* by the time The Donald became President.

Not surprisingly, Mexico's already cheap labor became that much cheaper in dollar terms. Thus, in 1991 and previous years US exports to Mexico slightly *exceeded* imports, meaning there was no bilateral imbalance worth mentioning, as shown in the chart below. By contrast, by 2017 the US was incurring a whopping *$69 billion* trade deficit. US exports to Mexico that year, in fact, were just $244 billion or 78 percent of the $313 billion of US imports from Mexico.

Yet that huge imbalance wasn't owing to removal of tariffs and other barriers under the NAFTA deal, which became effective on January 1, 1994. Nor was it owing to Mexican trade machinations thereafter. It was and remained a monetary and relative cost phenomenon.

Monthly US-Mexico Exports and Imports, 1985 to 2017.

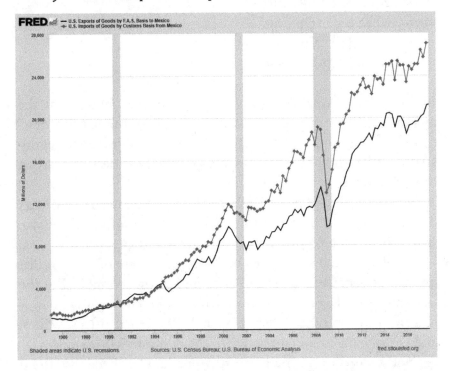

Nevertheless, The Donald's boasting about the NAFTA name change when he signed the new treaty in January 2020 was nothing less than fulsome:

> For the first time in American history, we have replaced a disastrous trade deal that rewarded outsourcing with a truly fair and reciprocal trade deal that will keep jobs, wealth and growth right here in America.

Then again, you would never know it from subsequent results. The US/Mexico trade deficit had already increased to $99 billion by 2019. But it has continued to head skyward since then, the allegedly awesome Trumpian trade deal notwithstanding:

US/Mexico Trade Deficit:
- 2017: *$69.1 billion.*
- 2018: $77.7 billion.

- 2019: $99.4 billion.
- 2020: $111.0 billion.
- 2021: $105.5 billion.
- 2022: *$130.5 billion.*

In short, The Donald might as well have been braying at the moon. All of his noisy expectorations about "shit-hole countries," trade cheaters, and allegedly the best new trade deal ever negotiated have had no impact whatsoever on the relentless increase in the US trade deficit with Mexico.

Moreover, the evidence for the truth that bad trade deals weren't the culprit lies in the other half of the Donald's anti-NAFTA crusade, where Trump got it entirely wrong about Canada, too.

To be sure, the Canadians had run their share of mercantilist promotion schemes, such as in dairy and forest products. But the Canadian exchange rate was not much different in 2017 than it had been in the early 1990s. Nor had its internal prices, wages, and costs changed much relative to the domestic US economy.

Not surprisingly, therefore, there had also been no trend change in the US trade balance with Canada. Both imports and exports had grown by about *3.5x* compared to their pre-NAFTA levels. In fact, during 2017, US exports to Canada totaled $283 billion and imports from Canada were $299 billion. Accordingly, exports at 95 percent of imports were probably close enough to balance for government work.

Stated differently, an allegedly "bad" trade deal led to wholly different outcomes as between the United States' NAFTA partner to the north versus its partner to the south. That is, a trade account hemorrhage with Mexico versus steady state balance with Canada.

So the cause of the imbalance with Mexico that Trump inherited in 2017 did not lie in the mechanics of NAFTA nor in nefarious betrayals by Washington trade officials, as The Donald persistently declaimed.

To the contrary, the cause of the exploding US trade deficit with Mexico was rooted in the systematic fall of the peso's

US/Canada Exports and Imports, 1990 to 2017.

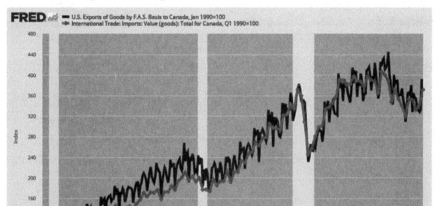

Sources: Census; BEA; OECD   myf.red/g/17UUp

exchange rate and its impact on relative wages, costs and prices between the two economies. That is, Mexico's exchange rate versus the dollar should have strengthened dramatically owing to its surging post-NAFTA surpluses with the US, but it was actually hammered into the sub-basement by the money-printers at its central bank, who made those at the Fed seem like pikers.

The divergent exchange rate history of these two NAFTA partners shown below—Mexico depreciated, and Canada didn't—thus provides a striking illustration of this phenomenon. By 2017 the US dollar was worth nearly 7x more pesos than in 1994, whereas it bought an identical amount of Canadian dollars.

Nor is the NAFTA case an isolated example. As we have seen, America's massive trade deficit problem and the resulting drastic decline of the US industrial economy during recent decades is a function of bad money, not bad trade deals. And with respect to that truth, the Donald's endless humbug about NAFTA provides ample proof that he was stone cold clueless.

To be sure, when other mercantilist nations used the flood of Fed dollars as an excuse to engage in persistent exchange rate suppression and dirty floats, it appeared that they were stealing production and jobs from American workers. But the solution to

Mexican Peso and Canadian Dollar versus US Dollar Indexed to 1994.

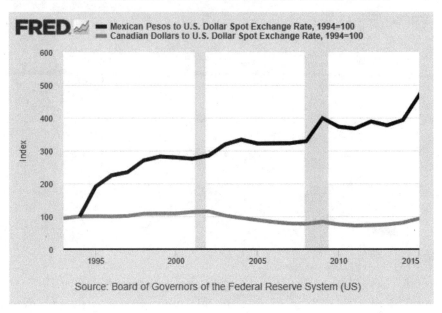

that was stern anti-inflation policies at the Fed, not loud protectionist hollering via the Oval Office's Twitter account.

Nor is this the half of it. Since January 2020 the long-standing trade balance with Canada has also gone sour—the Donald's spanking new trade deal notwithstanding. During the last year, before Trump claimed to be winning again with his new NAFTA deal, the 2019 trade deficit with Canada was still a modest *$26 billion*, with US exports to Canada still clocking in at 92 percent of imports from Canada.

Thereafter, however, came a "sucking sound to the north," as Ross Perot might have put it. By 2022 the US trade deficit with Canada had blown out to *$80 billion*—with exports of $356 billion representing only 81 percent of $437 billion of imports.

Alas, the explanation is not hard to find. More than 90 percent of this $54 billion three-year rise of the US trade deficit with Canada was due to an explosion of imports. After the greatest eruption of fiscal and monetary stimmies known to the modern world, US consumers were buying Canadian goods hand-over-fist, and, on the margin, funding these bloated purchases with newly minted public and private debt.

So again, trade deals had nothing to do with it, including The Donald's ballyhooed NAFTA name change. What actually made a mockery of the latter was the unhinged US spending, borrowing, and money-printing that the Donald himself had unleashed during his final year in office.

Chapter Ten

The Red Ponzi and the Folly of Trump's Big Chiiina Tariff

———

At the end of the day, Donald Trump was right about the horrific results of US trade since the 1970s, albeit he was totally wrong about the causes. In fact, he never got beyond a bombastic affection for seventeenth-century mercantilism.

Nevertheless, even giving the benefit of the doubt to free market economics, you do not get an $810 billion trade deficit worldwide and a 66 percent ratio of exports (*$1.55 trillion*) to imports ($2.36 trillion), as the US did in 2017, on a level playing field. And most especially, an honest free market would never have generated an unbroken and deepening string of trade deficits over the previous forty-three years running, which accumulated to the aforementioned sum of *$15 trillion.*

Better than anything else, those baleful trade numbers explain why industrial America has been hollowed-out and off-shored, and why vast stretches of Flyover America have been left to flounder in economic malaise and decline.

But two things are absolutely clear about the "why" of this $15 trillion calamity. It was not caused by some mysterious loss of capitalist enterprise and energy on America's main street economy after the early 1970s. In fact, the dramatic flourishing of the tech industry and the internet-based economy in the 1990s and after indicated the very opposite.

Contrary to The Donald's simple-minded blather, it was not caused by trade policy malefactors, either. After all, the basic framework of global commerce and trade deals under the WTO and other multilateral arrangements was established in the immediate post-war years and was well embedded in the 1950s and 1960s. Yet that was a time when the US was still running balanced trade accounts.

Those healthy post-war US trade surpluses, in fact, were consistent with the historical scheme of things during the golden era of industrial growth between 1870 and 1914. During that era of gold standard–based global commerce, Great Britain, France, and the US (after the mid-1890s) tended to run trade surpluses owing to their advanced technology, industry, and productivity, while exporting capital to less developed economies around the world. That's also what the US did during the halcyon economic times of the immediate post-war decades.

What changed dramatically after the mid-1970s, however, is the monetary regime, and with it the regulator of both central bank policy and the resulting expansion rate of global credit. In a word, Nixon's junking of the Breton Woods gold exchange standard removed the essential flywheel that kept global trade reasonably balanced and sustainable. So, without a disciplinary mechanism independent of and external to the central banks, trade and current account imbalances among countries never got "settled" via gains and losses in the reserve asset (gold or gold-linked dollars) accounts.

The destruction of Breton Woods allowed domestic monetary policies to escape the financial discipline that automatically resulted from reserve asset movements. The old regime of monetary discipline happened because trade deficits caused a loss of gold, which tended to shrink domestic bank credit, thereby deflating domestic demand, wages, prices, costs and net imports. At the same time, the prolonged accumulation of reserve assets owing to persistent current account surpluses tended to generate the oppo-site effects—domestic credit expansion, price and wage inflation, and an eventual reduction of trade surpluses.

Needless to say, as the issuer of the gold-linked "reserve cur-rency" under Breton Woods, the Fed was the first to break jail when this linkage was deep-sixed in 1971–1973. The Donald inherited the resulting mess but was unfortunately so far over his head that his primitive thrashing about with protectionist rhetoric and more than $100 billion of new taxes (tariffs) on American consumers only made it worse.

How Bannonism Begat More Welfare for The Rich

The Donald's lurch into unhinged protectionism and his subse-quent morphing into the Tariff Man only made the legacy of bad money even worse for Flyover America. When the full monte of the Trump China tariff, averaging nearly 20 percent (the weighted average of the 25 percent and 7.5 percent tiers) on $360 billion of Chinese imports, went fully into effect after 2018, the added cost to American consumers was more than $70 billion per year on a pure math basis.

But the economics of tariffs are actually more complicated than simple math. Since China was overwhelmingly the low-cost global supplier on most of the $360 billion of goods subject to the tariffs, the effect was the erection of a huge price umbrella 20 per-cent above the then prevailing market—and not just on the actual Chinese imports, but on the balance of supply in the entirety of these tariff-impacted product markets.

On average, China was supplying about 30 percent of the goods consumed by the US economy in the product categories in which it competed, with the balance sourced from other import-ers or domestic suppliers. So that meant upwards of $1.2 trillion of annual goods consumption in the US economy was directly subject to The Donald's severely inflationary tariff umbrella.

In some instances, where China had been the monopoly sup-plier (i.e., at or near 100 percent), US prices undoubtedly rose by the full 20 percent average tariff. In other cases, where there were alternative higher-cost foreign or domestic competitors, prices also rose but not necessarily by the full 20 percent. In these instances, the actual increase was dependent upon how aggressive competitors were in trying to capture market share from incumbent Chinese suppliers.

Unfortunately, we are aware of no detailed studies at the product line level showing how much market share the Chinese lost to un-tariffed suppliers and what the residual level of price increases was on the product lines subject to the Trump levies. But the aggregate data suggests that while China obviously lost share owing to the 20 percent up-charge on it products, non-Chinese importers didn't actually gain any share subsequent to the Trump tariffs. In the aggregate, therefore, China's share loss went to domestic suppliers, who, we are quite confident, did not hesitate to raise prices up to near the 20 percent tariff umbrella on impacted product lines.

Specifically, apparent US demand for all goods in 2017 was $4.21 trillion, reflecting personal consumption expenditures (PCE) for goods (durable and non-durable) plus the increase in business inventories over the prior year. The sources of supply and their share of apparent demand were as follows:

2017: Sources of Supply of Goods to US Market/Percent Share of Apparent US Demand:
- China: $505 billion/12.0 percent.
- Non-China Imports : $1.84 trillion/*43.5 percent.*
- Domestic Suppliers: $1.87 trillion/44.4 percent.
- Total Apparent Demand: $4.21 trillion/100 percent.

The same data for 2022 show $6.31 trillion of apparent US demand and the shift of shares among suppliers. Given the fact that domestic wages and costs rose by more than 20 percent between 2017 and 2022, domestic suppliers wouldn't have set prices much below the China-tariffed level in order to recapture business lost during previous years and decades. Likewise, the fact that non-China importers actually lost a small tad of share

(0.6 percent) suggests that they too largely took advantage of the price umbrella that The Donald graciously offered rather than grabbing more share at lower prices. The result, on net, is that the 3.5 percent share lost by China went to the highest cost suppliers based in the US.

2022: Sources of Supply of Goods to US Markets/ Percent Share of Apparent US Demand:
- China: $536 billion/8.5 percent.
- Non-China Imports : $2.71 trillion/*42.9 percent*.
- Domestic Suppliers: $3.06 trillion/48.5 percent.
- Total Apparent Demand: $6.31 trillion/100 percent.

These aggregate figures on apparent US demand for goods and the sources of supply include a lot more items than the $1.2 trillion sub-sector subject to the China tariffs. And there are also many inflationary and competitive cross-currents operative outside of the China goods sectors, as well. For instance, global oil prices nearly doubled over that five-year period, while the physical volume of imports declined by only 20 percent. On net, this would have pushed the share of apparent demand for goods attributable to non-China imports somewhat higher.

In any event, it would be quite conservative to assume that on average only two-thirds of the 20 percent Trump tariff umbrella was actually realized in the price of goods delivered to US consumers from all sources. Accordingly, that would have amounted to a 13 percent price rise on the $1.2 trillion of goods subject to the China tariffs or *$155 billion* per year.

That's not chump change! And it's also likely that it fell heavily on the bottom 80 percent of US households which essentially survive paycheck-to-paycheck on goods purchased at Walmart, Target, and other emporiums of imported merchandise.

Of course, The Donald's blunderbuss China tariffs did bring some production and jobs back to the US, as is implicit in the domestic share gains cited above. But that's what protectionism does—it returns some activity to the domestic economy but at a huge cost in inflation and other detriments to overall economic welfare.

At the end of the day, Trump's utterly erroneous diagnosis of what was wrong with the failing US economy led to trade policy actions that literally monkey-hammered the very rust belt voters who put him in office. In the meanwhile, his loud remonstrations against even the tepid steps the Fed was actually taking to normalize rates and its balance sheet prior to September 2019 were even more counterproductive.

The Donald's cheap money howling simply ensured that no action was taken to tether the central bank monster which caused the nation's massive trade deficits and loss of domestic production, jobs, and wages in the first place. In short, over the course of four years the Donald did virtually nothing to address the bread-and-butter grievances of Flyover America's economic left-behinds.

And yet, today's MAGA Republicans seem to think that giving him another shot will result in a better outcome. But they are surely delusional and fail to recognize the economic havoc The Donald sowed last time around. In some sense, the folly of Trump-O-Nomics is just getting started.

For one thing, The Donald's massive tariffs on China are totally sui generis in the annals of protectionist tomfoolery. All the previous historic flare-ups of US protectionism, such as the McKinley tariffs of 1890 or Smoot-Hawley in 1931 or Nixon's 10 percent import surcharge in August 1971, were generally directed against all imports, not just a single country in the complex nexus of global trade, which today totals more than $22 trillion.

The impact of stunting the China import tsunami has been a prodigious revenue windfall to the other major low-wage exporters, owing mainly to higher prices resulting from The Donald's tariff umbrella.

During this five-year period in which overall US imports rose by *38 percent*, imports from China were up by only *6 percent* while those from Vietnam have soared by *174 percent*. Obviously, some low-wage Chinese production moved a few hundred miles south, not 6,500 miles east to Wisconsin.

In fact, during that five-year period US imports from China barely crawled higher, rising from the aforementioned $505 billion to $536 billion. At the same time, imports from the other seven low-wage suppliers shown in the chart, led by Vietnam and Mexico, rose from $550 billion in 2017 to $920 billion in 2022 or by +67 percent. The Donald may well have lowered the boom on China, but the real winners were the rest of the low-wage global supply chain.

The Donald's Trade War against China—a Weird Exercise in Global Philanthropy

It goes without saying that The Donald's Trade War was a wholly different kettle of fish. Whether he understood it or not, his monster China tariffs amounted to a weird exercise in global philanthropy that should have left his MAGA followers hopping mad.

That's because the extra $155 billion of domestic costs owing to the China Tariffs largely came out of the hides of his Red State constituencies, which live hand-to-mouth at Walmart, Target, Dollar Stores, etc. For the bother of it, they ended up transferring foreign aid to Mexico, Vietnam, Bangladesh, and the others shown in the graph above!

Our recollection was that The Donald got elected by demonizing Mexico and other "shithole countries"—so the outcome of his tariffs is more than a little bit ironic. But at least the massive windfall reaped by Vietnam has a bit of logic: America probably does owe it some war reparations.

As to how this went down at the product level, just consider the top two categories among the thousands of the four-digit product codes which track US imports and exports. These two categories encompassed cell phones/cellular network gear and computers and related peripherals, where America imported $198 billion of stuff during 2017. Not surprisingly, China supplied $124 billion or 63 percent of that total. And laptops, iPhones, and other Apple products—made by more than 1 million Foxconn workers at $4 per hour in factories mostly in the interior of China— accounted for a goodly share of that figure.

But it isn't hard to guess who the next largest supplier was—Mexico at $31 billion, South Korea with $6.5 billion, and Taiwan with $5.5 billion. In all, the next three suppliers after China accounted for $43 billion of imports, bringing imports in these two codes by the top four suppliers to $167 billion and 84 percent of the total.

Likewise, the twenty-five largest four-digit product codes, which included the above two product categories plus tricycles and wheeled toys, furniture, monitors and television equipment, lamps and lighting fixtures, trunks and suitcases, printing machinery, video-game consoles, electrical transformers, footwear, numerous apparel categories, etc., resulted, in $286 billion of imports from China in 2017.

The key point is that these $286 billion of Chinese imports accounted for 52 percent of total US imports of $556 billion reported in these 25 categories. But when it comes to where the balance—the other $270 billion—of these goods came from and where they are positioned on the global labor cost curve, the answer is not surprising. The next $61 billion came from Mexico, followed by large volumes from Taiwan, South Korea, and a handful of other low-cost exporters.

Needless to say, when Chinese prices rose by 20 percent in these categories owing to The Donald's big tariffs, the next few countries on the global wage and cost curve picked up an immense revenue windfall and some additional volume, too.

And there's something else. The slickest way to beat The Donald's tariff hammer was for Chinese suppliers to ship—in lieu of fully assembled gadgets and products—an alternative package of quasi-finished "kits" to Mexico for final assembly, packaging and re-export to the US.

To prevent that kind of natural market circumvention, of course, The Donald's Trade Nanny operation had to drastically expand its rules-of-origin regulatory dragnet. Which is to say, more Swamp!

After all, consider the $556 billion of total imports in these top twenty-five mostly labor-intensive categories as of 2017. Exactly

$286 billion of those goods originating in China have been taxed at *an average of 20 percent,* while another $270 billion of virtually identical goods in the same categories originating from the rest of the world have been taxed at *0 percent.*

Can you say arbitrage? At the end of the day, The Donald's idiotic tariff-war-on-one-country caused more upheaval and dislocation in global trade channels than can scarcely be imagined. But for what?

Indeed, the net of it is stunningly perverse: US consumers got clobbered by the inflation part; low-cost foreign competitors got immense revenue windfalls and the re-located production and jobs; and the Red Ponzi "suffered" a market frozen at some $500 billion of exports to the US. That is, they perhaps lost a tad of profitability owing to modest price erosion, but still retained a massive level of US business.

This is all to say that The Donald's declaration of Trade War against China has proven to be one of the greatest of the many follies which transpired during his sojourn in the Oval Office. Yet how did we get to the point where an utterly uninformed cowboy in the Oval Office triggered this calamity almost unilaterally? And that includes retaliatory Chinese tariffs on $110 billion of US exports, which were mainly farm products (Trump voters again) and which represented more than 70 percent of total US exports to China.

Simple. The Donald accidentally discovered the imperial presidency can unilaterally raise tariffs virtually at will by abusing the rubbery enabling acts passed decades ago by Congresses which never imagined the Red Ponzi over there, nor the Orange Swan which arose therefrom over here.

So, the $700 billion of current two-way trade between the two largest economies on the planet has been subjected to an open-ended trade war that is truly unprecedented. Nothing of that magnitude has been remotely dreamed of by the protectionist lobbies in the past, but in today's memory-free fantasyland even much of Washington's purported free market GOP has gone over to the dark side of protectionism.

Indeed, with domestic inflation now raging on Joe Biden's watch, GOP orators would normally be pounding the tables against these inflationary levies on nearly $400 billion of goods coming into the US. But, alas, not so much when they are MAGA tariffs!

The Massive US/China Trade Imbalance—a Freak of Economic History

Given these baleful developments, the question recurs: How did a situation unfold whereby in 2017 US exports of $130 billion to China had amounted to only 25 percent of its $505 billion of imports from China? And if Trump's subsequent blunderbuss tariffs and trade war with China was the absolute wrong solution, then what is the rational route to its amelioration?

As it happened, US imports from China grew from $20 billion in 1993 to $505 billion in 2017 or by *25x* in twenty-five years. But nothing grows by *25x* in barely two decades in the natural order of markets, and most especially not in world merchandise trade where the US export side of the equation consistently stood at a tiny fraction of this staggering level of imports.

That is to say, there can be large trade imbalances between countries owing to comparative advantage and specialization, as well as to mercantilist trade practices like tariffs, quotas, and NTBs (non-tariff barriers). But imbalances this freakishly large and persistent over more than two decades cannot be attributed to either economics or conventional protectionism. As we have explained to the contrary, they are a function of money gone bad during the Fed-driven global central bank print-a-thon of the last several decades.

As shown in the chart below, the People's Printing Press of China had been a major contributor to the explosion of central bank balance sheets after the 1990s. Just in the first sixteen years of the twenty-first century, the world's combined central bank balance sheets had grown from $3 trillion to $19 trillion. That was a gain of nearly *12.5 percent* per annum—a rate of money printing that is just plain insane.

Freakish Evolution of the US/China Trade Imbalance.

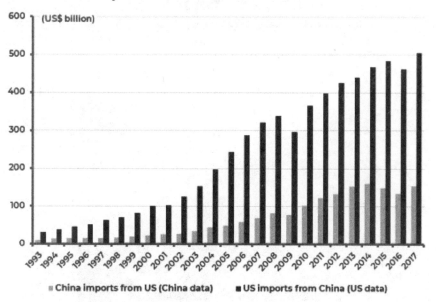

■ China imports from US (China data)   ■ US imports from China (US data)

But print they did, especially the People's Bank of China (PBOC), which grew its balance sheet at a red-hot 15 percent annual rate during that sixteen-year period. Moreover, that came after it had radically depreciated its currency by 60 percent in 1994 and had thereafter pegged the yuan to the dollar (rigidly between 1995 and 2004 and loosely thereafter). The purpose originally was to bolster its export sector and after that to prevent the yuan's exchange rate from soaring in the face of burgeoning trade surpluses with the US and the rest of the world.

The mechanism for this aggressive money-printing by the People's Bank of China was the acquisition of huge amounts of US Treasury debt and other FX reserves. To accomplish these purchases, the PBOC had to print yuan hand-over-fist to fund the buy-in of dollars and other foreign exchange as part of their pegging operation. Without these massive PBOC purchases of US debt, in fact, the dollar would have sunk like a stone against the yuan, thereby stemming the subsequent tsunami of China imports to the US.

More and more and more!
Aggregate balance sheet of large central banks, $tn & % of GDP

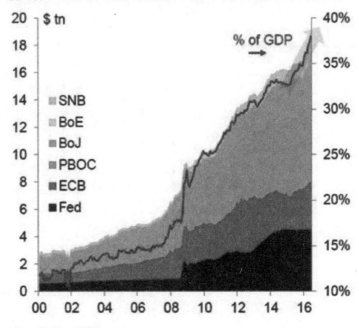

Source: Citi Research, Haver.

The consequence of this humongous dollar support operation by the PBOC was a massive explosion of domestic credit in China. The latter grew by *80x* or from $500 billion in 1995 to $40 trillion by 2018 (and upwards of $50 trillion today). By the lights of Keynesians and monetarists alike, of course, that was supposed to be their problem, not ours.

But what it really did was totally block the natural adjustment of trade balances which would have occurred under either a gold-based sound money regime or even under an honest free market–based floating currency regime.

The former case would have cost the US an immense amount of gold reserves, causing the domestic banking system to contract, credit-funded consumption and investment to be curtailed, and domestic wages, prices, and costs to decline until imports abated and exports picked up.

Alternatively, under an *honest free market float*, the adjust-ment would have occurred via big time appreciation of the yuan exchange rate versus the dollar. That would have dramatically reduced the competitive advantage of China's cheap labor econ-omy while opening the door to a higher level of US exports.

To be sure, China would have undoubtedly maintained a mate-rial trade surplus with the US owing to the inherent advantage of low-cost labor and newly constructed manufacturing plants and related infrastructure. But it would have been nothing like the trade balance aberration shown above, which is what drove the massive offshoring of American industry and the equally freakish election of Donald Trump.

That aberration, of course, was the direct result of the "dirty float" embodied in China's massive and chronic currency market intervention. But that was the outcome and symptom, not the cause of today's bad money-driven trade disaster.

The actual culprit was the US Federal Reserve, the issuer of the world's so-called "reserve currency." The dollar had played a legit-imate reserve currency role in the Breton Woods system because the US was supposed to hold the gold which anchored the sys-tem. In turn, this permitted others to use dollars as their reserve asset—given that these redeemable dollars were the equivalent of gold and were to be convertible at a fixed rate on the demand of non-dollar central banks.

In the 1960s, of course, the Texas Cowboy in the White House had found these convertibility obligations inconvenient to the conduct of his Asian war and the related "guns & butter" fiscal policy. So, the Johnson Administration had invented various temporizing expedients such as the London Gold Pool, which spared Washington of a massive gold drain for a few years. That is, until Tricky Dick Nixon came along and just pulled the plug on Washington's solemn obligation to cough up the gold.

But once the US went off the gold standard, and the world descended into Milton Friedman's putative nirvana of float-ing rates, the whole idea of a "reserve currency" became obso-lete. Under Uncle Milton's scheme there would be no need for a settlement asset between national trade accounts because floating or mobilized exchange rates were supposed to continuously clear the market, instead. And do so at the hands of free market currency traders on a 24–7 basis.

As it happened, the currency traders did make a handsome living plying the FX markets on a twenty-four-hour cycle around the planet. But like stock traders today, they didn't need to know a damn thing about the economic prospects for Sweden versus those of Canada, South Korea, China, or the US. Their job was to merely handicap the horses running the central banks—divining the next iteration of a moveable feast of dirty floats.

Needless to say, the most important horse by far was barned at the Eccles Building, where the Greenspan Fed absolutely eschewed the job assigned to it by Friedman's free market currency model. As we have indicated, under a regime of sound money the US would have experienced systematic and persistent internal *deflation* of prices, wages, and costs in the face of the mobilization of the latent east Asian labor force out of the rice paddies of subsistence agriculture and into gleaming new export factories.

That meant, in turn, that the Fed would have been required to accommodate a shrinkage of dollar liabilities, causing US interest rates to become painfully and persistently high. In turn, that was necessary in order to generate larger domestic savings and efficiency-driven investment, while sharply curtailing credit expansion to finance excess consumption and government fiscal stimulus.

Alan Greenspan, unfortunately, desperately aspired to be the toast of the town in Washington during the 1990s, not the monetary Scrooge who let the free market have its way, and which would have forced both Wall Street and main street to shed the inflationary fat that had built up during the two decades after Nixon's perfidy in August 1971.

The maintenance of honest money under a free-market currency regime would have eliminated any need whatsoever for the Fed's balance sheet of $200 billion (1987) to expand at all. Let us repeat: The Fed's balance sheet was already way too big in 1987 owing to sixteen years of monetary excess after August 1971. So, there was no reason for it to be expanded beyond $200 billion for years to come, thereby ensuring a dramatic halt to domestic credit growth and a resulting purge of the domestic economy's debt-inflated cost structure.

Indeed, the justification for an extended moratorium on Fed money-printing is strikingly evident in the chart below. Between June 1971 and June 1987 on the eve of Greenspan's arrival at the Fed, nominal GDP (top area) grew by *6.3x* while real GDP (bottom area) had risen by just *1.7x*. That is to say, most of the monetary excess which occurred after Washington's central bankers were freed from the shackles of gold-convertibility ended up inflating prices, wages, and costs in the US economy, not materially enhancing America's real output and wealth.

Index of Real versus Nominal GDP, 1971 to 1987.

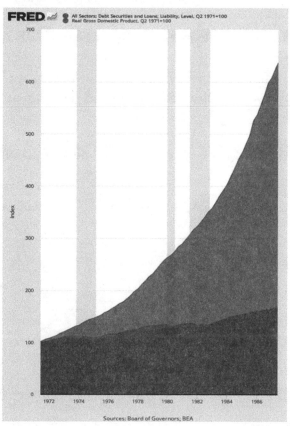

Sources: Board of Governors; BEA

The opposite of a money-printing moratorium actually transpired, of course. The Fed's balance sheet more than quadrupled
during Greenspan's nineteen-year tenure; and then it had been
off to the races under his successors, who brought it to a peak of
$4.5 trillion—a *23x* gain in barely thirty years—on the eve of the
Donald's inauguration in January 2017.

Excess dollar liabilities became America's number one
export—a plague on the world economy which naturally caused
the statist and mercantilist governments of Asia and the EM world
generally to massively intervene against the Fed's dollar tsunami
in desperate efforts to hold down their own FX rates and keep
their export factories in business.

The telltale sign of the Fed's culpability was the feverish
buildup of currency reserves in China and among other sur-
plus-generating exporters when there was no longer any real need
for monetary reserves at all.

Yet look at the freakish explosion of China's FX reserves pic-
tured below. It is exhibit #1 proving that the America's massive
trade deficit and economic hollowing-out began at the Fed and
must be resolved with a massive house-cleaning at the Eccles
Building.

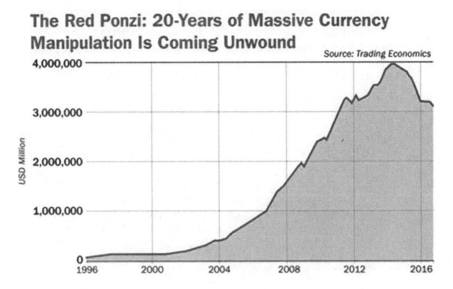

The Red Ponzi: 20-Years of Massive Currency Manipulation Is Coming Unwound

Source: Trading Economics

Greenspan's Greatest Export—Mercantilism and Central Bank Printing Presses Everywhere

Indeed, the Fed's culpability is truly staggering. It was the source of the massive and chronic FX interventions of China and the EM economies linked to it, which, in turn, ended up fueling out-of-this-world credit growth in their domestic economies. In turn, that ultra-cheap capital confected by the EM central banks funded an explosion of industrial infrastructure, factories, warehousing, and distribution capacities that became a mortal competitive threat to the inflation-racked industrial base of the US.

Indeed, the Keynesian geniuses at the Fed managed to batter the American industrial belt with an actual double whammy. It first drafted the cheap labor in China's hinterlands into new export factories; and then, on the back of cheap debt printed by the PBOC to buy-in dollars, filled these spanking new industrial zones with state-of-the-art manufacturing plants, highways, warehouses, airports, shipping terminals, and the advanced back-office technology to service the world with merchandise goods.

For avoidance of doubt, consider the graph below. Between the year 2000 and 2018, credit outstanding in the non-government,

18X Explosion of Business Credit Growth in The Red Ponzi.

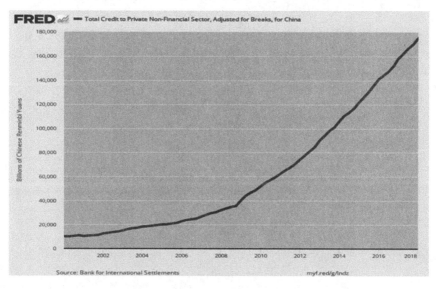

non-financial sector of the Chinese economy grew from 10 trillion yuan to nearly 180 trillion yuan ($26 trillion).

That's an *18x* growth in eighteen years and is what turned China into a freaky industrial behemoth. That is to say, a state-directed, debt-fueled economic madhouse that only resembles a capitalist economy because Beijing is pleased to keep up the pretense; and because Wall Street long ago lost its capacity to assess reality.

Given China's insane credit growth since the mid-1990s, it is no wonder that the Red Ponzi consumed more cement during its three peak growth years before The Donald's arrival in the White House (2011–2013) than did the US during the entire twentieth century!

That's right. Enabled by an endless $40 trillion flow of credit from its state-controlled banking apparatus and its shadow banking affiliates, China went berserk building factories, warehouses, ports, office towers, malls, apartments, roads, airports, train stations, high speed railways, stadiums, monumental public buildings and much more.

If you want an analogy, 6.6 gigatons of cement is 14.5 trillion pounds. The Hoover dam used about 1.8 billion pounds of cement. So, in three years China consumed enough cement to build the Hoover dam *eight thousand* times over—160 of them for every state in the union!

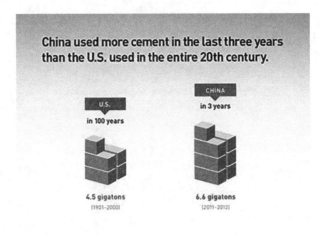

China used more cement in the last three years than the U.S. used in the entire 20th century.

U.S. in 100 years — 4.5 gigatons (1901-2000)

CHINA in 3 years — 6.6 gigatons (2011-2013)

SOURCES: USGS, Cement Statistics 1900-2012, USGS, Mineral Industry of China 1990-2013

Thanks to the Fed, therefore, the Middle Kingdom had been reborn in towers of preformed concrete. They rose in their tens of thousands in every direction on the horizon. They were connected with ribbons of highways, which were scalloped and molded to wend through these endless forests of concrete verticals—all with scant regard for economic returns.

Some of them were occupied, a lot of them were not. In fact, there were upwards of 65 million empty housing units in China in 2017, enough to house the entire nation of Italy with rooms to spare. They stood as a tribute to the bubble-borne notion that unrented real estate is a wonderful investment because it never stops appreciating and the government will never let prices fall— even if the implied rental yields are unaffordable to the over-whelming share of the population.

The point is, China's economy was a complete artifact of the craziest credit expansion in recorded history. Yet The Donald had no clue at all that the place to bring this monstrous threat to American prosperity to heel was just ten blocks away at the Federal Reserve Building.

Chapter Eleven

The Rising Tide Which Lifted All the Yachts

A s we have seen, The Donald's economic policy actions and nostrums were thoroughly wrong-headed and counterproductive. But the opposite assumption—that market capitalism was working according to the texts penned by Adam Smith—was also dead wrong and had been for decades. Today's bailout-ridden crony capitalism is not remotely the real thing, and that's especially because free markets can't function efficiently and productively when they are flooded with cheap credit printed by the central bank.

The ill effects of these perversions are legion, but one of the most obnoxious is the massive financial windfall to a tiny elite of the wealthy and a concomitant depletion of the middle class. Ironically, The Donald was elected and heralded by the latter, but his policies did absolutely nothing to change the system's long-standing windfalls to the rich.

Here is but one of the smoking guns that can be offered in evidence. To wit, in 1989 the collective net worth of the top 1 percent of households weighed in at $4.8 trillion, which was *6.2x* the $775 billion net worth of the bottom 50 percent of households. By Q1 2022, however, those figures were $45 trillion versus $3.7 trillion, meaning that the wealth differential was now *12.2x*.

In round numbers, therefore, the top 1 percent gained *$40 trillion* of wealth over that thirty-three-year period compared to the mere *$3 trillion* gain of the bottom 50 percent. Stated differently, there are currently 65 million households in the bottom 50 percent, which have an average net worth of just *$56,000*. This compares to the 1.2 million households in the top 1 percent which currently sport an average net worth of *$38,000,000*.

Needless to say, there is no reason to believe that left to its own devices free market capitalism would generate this *680:1* wealth differential per household. Indeed, three decades ago—and well before the Fed went into money-printing overdrive—the per household wealth differential between the top 1 percent and the bottom 50 percent was *barely half* of today's level.

Back in the heyday of America's post-war prosperity, in fact, President Kennedy's famous aphorism that "a rising tide lifts all boats" was repeatedly confirmed. But once Alan Greenspan inaugurated the current era of rampant central bank money printing, stock market coddling and egregious bailouts, the more accurate characterization is that a rising tide mainly has been lifting all the yachts. And it goes without saying that only a teensy-tiny number of MAGA red caps were to be found actually lounging aboard these vessels.

The truth is, Donald Trump's tenure in the Oval Office witnessed the steepest climb ever in the wealth of the top 1 percent. Nor is that surprising. The Donald was relentless in demanding that the Fed push interest rates ever lower and run the printing presses ever faster. Most of the billionaires, however, have never bothered to thank him for the resulting windfall.

There is no mystery, of course, as to why capitalism lost its historic middle class growth mojo during recent decades. Or why that occurred even as financial markets became bubble-ridden fountains, pumping egregious amounts of windfall wealth to the very top of the economic ladder.

The culprit was "financialization." By inducing relentless debt creation and leveraged speculation, the Fed and other central banks have bloated the financial asset sector out of all historic proportion to the real economy.

Net Worth of Top 1 percent versus Bottom 90 percent, 1989 to 2022.

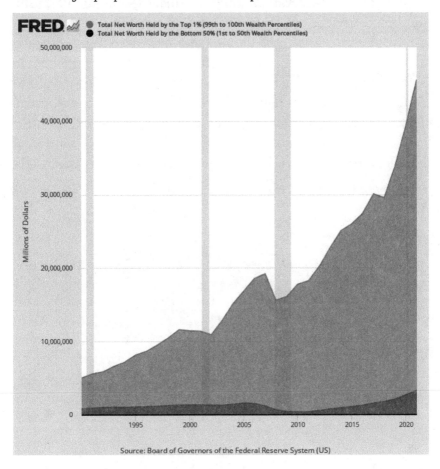

Source: Board of Governors of the Federal Reserve System (US)

Thus, between 1954 and the mid-1990s, total household financial assets oscillated around 2.5x–3.0x GDP, as tracked by the purple line below. But once the Fed's printing presses went into high gear under the Greenspan "wealth effects" doctrine and the serial bailouts that flowed thereafter, the ratio escalated steadily skyward, reaching nearly 5.0x GDP in 2021.

The fact is, there was no sustainable or sound basis for the eruption shown in the chart below. As we indicated with respect to total assets in Chapter 2, this ratio amounts to the price-earnings (PE) multiple for the entire economy. And since the trend rate of economic growth and productivity has deteriorated notably since the turn of the century, if anything the macroeconomic PE multiple should have been falling, not rising.

Nor is this eruption of the de facto macroeconomic PE ratio merely an academic curiosity. At the 1954–1987 average of 2.7x GDP, household financial assets in 2021 would have totaled $64 trillion, not the actual level of $114 trillion. That is to say, financialization has generated upwards of *$50 trillion* of extra household financial assets out of thin air. And about three-fourths of that bloated asset total is held by the top 10 percent of households.

Financialization of the US Economy: Financial Assets as Multiple of GDP, 1948 to 2021.

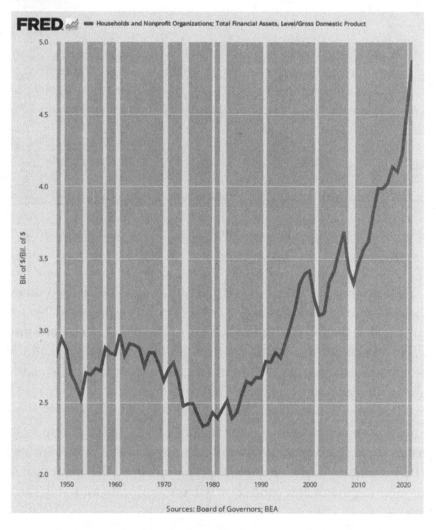

Sources: Board of Governors; BEA

What has kept the financialization ratio trending skyward was the very opposite of sound, sustainable economics. After 1990 the savings rate dropped precipitously, even as the debt-to-GDP ratio rose to new heights. America did not save its way to solid financial prosperity but borrowed its way to a fantasyland of phony wealth for the few and deteriorating economics for the many.

The cornerstone of long-term growth and wealth creation is net savings from current economic output. The latter measures true savings or the amount of economic resources left for new investment in productivity and growth after government borrowings have been subtracted from private household and business savings.

But as to the current trend, fuhgeddaboudit. This measure averaged a healthy 7.5 percent to 10 percent of GDP in the economic heyday before 1980. But especially after the money-pumping era of Greenspan and his heirs and assigns commenced in the early 1990s, the net national savings ratio headed relentlessly south. By 2022 the ratio was an anemic *1.0 percent* of GDP—a sheer rounding error in the sweep of post-war history.

Again, the actual net national savings in 2022 was just $260 billion, but that figure would have computed to $1.96 trillion at the 7.5 percent net savings rate of the pre-1980 period.

That *$1.7 trillion* of net national savings has gone missing, of course, does make a huge difference. Gross savings by the private sector had fallen sharply, and then The Donald came along and enabled governments to scarf-up most of the available new savings to fund massive, serial budget deficits.

So, the obvious question answers itself. A true MAGA policy would have reversed the Fed's long-standing war on savers via dramatically higher, normalized interest rates, while at the same time getting the US Treasury's sharp elbows out of the bond pits by balancing the federal budget.

That would have generated the surge in net national savings needed to revitalize investment in productivity and growth. Alas, sound money and fiscal rectitude were not terms that the Donald had any familiarity with whatsoever. In fact, his stance on these crucial matters was worse than that of every Democrat president of modern times, starting with Joe Biden and going all the way back through Obama, Clinton, Carter, Johnson, Kennedy, Truman, and FDR.

That's right. At the end of the day, The Donald's monetary and fiscal policy bacchanalia amounted to an outright war on capitalist prosperity. That alone should disqualify him from another berth on the Republican ticket and term in the Oval Office.

The nation can ill-afford four more years of The Donald's apostasy on the core issues of central banking and the public debt. That's because neither public nor private debts liquidate themselves over time. If the badly unbalanced income/outgo relationship is not addressed, chronic cash shortfalls from current operations just cause debts to accumulate and compound.

It is not surprising, therefore, that during the past half century the nation's combined public and private debt-to-income (GDP) ratio soared skyward. In fact, the 150 percent debt-to-GDP ratio which had prevailed through the 1970s went vertical thereafter, reaching 358 percent by the time of the Great Financial Crisis, where it remains stranded to this day.

As it happened, once the Fed got into the money-printing business after 1970, everybody joined the debt accumulation parade—governments, businesses, financial institutions, and households, too. Accordingly, the *$1.7 trillion* of total public and private debt outstanding on the eve of Nixon's dollar default in August 1971 rose to $10.7 trillion upon Greenspan's arrival at the Fed in August 1987; and it then reached $50.0 trillion on the eve of the Great Financial Crisis in late 2007, stood at $66 trillion when The Donald was sworn in, and totters at just under *$95 trillion* at present.

In effect, continuous Federal Reserve money-printing has resulted in what amounts to a massive national leveraged buyout. Just during the thirty-six years since Greenspan took over the Fed, total public and private debt (i.e., held by households, businesses, and financial institutions) has soared by a factor of 9.2x. By contrast, America's nominal income (GDP) rose by just 5.6x during the same period.

Again, we are not talking about mere academics. Had the red line in the chart remained at its 1.5x level of historic times, which ratio was pretty much constant all the way back to 1870 and which had accompanied the greatest century of economic growth and middle-class prosperity in human history, the nation's total debt today would be about $40 trillion.

Accordingly, the aforementioned actual figure of $95 trillion means that the main street economy is now lugging around an incremental debt burden of *$55 trillion*. And that's why aggregate economic growth and middle-class prosperity is faltering badly.

Yet, did Trump—the King of Debt—have a clue during his presidency or after?

He most definitely did not.

National Leverage Ratio: Total Debt to GDP, 1947 to 2022.

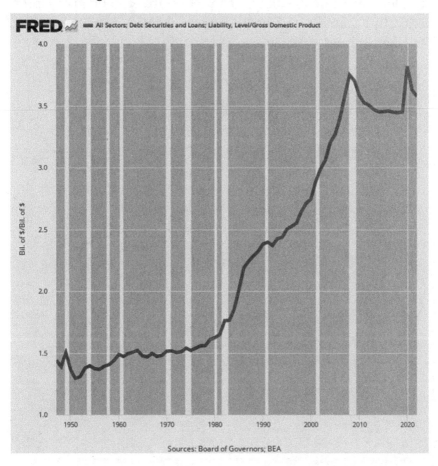

Sources: Board of Governors; BEA

In fact, real economic growth has dropped from a trend rate of 3.5 percent per year before the turn of the century to barely 1.5 percent per annum since then. And the reason for that is real fixed private investment has stopped growing because the meager private savings available have been channeled into private speculation and public debts.

Since the year 2000, real net fixed private investment—which strains out the inflation and the annual depreciation from the gross investment figures—has dropped from $933 billion to just $621 billion during The Donald's final year in office. Relative to national income, this figure plunged from 7.1 percent of GDP at the turn of the century to 3.4 percent in 2020.

Stated differently, main street has experienced a continuing deterioration in the share of national income being plowed back into new investment—the motor fuel of growth and rising prosperity. But then again, Donald Trump's MAGA notwithstanding, the 1 percent did get their yachts.

Real Net Private Investment Percent of Real GDP, 1997 to 2020.

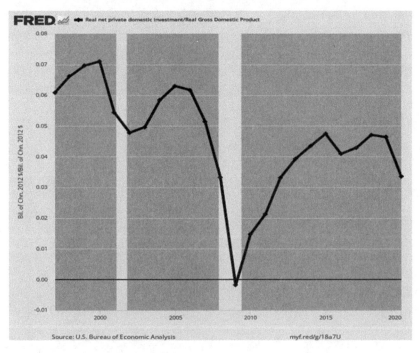

The Sound Money Road Not Taken

Had he accepted it, the true mission of the Low Interest Man was to make the dollar good as gold again. That meant big budget surpluses, high interest rates, a tumbling stock market, the end of financial engineering in the C-suites, and the painful sweating out of inflation that became embedded over the last several decades in wages, prices, costs, house prices, and much more on main street.

Those were the things which draining the Swamp was actually all about.

But none of that was in The Donald's DNA. Not even remotely. Nevertheless, deflationary austerity was and remains the only viable alternative to the failed spend, borrow, print, and inflate economic policies of the Washington uniparty—the embedded groupthink apostasy that Donald Trump embraced with unreserved gusto.

The truth is, all of today's maladies—low growth, high inflation, a shrinking middle class, and the concentration of vast windfall wealth at the tippy-top of the economic ladder—stem from the central bank's basic modus operandi. That is, the Fed's overwhelming presence in Wall Street money and capital markets via massive bond-buying, interest rate pegging, yield curve manipulation and price keeping operations designed to prop-up equities and other risk assets.

This modern form of Wall Street–centric central banking has been an abject failure and not just because it is anti-growth, pro-inflation, and deeply biased in favor of the super-rich, who own most of the financial assets which have been inflated to a fare-thee-well. Its even more fatal defect is that it led to near total *capture of the Fed* by Wall Street operators, traders, speculators, and their shills in the financial press.

The result was crony capitalism in capital letters. And that put the Eccles Building at the very epicenter of the Swamp.

There is no mystery as to why this is the case—even crediting the arguably good intentions of the twelve people who serve on the FOMC (Federal Open Market Committee). With every Fed meeting there are extant literally tens of trillions worth of bets that have been placed by Wall Street's fast money-operators based on the expected FOMC policy announcement. The latter include changes in money market rates by as little as twenty-five basis points, guidance on the monthly rate of bond-buying or selling to the nearest $5 billion, and hints in the post-meeting statement and chairman's press conference as to what hairline maneuver the FOMC might undertake at the next monthly meeting and in the months immediately beyond that.

In a word, the rise at the Fed of what Alan Greenspan called "the wealth effects doctrine" has fundamentally changed Wall Street. In days of yore it *invested* based on the facts embedded in the flow of business and financial information on the free market. But now it *trades* overwhelmingly on the flow of monetary policy tweaks coursing through the brains of the twelve FOMC members and a handful of Wall Street gurus who attempt to divine their latest revelations and intentions.

Accordingly, the Fed dare not disappoint the momentary Wall Street consensus because its entire "policy transmittal" process works through the Wall Street–centered financial markets, not the main street banks and S&Ls of times gone by. Under today's Fed model, prices in the money, bond, stock, and real estate markets are actually the transmission mechanism which purportedly conveys the Fed's policy signals and intentions to main street.

So, for want of a better term, Wall Street has the FOMC by the short hairs. And it never lets go. Doing Wall Street's short-term bidding at meeting after meeting after meeting leads to nothing less than permanent policy capture of the Fed by traders and speculators.

And we do mean traders, not investors. In theory the latter were historically happy with honest market-based pricing of financial assets on Wall Street and a convertible dollar linked to a fixed weight of gold. After all, old-fashioned "investors" were in the business of picking profitable investments for the long-haul based on the intrinsic facts of the instrument in question.

That's not the case with today's Wall Street traders. Not by a long shot. To the contrary, they make their money through Fed subsidized carry trades or options market positioning based on zero or negative cost of capital in real terms, and also via artificially low cap rates (i.e., long-term interest rates and their reciprocal in the form of higher P-E ratios). So if you are invested in assets that are appreciating due to rising valuation multiples and are funding them to the tune of 80 percent or more in zero cost overnight debt markets, it is truly a case of shooting fish in a barrel.

This proposition cannot be overstated. Dwelling down in the canyons of Wall Street cheek-by-jowl with the traders and speculators, the members of the FOMC lose all contact with the long-term trends they are fostering through their day-to-day capitulation to the demands of the fast money. For instance, the overnight interest rate (Fed funds and money market rates which track it) is of little use to main street because prudent businesses do not wish to finance either fixed or short-term capital in overnight markets that can be here today and gone tomorrow in terms of rate levels, conditions, and availability. And that's for the obvious reason that their funded capital—buildings, machinery, inventory, receivables, etc.—is not highly liquid or capable of being monetized at book value on a moment's notice.

Besides, their capital stock is designed to support the long-term capacity of an enterprise to produce goods or services. It's not there to be liquidated in order to pay off short-term funding that can't be rolled over. So the Fed's number one policy tool—the Fed funds rate—is essentially irrelevant to the main street economy.

But in contrast to main street businesses, Wall Street traders' books are far more liquid, meaning that assets can generally be quickly liquidated, even if it involves a mark to market loss, if funding is interrupted. It also means traders are inherently incentivized to borrow short and cheap and to invest in longer term assets with more yield and and/or appreciation potential. In this context, therefore, cheap carry trade finance is the mother's milk of speculative riches.

As it turns out, during the years of egregious money-printing, the inflation-adjusted or "real" cost of carry trades has been negative during the preponderance of time. For instance, during the 108 months between February 2008 and Trump's arrival in the

Oval Office, the real federal funds rate was negative every single month. And when that span is extended out to the present—184 months—the data shows it has been negative 96 percent of the time.

So, if you were a fast money operator on Wall Street you made profits by borrowing on the money market and rolling it over day after day, even as the longer-duration assets being funded were producing higher yields or better rates of appreciation and therefore a positive spread on the carry.

In the great scheme of things, this was damn near criminal. It showered Wall Street speculators with hideous riches, and provided a giant incentive for capital and talent to flow into financial speculation. And also, for the corporate C-suites to indulge in massive financial engineering—huge stock buybacks, overvalued M&A deals, leveraged recapitalizations, etc.—in lieu of productive investment on main street.

The latter point cannot be emphasized strongly enough. The Fed's day-by-day Wall Street coddling, subsidizing, and price-supporting actions have turned the capital markets into a casino where short-term trading is everything, and investing for the long run is hardly an afterthought.

Unfortunately, stock options–endowed corporate executives cannot resist the resulting temptation to get richer quicker. That is, the opportunity to goose options' value via financial engineering machinations that generate stock price gains in the short-run, even as they undermine long-run earnings growth through too much debt accumulation and too little investment in plant, equipment, technology, and human capital.

A succinct word for this perverse process, of course, is financial strip-mining.

The question therefore recurs. How did the monetary policy mechanism work before the Fed fell into bed with Wall Street after Greenspan's post Black Monday bailouts in October 1987? And why in those now forgotten earlier times did the US economy thrive just fine absent the heavy hand of Fed micro-management of the nation's total GDP?

The answer is that even Volcker did not target interest rates or attempt plenary management of the GDP. His goal was the restoration of sound money and returning goods and services inflation to absolutely minimal levels. Likewise, the great William McChesney Martin before him had no pretense that he and the FOMC were running the US economy. He knew that was the job of businessmen, investors, savers, workers, consumers, and even speculators pursing their own best interest on the free market.

In short, for the Fed's first seventy-three years of existence up until Greenspan's arrival in August 1987, its modus operandi had not strayed too far from the original vision of its legislative author, Congressman Carter Glass. The latter's vision was that the Fed's purpose would be to safeguard sound money and to ensure that the commercial banking system remained liquid as the US economy expanded in the normal course or encountered temporary rough patches from time to time.

But the watchwords were sound money and a well-functioning banking system. The pre-Greenspan Fed was not in the jobs, growth, housing, business investment, and 2 percent inflation business. All that claptrap was invented by Greenspan and his heirs and assigns based on the excuse that the misbegotten Humphrey-Hawkins mandates of 1978 made them do it.

The latter did not—there are no rigid inflation or unemployment targets in the legislation, just a motherhood-type aspiration for full employment and low inflation. But the Fed's subsequent mission creep into outright monetary central planning has now gone so far that the damage can only be undone by returning to a strict Carter Glass approach to central banking.

That is to say, the one decisive reform that is needed is to jettison the FOMC and all activist day-to-day Fed intervention in financial markets and return to a passive discount window modality. That shift and that shift alone would rescue the Fed from its captive status deep down in the bowels of Wall Street.

To be very clear, under this alternative monetary regime the banking system could get liquidity when it was needed, but only at a penalty spread above a market-driven floating rate at the Fed's discount window. Under a revived Glassian model the money market, not the FOMC, would set the discount rate based on the supply of savings and the demand for borrowings. And the discount window would be open for business one commercial bank-borrower at a time, day in and day out.

There would be no monthly Fed meeting drama—endlessly amplified by financial TV—about the Fed funds rate and level of bond-buying. Nor would there be a massive concentration of bets (i.e., front-running) around the Fed's expected action because policy-action would be delivered in tiny fragments and via continuous pricing bits at the market-driven discount window, not via a "breaking-news" flash on bubblevision ten times per year.

Moreover, the remit of the Fed under the Glassian model would be strictly limited to support for commercial bank liquidity. Period. The private economy would take care of growth, jobs, and the other elements of GDP. And White House bullies like LBJ and Donald Trump could huff and puff at length about easier money, but to no avail because there would be no FOMC or monetary politburo to heed their wishes.

At the same time, there would be no financial bubbles or main street goods and services inflation, either. That's because the mechanism by which the Fed fosters financial bubbles and CPI inflation—artificially low interest rates and inflated financial asset prices—would be disabled.

The vast unearned windfalls garnered by the super-rich in recent years were not the natural product of capitalism at work. Bubbles happen when the central bank subsidizes debt and coddles speculation. This inherently attracts talent and capital to the speculative trading pits, leading to even higher asset prices and ever larger speculative bubbles.

However, under a Glassian model, attempts at debt-fueled speculation would self-correct. That's because the interest rate at the discount window would automatically rise in response to surging demand for credit, and appreciably so. That was effectively demonstrated by the Volcker interlude in the early 1980s when Tall Paul essentially enabled the Fed funds rate to find its own market-clearing level. It did—at 22 percent in the face of the virulent inflation that had been unleashed by the money-printers during the previous decade.

At the same time, the banking system would not be left high and dry. But instead of validating the Wall Street canard that discount window borrowing is a bad thing because it taints the reputation of the bank obtaining the Fed advance, such discount borrowing would become par for the course. It would become the one and only source of sound money liquidity injections into the banking system to support real growth and productive main street investment.

In the historic monetary literature this was called a "mobilized discount rate." This kind of free-ranging market rate not constrained by the Fed's heavy foot would choke off excess demand for credit, and do so long before today's plague of Fed-subsidized financial asset inflation had time to build up a head of steam.

One more feature of a restored Glassian discount window model is crucial and would guarantee that its modus operandi would be non-inflationary at the CPI level, as well. Glass never intended for the Fed to be in the business of buying and holding Uncle Sam's debt paper, thereby subsidizing the government borrowing rate and encouraging the politicians to run-up the public debt. Government debt came to dominate the Fed's portfolio only by the accident of enlisting it to finance WWI.

By contrast, Congressman Glass was a believer in what was called the "real bills" doctrine back in the day. In simplified terms it held that bank loans backed by already produced goods (i.e., finished inventory or receivables paper due for settlement within a set period such as ninety days) were the only suitable collateral for loans at the Fed discount windows. Accordingly, when the Fed printed new money to advance a discount loan to a commercial bank member, the associated collateral would signify that new supply of goods had already been brought into existence to match with the expanded credit.

To be sure, the real bills route to Fed liquidity support for the banking system was not perfect. But it stands head and shoulders above the current defective arrangement where the Fed creates endless amounts of new credit by buying government paper without regard to the supply-side of the economy.

For this to work in the present era only one change would be needed, and it would bring the Fed inflationary money-printing spree and endless showering of windfall wealth on the 1 percent to an abrupt hall. *A present day Glassian Fed would accept only secured commercial loans as collateral for new Fed credit.* It would therefore cap its current holdings of federal debt and guaranteed housing paper at the present $8.3 trillion level and undertake a fixed plan of paydown.

For example, as long as it was fixed and irrevocable, the Fed's current rate of $95 billion per month of government debt liquidation (called quantitative tightening or QT) would result in an end game of zero holdings of government and GSE paper roughly seven years down the road. Under that scheme the Fed would never buy another US Treasury bill, note, bond, or guaranteed GSE security, ever again.

Accordingly, the Fed's heavy-handed price supports for Uncle Sam's debt emissions would end and legislators would have to service the public debt in the bond pits out of private savings at honest market rates. Upon the Fed's ending of public debt monetization, therefore, yields on Treasury paper would soar, causing profligate spending by the Washington War Machine and the domestic stimulus racketeers to come to an abrupt halt.

That would also end the current inflationary disconnect between excess demand fueled by US Treasury debt monetized by the Fed and the available supply of goods and services. Under a Glassian discount model, Say's Law would prevail: new supply would come into being first and only then could new central bank credit follow.

Equally important, the cavalcade of money-printing central banks that have enabled the collapse of America's trade accounts and industrial economy would undergo a decisive *volte-face.* Dollar-denominated interest rates would rise, causing the dollar's FX rate to sharply strengthen. And that would be unrelenting bad news for the mercantilist exporters, which, as The Donald so unartfully described it, were stealing production and jobs from America.

More precisely, these great mercantilist production machines have had one Achilles heel all along. Namely, they converted their dollar-based imports of energy, metals, and myriad other commodities into processed goods and finished manufactures and components, which, in turn, were resold to the US and other advanced economies at a profitable mark-up. However, were these goods converters to allow their currencies to abruptly collapse in the face of a newly hardened dollar, their domestic economies would face gale-force inflation as the domestic currency cost of imported supplies soared.

At length, China and the other mercantilist exporters of the world would need to severely tighten their monetary policies by raising rates and shrinking their own domestic money supplies. This would be necessary in order to support plunging FX rates and thereby counter the severe imported inflation that would be generated by a strong global dollar. Even then, local wages would have gone up with rising domestic inflation, while debt service and capital costs would also rise owing to higher interest rates and credit scarcity. In short order, the artificially competitive advantage that had materialized during the Fed's money-printing era would be substantially vaporized.

In a word, a sound dollar has been the key all along to reversing the accumulating main street disaster in trade, industrial production, jobs, and middle-class incomes. And yet, Donald Trump was and remains surely the most pig-headed dollar-trasher to rise to the top of American politics. Ever.

The current roadblock to fixing the Fed, and therefore fixing the American economy and restoring sustainable prosperity, is that the conservative party in America has come under the thrall of a dangerous protectionist, statist bully, and monetary quack. Unless he is sent to the showers decisively there is literally no hope for an outcome that does not end in financial, fiscal, and economic disaster.